REMEMBERING
HOOKESY

Published by
Swan Sport Pty Ltd
PO Box 80, Isle of Capri, Qld 4217 Australia
Fax: (07) 5531 7986 Email: swan.sport@bigpond.com

© Swan Sport Pty Ltd 2004

Produced on behalf of the publisher by
Media 21 Pty Ltd
30 Bay Street, Double Bay, NSW 2028
Tel: (02) 9362 1800 Email: m21@media21.com.au

National Library of Australia Cataloguing-in-Publication entry
Remembering Hookesy.

ISBN 1 877082 43 0

1. Hookes, David.
2. Cricket players - Australia - Biography.
3. Cricket captains - South Australia - Biography.
4. Cricket - Batting.
I. David Hookes Foundation.
II. Title.

796.358092

Cover design by Michelle Wiener
Text design by Sharon McGrath
Colour reproduction by Clayton Lloyd

Printed and bound in Australia by Griffin Press

REMEMBERING
HOOKESY

SWAN
SPORT

VALE DAVID HOOKES
1955-2004

We are all overwhelmed by the generosity of families who, in the midst of grief and suffering following a sudden and tragic death, are able to think of the pain of others and consider organ donation.

The decision about organ donation for family members happens in unexpected and traumatic circumstances. Thinking about organ donation and discussing your wishes with your family helps make the decision, at this time, a little easier.

You are encouraged to register; visit the website www.davidhookesfoundation.com and follow the online prompts; to access the Australian Organ Donor Register call 1800 777 203 or visit a Medicare office.

Contents

OBJECTIVES

• To increase the number of organ donors
• To increase the public awareness of the need for organ donors
• To educate families to support the decision of their loved one to donate organs

Acknowledgements

Any surpluses from the sales of this book will go to the various State Organ Transplant Units.

The publisher wishes to thank the following people for their assistance in ensuring the success of this project: Robyn Hookes and her children, Caprice and Kristofer, Rob Zadow, long-time friend, former team mate and manager of "Hook"; the many other friends of David Hookes, whether they be in business, sport or the media; Denis Brien, who spent quality time with the young "Hookesy"; the contributing members of the media, sporting and general, who waived their professional fees to express their feelings about David, his career in cricket, his attitude to life, and his untimely and tragic death; Robyn Reilly and Jackie Miller, who so poignantly brought us closer to understanding the grief of Robyn Hookes and the pain and joy of Jason Grey; young Ben Shipperd, who was so touched by the death of his new friend; News Limited and ACP, which kindly donated all photos; Getty Images, which agreed to reduce its fee for the use of its photos; *The Age* newspaper, which allowed reproduction of extracts of David Hookes's columns; Lauren Webb for her assistance in coordinating the editorial; the Nine Network and Fox Sports for publicity and promotion in the electronic media. Also to the many regional television stations who helped, in particular NBN and WIN TV. To News Limited, many thanks for their support in promotion of the book and undertaking to sell and market the special Limited Edition leather-bound publication. To SAI Private for their support in establishing and promoting The Foundation. To all the media in general, both in capital cities and regional outlets. And to the radio stations, too many to mention, who got in behind the book to offer their support and publicity.

Contributors

Mike Gibson is a commentator with Fox Sports and a sports columnist for Sydney's *Daily Telegraph* newspaper.

Denis Brien has been a close friend of the Hookes family for 36 years and played club cricket with the very young Hookes at West Torrens: "Many pleaded with me to alter his style ... adjust his hands, fiddle with his feet ... but David was enriched with so much talent that it seemed unnatural to curb it."

Ian Chappell recalls a chilling moment that might have wrecked a career: "David Hookes was playing a blinder in the second World Series Cricket Super Test in 1977-78 ... it came as a shock when he suddenly missed an attempted hook shot from the bowling of Andy Roberts and crumpled in a heap, spitting out blood and broken teeth."

Ian Edgley was the West Torrens A grade captain in Hookes's third season. He soon observed the left-hander's powerful talent to change the course of a match by hitting sixes in clusters: "One of them (a six) cleared the club house and crashed into the wall of the nearby Church of Christ as worshippers were leaving the building."

David Raggatt played youth football with "Hook" and later in life used to have a few beers with him when watching the local footy team the Eagles: "He became an internationally renowned sportsman but never forgot his mates, Duges and Jenny, Zakka, Banger, RB, Sweety and Cass ... 'still your buy, Cass,' as Hook would say!"

Mike Coward is a cricket correspondent for *The Australian* newspaper. He well remembers Hookes's debut in the Centenary Test: "Five daring and consecutive shots to the boundary off the England captain, Tony Greig, by a boy on a stage that tested the nerve of older and hard-bitten men, vested David with a new identity."

Jack Fingleton. The late Jack Fingleton was an outstanding cricketer, who subsequently developed exceptional talent as a cricket correspondent, just as Hookes did in the modern media. From Fingleton's report on the Centenary Test: "Greig took his sweater, pretended to crawl into it, cringing away from the setting ... "

Tony Greig is a cricket commentator with the Nine Network. Of the lead-up to that moment in the Centenary Test, he says: "I went straight to silly point, and it wasn't long before I had my first conversation with young Hookes. It was time to indulge in a little sledging. I said to the fresh-faced young Hookes, 'Tell me son ... '"

Sam Loxton was a member of Bradman's famous 1948 "Invincibles" and, as did

Bradman in retirement, devoted himself to the role of Australian selector. He was on the panel that chose Hookes: "I watched as he tried to come to grips with the situation (his Centenary Test debut), realising that he had a technique problem … "

Len Pascoe was on Hookes's first Ashes tour in 1977: "More than half the team had signed for Kerry Packer's World Series Cricket. It was a time of great secrecy, opportunity and sacrifice and David made that sacrifice. If he had stayed with the cricket 'establishment' he'd have been a megastar, a future Test captain."

Richie Benaud: "There have been players around the world who have laboured under the burden of cricket followers believing they should have done better. I think David was one of these; the idea probably had its birth right at the start of his career when he hit those five centuries in six innings, then played the Centenary Test and joined World Series Cricket."

Greg Chappell: "His captaincy was creative and instinctive, and a shrewd cricket brain was often in evidence whether when opening the bowling with one of his spinners or, when taking deliberate short runs to keep the strike when batting with the tail in a tight run chase."

Rod Marsh and David Hookes were on the World Series Cricket tour to the Caribbean in 1979: "It was decided David should be called up before the fines committee to see what he would say if accused of causing the mass evacuation of the hotel. He was duly accused and, to everyone's amazement, pleaded guilty without any hesitation."

Phil Wilkins was a cricket correspondent with *The Sydney Morning Herald* when Hookes was at the peak of his powers: "He was the first to profess he was no champion, but David Hookes was a man spectacular of personality, an irresistible character, a wonderful cricketer, and he bore an aura. He glowed in a crowd."

Rick Darling opened the batting for South Australia and Australia. He was batting at the other end when Hookes made a century off only 34 balls in a Sheffield Shield match: "Hookesy had fire in his eyes after a verbal confrontation with the Victorian captain Graham Yallop; after six overs he'd scored 83 runs, I had seven."

Paul Nobes was a batsman with a similar aggressive streak to Hookes and was as much influenced by his captain as Hookes was by Ian Chappell: "As a left-hander, he had a theory about leg spinners – there was no such thing as a good leg spin bowler, simply because the ball would always be coming into him and he could slog it."

Wayne Phillips and David Hookes were best mates, and team mates: "He would want us to move on with our lives … but he would be thrilled to know that if, when stumps were next drawn, you grabbed a beer and headed next door to talk and learn about the game, to ensure the spirit of the game was being strengthened."

Barry Gibbs was the chief executive of the South Australian Cricket Association from 1987 to 1997. Prior to that he was the Australian Cricket Board's Code of Behaviour commissioner from 1984 to 1988, secretary of the Queensland Cricket Association from 1961 to 1966 and a freelance cricket writer for more than 30 years.

Allan Border remembers Hookes liked to scheme: "Look like you are drinking one-to-one with everyone but skilfully pour half the contents into a nearby pot plant; towards the end of the night tell everyone that you are going to the toilet, but instead sneak out (generally this is known as 'doing a runner' but in cricket it's 'doing a Hookesy').''

Greg Ritchie shared an Australian dressing room with Hookes in the 1980s. On the way home from a West Indies tour they shared the surf at Waikiki: "Hookes was wearing stubby shorts, not board shorts; he wasn't bald then, but the only thing that made him look like a surfer was the fact that he had a little bit of blonde hair ... "

Dennis Lillee: "When you reach Test level you've got to change your style. It doesn't have to be a major step, but it has to be done. But a bloke like Hookesy, whose style was outright attack, would have found it difficult to play more defensively. It seemed Hookesy wanted to make a statement every time he went out to bat."

Jeff Crowe played youth cricket and Sheffield Shield with Hook before he played Test cricket with New Zealand: "I will miss him ringing me at some ungodly hour when I am living on the other side of the world just to say he's eating a 'cop the lot' hamburger from Fast Eddie's in Perth."

Rodney Hogg, former Australian fast bowler and bowling coach with Victoria, says Hookes was part of an Australian cricket fraternity in which his idol, former captain Ian Chappell, passed on a certain cricket knowledge. Hookes then did exactly the same for Darren Lehmann, now Australia's premier middle-order batsman.

Jim Maxwell is the ABC cricket commentator who interviewed Hookes after he was caught in a "sting" at the SCG: "Hookes's on-air performance inspired letters from listeners, some of whom were still upset by the appalling example he set for youngsters within earshot of his expletives; others reckoned he had a career as a barrister or politician."

Ian McDonald was the manager of the Australian cricket team in the 1980s: "It has always been an intriguing selection mystery as to why he played only 23 Tests between his blazing debut in the 1977 Centenary Test at the MCG, and his final Test nine seasons later on India's 1985-1986 tour of Australia."

Graham Cornes is a former star Australian rules footballer: "Throughout his playing career Hookes had flirted with the media, but it was always in the role of the subject rather than the commentator. With maturity as a man and status as an International sportsman came the confidence to front the camera and speak into the microphone."

Gerard Healy was co-host with Hookes of Melbourne's top-rating Saturday sport show: "His controversial opinions made good talkback radio; he once opened the program with 'Welcome to Melbourne Park ... where Sports Saturday will take you live to the battle between the half-man, half-woman of France versus the little lady from Switzerland.'"

Ken Cunningham was on radio with Hookes: "There was a lot of debate about Kim Hughes's captaincy ... I asked Hookesy the simple question, 'Who would make a better captain, Kim Hughes or Rodney Marsh?' It was the question any interviewer worth his salt would ask ... I thought David would be diplomatic for once ... "

Terry Jenner: "We played a golf Test series between the Australian and South African media. Playing for the South Africans was Graeme Pollock, the man whose batting style so many compared to that of David Hookes. One thing they definitely had in common was their lack of length off the tee!"

Jeff Thomson: "Few people would know that Hookesy was still getting the better of Tony Greig more than 25 years on from the Centenary Test ... on the golf course. Greigy is not real good standing over a two or three-foot putt and it was only natural, given the 'needle' in the contest, that Hookesy and I had stored away that little bit of knowledge ... "

Darren Berry captained Victoria when Hookes was the coach: "We pulled off that amazing win over New South Wales, scoring 455 in our second innings against impossible odds, and although David Hookes was a South Australian deep down, the occasion made him so proud of his boys that he really became one of us."

Greg Shipperd was Hookes's assistant coach at Victoria: "He reminded us, after having completed an appointment with the ill, needy or dying, how privileged we were to enjoy what we had, a lesson that now shapes the thoughts of many people affected by his untimely death."

Shane Warne remembers a first day in the nets with Hookes: "I came in and bowled a pretty good leg break to him, but too straight, too much on leg. He took one hand off the bat and hit the ball back to me from behind his back. He looked down the pitch at me and said, 'Don't bowl there, son.'"

Alan Shiell is a cricket journalist and a former South Australian cricketer: "As hard as it is for those who loved Hookesy to come to terms with their loss and the tragedy that befell him, there are now thousands of people who will benefit from the philanthropic decision he made in respect of organ donation."

Ben Shipperd is the teenage son of Greg Shipperd: "This is my reflection on a time of my life that was full of great difficulty and wavering emotions and is written to help people that have never experienced a death in their family to better understand the pain and helplessness an individual feels during a time of death."

Darren Lehmann: "Kandy is the only venue where David made a Test century ... thoughts of him overwhelmed me after the Second Test there when we had won ... I sat out on a ledge at the front of the change rooms for an hour or more and cried. I kept thinking, 'Is it all worth it?' I was going through all these emotions ... "

Peter FitzSimons is a columnist with *The Sydney Morning Herald* and worked with Hookes on television: "At the moment David's body left the turf of the Adelaide Oval for the last time, slowly exiting beneath the Victor Richardson Gates on the far side of the ground, someone began to clap. Then another joined in. And it spread from there."

Les Burdett is the Oval Manager at the world famous Adelaide Oval, a job he has enjoyed doing since 1979 and has been a member of the SACA staff since 1969. He and Barry Gibbs were great mates with Hookes. Hookes's death abruptly ended the friendly banter and the "taking the mickey" that inevitably occurred when they got together.

Terry Cranage is David Hookes's only brother; Caprice and Kristofer Gellman are Robyn Hookes's children; Dr Leonie Zadow is a close friend of the family. Each spoke eloquently and lovingly in eulogies at the memorial service at Adelaide Oval.

Robyn Reilly is a journalist with Melbourne's *Herald-Sun*. She spoke with Robyn Hookes about life with David, and the decision that had to be made whether or not to donate his organs: "When the children were going for their driver's licences David told them it was their decision on donation, but would always add, 'What do you need your organs for after you're dead?'"

John Singleton is a businessman: "As one we agreed we ought to form The David Hookes Foundation and use his senseless death to give life to others through increased awareness of organ donations. The phone calls flowed … "

Jennifer McGuirk OAM was chaplain for Pastoral Care and Counselling at the Victorian Liver Transplant Unit for 15 years: "Out of this seemingly senseless death countless other people stand now on the threshold of new life through successful surgery, and many more wait with deepening hope."

Professor Don Esmore is the head of the State Heart/Lung Transplant Service at The Alfred Hospital in Melbourne: "Solid organ transplantation remains a miracle of 20th century medicine."

Jackie Miller is a freelance journalist. She and husband Mitch were part of a Kidney Foundation Safari through the outback in 2001 to raise funds for organ donation research, and public awareness programs. She tells the story of Jason Grey, a triple transplant recipient. Jason: "It was about 8.30pm when Dr McNeil came into my room, put his hands on my feet and said, 'Guess what – we may have found a donor for you.' My mind was churning: Is this the end? Will I survive?"

Fiona Coote is one of Australia's first heart transplant recipients: "The real miracle is that there is enough love in the world that hundreds of unrelated people join together every day to deliver the miracle of life to people they've never met, to people they may never know. Every day for the last 15 years I've enjoyed and appreciated the second chance at life that organ transplantation has provided to me."

Rob Zadow is a long time friend of the Hookes family: "You scratched the surface of David Hookes and you may have gotten bitten, but if you kept going you would always hit gold." Zadow's eulogy at the Adelaide Oval memorial service is a fitting epilogue.

Ross Dundas is one of Australia's leading cricket statisticians. He has detailed Hookes's career, starting with the Centenary Test magic: "Hookes's famous tilt with Tony Greig began at 2.18pm, the 57th over of the innings. Australia were five for 223, Hookes on 36, Marsh 19. This is how history unfolded … "

Ian Edgley was assisted by Denis Brien; Darren Lehmann by Malcolm Conn of *The Australian* newspaper; Jeff Thomson by Jim Tucker of *The Courier Mail* newspaper; Dennis Lillee by Jim Woodward; Rodney Hogg by Austin Robertson. Jack Fingleton's comments were excerpted from a report in the *Australian Cricket Yearbook 1977*. Sam Loxton's comments first appeared in the David Hookes Testimonial booklet.

Foreword

HIS EXCELLENCY
MAJOR-GENERAL MICHAEL JEFFERY
AC CVO MC (RETD)
GOVERNOR GENERAL OF
THE COMMONWEALTH OF AUSTRALIA

I watched David Hookes at the crease with a sense of anticipation because he made things happen. He had the ability to make a genuine difference. His flamboyant five boundaries in the Centenary Test against England in 1977 at the Melbourne Cricket Ground propelled him into cricketing folklore – five successive blows which defied convention. Here was an individual, courageous and decisive, inspirational and willing to lead the way. It was no surprise that as a coach those same qualities emerged as he influenced others to achieve certain goals. Since David's life was cut short in tragic circumstances, his name and willingness to show the way have taken a new course, more profound than sporting endeavours; a journey whereby others are being encouraged to examine the value of life. Because David had made abundantly clear his views on organ donation, his family was able to ensure he left gifts more valuable to the recipients than the memories of his cricketing feats, still cherished by people around the world.

As Patron of Transplant Australia, I firmly believe we all can, and should, contribute to this worthy cause because Australia needs to take urgent action to ensure transplants are available to all those in need. Our nation has one of the highest medical success rates for transplantation, but we have among the lowest donor rates in the western world. Projects such as this fine book will help raise public awareness, and as part of that process my wife, Marlena and I, having consulted our children, have registered as organ donors. I hope many others will recognise that like David Hookes, they also have that ability to make a genuine difference, not only to improve the quality of life, but very importantly to save lives.

Preface

BOB MERRIMAN
CHAIRMAN CRICKET AUSTRALIA
PRESIDENT CRICKET VICTORIA

David Hookes was an exciting player and an outstanding team member. His deeds in the Centenary Test are well known around the world, however his leadership, participation in the team environment, and his ingenuity will be my lasting memory of him. To smash a century off 34 balls in a Sheffield Shield match whilst Ricky Darling, a very aggressive player, could only score nine runs at the other end demonstrated a rare gift. David's ability with the one-liner and to quickly think of a way through a problem was well demonstrated with the "short run incident", a plan by which he retained the strike against the odds. His legal action prompted a change to a law of cricket.

His value as a team player was best demonstrated in a Test match in Sydney in 1986 when, for the first time, the young players under Allan Border's leadership were on the brink of victory and a collapse occurred in Australia's second innings run chase. David sacrificed his natural game to get Australia over the line. The photograph showing Allan and David on the ground celebrating the win is very significant because David knew his Test place was under threat.

His last two years in Victoria were seen by many as a huge gamble; in February 2002 Geoff Tamblyn, Chairman of Cricket Victoria, urged by Shaun Graf (one of his overs cost 18 runs in David's 34-ball "ton"!) and fully supported by Shane Warne, decided to appoint David coach of Victoria. David's success with the team is now history, but what cannot be measured is the public awareness of the Victorian team, and cricket, during David's term as coach.

Introduction

MIKE GIBSON

I've been in the media for 46 years. Started out as a kid of 17. Yet last night at Fox Sports was the saddest working moment of my life. I was sitting hosting *The Back Page*, our Monday night gabfest where sportswriters and commentators chew the fat. And the news came through, the news that we had been dreading all day. David Hookes had passed away.

Like everything yesterday, from the moment I first turned on the radio in the morning, there was an air of unreality about it all. "Victorian cricket coach David Hookes has been assaulted outside a pub in the Melbourne suburb of St Kilda. Hookes was taken to hospital where he is feared to be suffering permanent brain damage."

Hey, come on. How can it be? Not the former swashbuckling Test batsman. Not our colleague at Fox Sports. Not our cheeky mate. Not Hookesy. He is so full of life, how could he be clinging to it by a thread? How could that nimble mind of his be locked in a coma from which he might never awake?

Disbelief. Sadness. Then anger. This was how I felt as the tragedy unfolded, as further news bulletins during the day revealed the gravity of his condition.

How could this happen? How could a bloke like Hookesy, with so much to offer, be the victim of such senseless violence? How could he have lain there on the street outside a pub, his life slipping away? How could he be lying there in intensive care, being kept alive by a machine?

Quick? He was quick all right. When Hookesy appeared on our sports show, his brain moved as fast as he talked. Ratatat. Like he used to score runs. An incisive

This article, "Disbelief over Fate of Our Great Mate", appeared in the Sydney *Daily Telegraph* on Tuesday 20th January 2004.

comment. An impish grin. A roll of the eyes. He was never short of an opinion. That's the business he was in. Ask Hookesy what he thought and he'd tell you. Straight out.

Ask Steve Waugh. Last summer, Hookesy declared that the Australian Test captain should call it a day. We all saw what happened. Waugh replied with that unforgettable century at the Sydney Cricket Ground. Hookesy just shrugged and congratulated Waugh on a wonderful innings. Egg on his face. Hookesy couldn't care less.

But what a staunch mate he was. Despite all the trials and tribulations Shane Warne has faced during his career never once did Hookesy waver in his defence. "Come on," we'd josh, as Warne lurched from one disastrous headline to another. "You must be joking. How can you keep backing this bloke up?"

"You bastards from the media," he would reply. "You never let up on him. All you do is keep trying to knock him down." So unswerving was his support for Warne that Hookesy found himself joining his mate in the headlines last year when a South African woman claimed to have had a liaison with the beleaguered spin bowler.

Leaping to Warne's aid, Hookesy publicly dismissed the complainant as some "hairy-backed sheila". "You're kidding, Gibbo," he chuckled. "I just said what most blokes were thinking." So now we're all thinking. Thinking of our great mate, asking why this has happened, and trying to comprehend that he has gone.

CHAPTER
I

Whenever a Test match was televised young David Hookes would take the mirror off the lounge room wall and put it opposite the television set so he could watch his right-handed heroes as if they were left-handers. He then imitated the shots they played. He was innovative even at Primary school.

Barefoot ...
But, Oh Boy

DENIS BRIEN

D avid William Hookes was born on the fifth of May 1955, at Mile End, a suburb, as
the name suggests, one imperial mile from the Adelaide CBD. The happy event
took place at the Thebarton Community Hospital in Lurline Street. His parents, Russell
and Pat (nee Osborne), lived in the family home in Clifford Street, Torrensville, built by
Pat's parents in 1930. From her previous marriage to Les Cranage, Pat had another son
Terry, who was 13 years David's senior.

Terry was a leading South Australian junior tennis player. He contested every State
junior final from Under 12 to Under 17, before eventually beating Peter Harris for the
latter. In 1960, he was selected to captain the South Australian team in the Under 19
Linton Cup, against all other states. As the No.1 player he was forced to contend with
John Newcombe and Owen Davidson and, at the age of 16, lost the South Australian
Under 19 title to Newcombe, two sets to one. In 1961, Terry was ranked No.10
Australian junior. Clearly the Osborne gene pool was weighted heavily with the
characteristics of ball skills and hand-eye coordination.

The two brothers were extremely close from the day David and Pat arrived home
from hospital. Terry would roll balls across the floor to his crawling brother, who would
invariably stop them with his left hand. Already he was showing exceptional
coordination. So, not surprisingly David's first love became tennis and even as a pre-
schooler he played paddle tennis with Terry in the driveway of their home, using a
sprinkler system as a net. It's possible young David may have developed into a
Wimbledon contender rather than a Test cricketer had Terry not left for Melbourne in
1961 to be coached by Harry Hopman.

David was born with the arches of his feet not completely horizontal, rather they tilted upwards from inside to out and, at the age of three, it was discovered that one leg was slightly shorter than the other. These problems in turn caused his legs to be severely bowed. An orthopaedic specialist gave his parents a choice of remedial treatment, either wearing leg irons or going shoeless. They chose the latter. David didn't begin to wear shoes until the age of five, and then only to Thebarton Primary school. There was a fair bit of teasing from other kids about his lack of footwear, but playing all sports barefooted didn't seem to worry him – only his family.

Pat enrolled David in the Church of Christ Sunday school, which was in the same street as their home, and which he attended throughout Primary school. This local church proved advantageous to him in more than one way. The hall attached to the church had a large sidewall, which was perfect against which to hit, bowl or throw a ball. Here young David would spend hours honing his coordination against the rebounding ball. Unfortunately the wall also had numerous windows, and all were smashed at one time or another. Eventually the church could no longer fund the repair bill for glass panes; young Hookes was allowed into the church grounds for religious business only! Undaunted, he moved on to the Smalls furniture factory in Meyer Street. Its wall had as much rebound and, importantly, no windows! Coincidentally, that was the same wall against which Terry had sharpened his volleys and ground shots.

From the Hookes family home in Clifford Street it was a 50 metre sprint to the corner and then a long, 500-metre haul up Meyer Street straight to Thebarton Oval. It was a comfortable four-minute stroll for most, but the barefooted Hookesy would do it in two. "Thebby" Oval, as it was known, was officially the headquarters of the Eagles, the West Torrens Cricket and Football Clubs, and in Torrensville folklore it was the acknowledged Mecca of sport. To the local youngsters, though, it was the Land of The Giants, the home of legendary football Magarey Medallists Bob Hank and Lindsay Head, who had also participated in A grade cricket premierships.

Thebby was the sporting birthplace of Phil Ridings, State cricket captain and Australian selector, too; of Ron Hamence, a member of Bradman's 1948 Invincibles and, scorer of a century in his first and last State games; of Bruce Dooland, the leg spinning magician who took 1,016 wickets for Australia, South Australia and Nottinghamshire.

Soon, it was the new outlet for the unquenchable enthusiasm of the young Hookes, now aged 11 and a bat and ball fanatic. There, he was the barefoot retriever of cricket leather hit into the long field by audacious or frustrated net batsmen during their Tuesday and Thursday evening practice sessions. He was always extremely respectful, calling "I'll chase it for you, mister", rather than using their nicknames like "Banga" or "Rocka" or "Zac". At that time, club coaches were fairly uncommon and it was up to the captains to manage practice sessions.

At one practice the A grade captain, Brian "Banga" Flaherty, asked David whether he would like to have a bat at the end of the night. David was overwhelmed and immediately raced home to tell his parents that "Mr Flaherty said I could have a hit on the turf pitches". He was back in a flash with his own equipment and, at the end of training, he went into the A grade net. Banga, and a few others, bowled to him off a couple of paces because he was just a young kid on whom they took pity. After four or five balls the feisty fair-haired midget walked down the pitch and demanded of the experienced A graders, "Are you guys gonna bowl properly or what? Because I don't want you bowling that slow crap at me!" So they got a little more fair dinkum and David showed his talent with straight and cover drives, cuts and pulls and leg glances. He had the makings of it all then, even the turn of phrase.

David wrote with his right hand and always hit and threw with his left, but his father Russell was adamant he should be a right-handed cricketer. He was always telling David that it was a right-hander's world. "You never see a left-hand screw driver," he would say. So, Russell asked State player John Causby to have a look at David playing right-handed. "Caus" took David to the nets under the old John Creswell Stand at Adelaide Oval and made him bat right-handed, then left-handed; he then told Russell that David should remain a southpaw. David always believed he was a left-hander. When there was a Test match on television he would take the mirror off the lounge room wall and put it opposite the TV set, and watch his right-handed heroes as though they were left-handers. He would then try to emulate the shots they played. He was innovative even at Primary school.

His first foray into club cricket was to try out for the West Torrens Shell Shield team. This was a team that played in the South Australian Cricket Association (SACA) competition over 12 days during the January school vacation and was restricted to school students who were under 17 years of age. I was a schoolteacher, so qualified as the manager/coach by default. It was October 1968, and as I was addressing a milling throng of enthusiastic could-be champions at the rear of the old stand, a woman calling herself "Mrs 'Ookes" pushed her way through and thrust a blonde and barefoot urchin at me. "This is my son David. He wants to play cricket. Look after him, I'll be back later," she announced.

He was 13 and, for his age, small in stature, but my immediate reaction was that if he had his mother's determination he'd be all right. I had reservations about the lack of footwear, but by the time we had reached the practice nets the barefoot boy had produced the only pair of spikes amongst the hopefuls! I have no illusions about my role in the development of the young Hookes. I was more of a mentor, a guide. Nobody coached Hookesy. Many observers, including the SACA stoics, pleaded with me to alter his style: "Change this, change that, adjust his hands, fiddle with his feet." I resisted, believing I was hardly qualified to change what God had spent so many hours putting in – or leaving out. David was enriched with so much talent that it seemed unnatural to curb it, bar the odd criticism of rashness. Maybe I was wrong, but who's to say wholesale changes in his early youth would have given him a better defence, or introduced dourness? Conversely, such advice may have robbed him of flair and charisma and the consequent entertainment value.

David was selected for that January 1969 carnival. The history of the competition indicated that it was good for a boy to play two years, or three years if he was exceptional. David looked so talented, despite his age and stature, that he immediately had to play some games for experience; he therefore appealed as a four-year person, quite unique! On the morning of the first match I picked him up in my dilapidated, obsolete Simca, and on the journey to the ground explained to him he wouldn't be playing in this particular match. His eyes welled up with tears at this disappointment – he was confident he'd have been required for every game! It was a confidence which never left him, and served him well. That season, as a 13-year-old, he played at Underdale High school and, occasionally at Under 15 level for the Grange Cricket Club, once taking ten wickets in a match against Pennington.

Of course, at that stage the club had no idea that little David Hookes would become arguably the most talented player produced at Thebarton, and would play more Tests (23) than any other locally reared son. Jeff Crowe, also an Eagle, played more Tests, but he is a son of Auckland and played for his native country New Zealand (39 Tests). But Hookesy was a freak who could smash an attack into oblivion, take the new ball or bowl his left-arm orthodox spinners and "chinamen", pluck catches from anywhere and throw down the stumps at will. He was to become the closest that West Torrens would ever have to a Sir Garfield Sobers.

Yet, for all his natural talent David's A grade debut at the age of 17 years and 192 days seemed to come frustratingly late. He had to wait until the 1972-73 season, his fifth at Thebarton, and the road was arduous. The sages at Thebarton appreciated his natural ability, but thought he lacked the physical strength for a more meteoric rise. He was practising regularly with the seniors while still in year nine at Underdale High school but, because the SACA had no junior teams other than the Shell Shield, his father Russell had to secure him the occasional game in the local hard wicket association.

His break came in January 1969, when he was first selected in the West Torrens C grade side. He compiled a solid 39 not out on debut, and then 48 not out in a score of five for 362 batting with veteran player, and club president, Daryl Wood. But they were the only occasions on which he reached double figures in his five consecutive games, and he was dropped for the finals. The explanation, that he was replaced for the major round by older more experienced players moving down from B grade, hardly softened the emotional blow to a 14-year-old bent on securing a "baggy green" cap.

During the winter of 1970, David had an enormous growth spurt and added 15 centimetres in height and, with that, came added strength. In the season that followed he scored his first century in the Shell Shield, and won a place in that competition's SACA team of the year. He was promoted to B grade near the end of the season where he was a little overawed and scored only seven runs in three innings.

In the 1971-72 season he earned a regular place in the West Torrens B grade team. I'd watched him for three seasons, now it was good to play a season with him. He was selected in the South Australian Under 19 side for the Australian carnival in Adelaide and became captain of the West Torrens Shell Shield team. Once again he was chosen in the Shell team of the year, but this time it was mainly through his bowling. His physical development now allowed him to dominate in this discipline and he took 25 wickets at an average of six. And, he began to assert himself as a leader.

The year 1972 was as bitter as it was sweet. He became particularly friendly with Roxanne Hewett, one of his Underdale High school mates. She was a year his junior but they began to see much of each other. The latter part of the year, though, was particularly traumatic for David. In November, while trying to cope with the workload of his matriculation year, he was selected for his first A grade match, a source of great jubilation. But almost simultaneously, his parents Pat and Russell, separated. Within an hour of Russell leaving, Pat and David were bellringing at our home, Pat bitter and David in tears. This was the last time that I saw him cry. For the rest of his life he developed an unemotional cocoon around himself, which conveyed the message that adults don't cry, something akin to his mother.

[In February 2003, I went with David, his wife Robyn and son Kristofer, to say farewell to a dying Pat, who was in intensive care at the Royal Adelaide Hospital. She was unconscious, and had precious little time left. We constantly went in and out as a group, and finally, individually. When I squeezed her hand and thanked her for what she had done for my family, tears rolled down her cheeks and fell on my hand. I had never seen her cry before. That was her last response. She was stubborn and tough, but a wonderful, caring and articulate woman. After he had said his goodbyes, Hookesy rejoined us and uttered a quivering, "Let's get out of here". Robyn, Kris and I all had watery eyes. Not David. After a few beers at The Royal, the closest pub to Clifford Street, and dinner, we retired to my home. At 11.30pm Robyn suggested that they look in on Pat on the way home. David refused; he felt that Pat might rally for an hour or two and that would prolong her agony. At 1.30am he rang to say that Pat had passed away. I could tell he was upset, but relieved. After Pat's funeral he was observed having a quiet cry in private but very soon composed himself. He was a warm and generous person who hated to see suffering in a loved one or a friend, but he was intensely private when it came to showing emotion.]

David retained his place in the Eagles A grade line-up for the rest of that 1972-73 season and, was selected for the second time in the South Australian Under 19 team to play in Canberra. He only once ever returned to B grade. It was in January 1987, and he was 31 years old and the captain of the South Australian Sheffield Shield team. He did it as a protest. He had been angered by an antiquated district cricket by-law which prevented elite players from participating in a club match if it overlapped with a representative match. On the second weekend of a club match, the South Australian team was to be in New Zealand to play a four-day game against Martin Crowe's Central Districts. The entire State team had to sit out the first weekend of the club match because the by-law stipulated they couldn't be replaced on the second Saturday. So, concerned that his protest would compromise the standing of the A grade, Hookesy decided to play B grade!

Against East Torrens at Thebarton Oval he smashed 118 from 125 balls, including eight sixes and six fours, and took one for five from five overs. The Eagles, who could only field 10 men on the second week, lost the match but the protest had the desired effect. The by-laws were soon changed. Throughout his adult life Hookesy wouldn't tolerate crusty panjandrums who denied change or defied logic to prolong some staid or archaic tradition. He would fearlessly fight pomposity.

He now spent a lot of time at our home because neither Russell nor Terry were around, leaning on me as a male role model and treating our children, Seamus and Megan, as younger siblings. Often, he would play with the kids in our street and once, after he had been selected for South Australia, he decided we would play a match in the backyard. He won the toss, decided to bat and assumed that he would remain ensconced for the rest of the afternoon. Using eight-year-old Seamus's small bat he proceeded to smash the ball all over the place. Loud bangs resounded as his hits crashed the ball against the galvanised iron fences and, within five minutes, the kids from half the neighbourhood were in the yard. It resembled an orphans' picnic.

Within 10 minutes he had broken the bat. I expected Seamus to burst into tears, but his mates surrounded him, chirping, "How cool is that, Seamus, Hookesy has broken your bat." I think it must be the only time a kid has become an instant hero because someone else has broken his cricket bat. To David's credit he had another sturdier bat handcrafted by Gray-Nicolls for Seamus. When our family gathered together on the night of David's death, Seamus remarked, "When I was growing up, I had two super heroes, David and Spiderman; now only Spiderman is left." Such was the adulation with which his young admirers held David.

David was dismissed in controversial circumstances in his first A grade game. He went to the wicket to take strike to former State allrounder Mick Clingly. David asked for the sightscreen to be shifted, as Mick had changed his bowling approach. Mick said, "Don't be silly, son. Your old man wouldn't want it shifted and you've got better eyesight than him." David stupidly, and probably nervously, agreed as Mick was a good friend of Russell's and David had always called him "Mr Clingly". He kept the first ball out, tried to sweep the second and was out, bowled. He didn't walk, as he felt the ball rebounded off former Test wicketkeeper Barry Jarman's pads, and he waited for the umpire to give him out. After the day's play, Barry remonstrated with Brian Isaac, David's captain and the non-striker at the time of the incident, about the lad's attitude. Brian quickly reiterated that he believed David was correct and that the ball did ricochet from the wicketkeeper. Jarman was none too pleased with that reply, and all participants have never changed their own opinion about the dismissal.

The young Hookes was now maturing mentally. On Tuesday evenings at training he would often ask the A grade captain, Brian "Zac" Isaac, whether he would be at home the following evening. If Zac assented then, after his evening meal, David would mount his old pushbike and ride a few kilometres to Zac's home at Flinders Park, always with two "long necks" of West End beer in a brown paper bag under his arm. The old sage and the young colt would then sit on the back lawn and talk cricket, or general sport, until the four bottles were empty, and then it was time to bike it home to Torrensville.

Most alternate Thursdays were selection nights at Thebby Oval. Immediately after practice we would venture into the dilapidated change rooms under the old stand, someone would throw a lighted newspaper into the showers to scare away the cockroaches, the social committee would cook a barbecue and sell long necks of cold beer, and the camaraderie and idle banter which permeated the club would begin. After the announcement of teams for Saturday there would be the normal jubilation and dummy spitting, and then the senior players would break out the cards and wallets, drink the long necks, and tell apocryphal stories of their youth to anyone who would listen. David would listen, avidly. He would fetch the long necks and, as his confidence increased, he stayed later and later and would eventually join in the revelry and have a few beers himself. As well as enhancing his off-field sporting education these moments spawned a gregarious lifetime of story telling.

Zac and I kept close tabs on David; after his estrangement from his father, Russell had asked that a tight rein be kept on the boy, that he not be allowed to get away with anything untoward. It was about then in his life that the tenacity and will to succeed, so evident in Pat, emerged. The early promise of great deeds was being realised. He won the West Torrens batting aggregate and average (without a century) for the 1973-74 season, and also took 16 wickets with his slows. In January 1974, he was appointed vice-captain of the South Australia Under 19 team and won batsman and player of the championship.

To watch him play against Western Australia in the last match of that Under 19 Championship was a gratifying experience. Western Australia and South Australia were undefeated and the winner would take home the Kookaburra Shield. A spin attack of Hookes, bowling "chinamen", and John Frick (another future State player) bowling left-arm orthodox, kept Western Australia to a moderate score. South Australia started badly. Terry Alderman had two quick wickets but a brash Hookes strode to the wicket and blasted Alderman out of the attack. If the club had allowed him to continue to develop his left-arm over-the-wrist spinners, so good was his "wrong-un" he may have become one of the State's great all-rounders, rather than just a great batsman.

David began work at the South Australian Lands Department in 1974, and his cricket continued to blossom. He scored his first century in senior cricket, 110 against Student

Teachers at Thebarton in the home and away games and 104 in the limited-overs competition and took six wickets against Prospect at Prospect Oval. He was rewarded with selection in the South Australian Colts team, chosen as twelfth man in one Sheffield Shield match, and named District Cricketer of the Year (now the Bradman Medal) and retained the West Torrens batting aggregate and average.

Although maturing quickly as a cricketer, he was still a teenager at heart and bought an old Vauxhall car that was too old to be classified second-hand; it was past its use-by-date. But Hookesy was intrigued by its paintwork, which was an off-white colour and illustrated with large, black footprints climbing over the car body, beginning on the boot and moving over the roof and finally down, across the bonnet to the radiator. Its top speed was a marathon runner's pace. On Saturday mornings, he would collect Zac Isaac and then his teenage mate, wicketkeeper Greg Quinn, and they would set off for the ground. The 32-year-old Zac was forced to sit in the back seat listening to teenage gibberish for the whole of the journey. He likened it to "talking in tongues", some unknown language. Hookesy was no geographer. He knew the Adelaide metropolitan area road system like Yasser Arafat knows the Vatican. On a trip to play at Salisbury, "Quinnie" noticed they were going past HM Yatala Labour Prison, which was many kilometres from their destination, and they were heading east rather than north. A quick u-turn and much experimentation enabled them to be at Salisbury Oval in time for the match, but not the warm-up.

Hookesy was fortunate to inherit valuable characteristics through both his maternal and paternal genealogy; his father Russell's began to show in his late teens. He was always full of fun, but now a keen sense of humour was emerging, as was the indelible laughter when taking the mickey; a desire to question was noticeable, and he began to make his own way through the conformity of the cricket world.

As he grew older he developed self-analysis and self-reliance and, of course, those captious subtleties in his conversation. How I loved his pedantry and the semantics. Hookesy could really entice you into his web, have you crash in a heap, and then you would both convulse with laughter.

I recall telling him how proud I was of completing a half marathon at the age of 44. He simply replied, "You couldn't have." I was quite deflated, having expected adulation or, at least, a compliment. Let down, I replied, "David, I did, I actually completed a half marathon." Again he retorted, "Did you also enter the half high jump and the half triple jump? Have you ever run a half 800 metres, or half 200 metres? They don't have half premierships or half Test matches do they? I accept that you completed the 21 kilometre race but a half marathon means that you pulled out of the marathon half way around." My ego returned and we sat down and pissed ourselves laughing.

At the end of the 1974-75 season, his West Torrens club mate and later South Australian team mate Kevin Lewis, persuaded him to travel to England to play for the Dulwich Cricket Club in the Surrey League. "Lew" and Hookesy, along with another

West Torrens team mate Rick Walsh, took a flat in Streatham, a suburb next door to Dulwich. They all played at Dulwich and drank at The Greyhound, a pub in Streatham once frequented by "great train robber" Ronnie Biggs. Lew was a groundsman at the club, while Hookesy secured employment as a lift driver at Harrods in London. Twenty-five pounds in salary was reduced to twenty by travel expenses so he left after two weeks, but not before the famous department store had supplied a larder of cheese, meat and bread for the Streatham flat.

He made ducks in each of the three pre-season trials for Dulwich, which threatened his place in the first eleven, but he survived. In the first game of the League season, with Dulwich reeling at three wickets for very close to the minimum, he took the opposition attack apart, led the victory charge and set the club on course for another premiership. He had a good all-round season particularly with his medium pacers and left-arm orthodox spinners: he scored 381 runs at 23.81 and took 25 wickets at 13.92. A few games with Surrey Second XI were an added bonus. Hookesy endeared himself to Dulwich because of his personality and attitude. In a Sunday fixture against Bexley Heath he provided the sun-drenched spectators with fine entertainment when he lifted the left-arm "darts" of a hapless Geoff Burton into the adjoining tennis courts for six sixes from the same over.

John Soldan, the Dulwich club captain formed such a close liaison with Hookesy that he flew the 22,500 kilometres for the funeral. That affinity with his Dulwich team mates was well illustrated, too, in other notable moments of confidence, bravado and a devil-may-care attitude. Lew and Hookesy, and a few of the Dulwich boys, planned a day trip to France: train from Victoria Station to Dover, ferry to Calais, and idle hours imbibing ales on board and in a local cafe was their idea of a big day out. On the return trip across The Channel an inebriated Lew got up to some horseplay. He removed Hookesy's passport from his hip pocket, hid it under a pillow in the ship's bar and, promptly forgot about it. Hookesy discovered his loss as he approached customs and immigration about 200 metres from the ship. Undaunted, he strode onwards and up to the counter, promptly engaged the officials in some banter, then proceeded to pass through the barrier. Only "DWH" could talk his way into England, minus a passport!

On another occasion Hookesy met a girl from Swindon, a town some distance to the west of London. He was rather taken with the young lady and decided to visit her for the week and, for the occasion, he borrowed Lew's battered Mini Minor, which had seen many a better day. On the Friday he arrived back to play for Dulwich – by train. Lew inquired as to the whereabouts of the Mini. Hookesy told Lew that it had broken down, but was quick to assure him it was on a motorway somewhere between Swindon and London, although he was unsure of the exact location. No retrieval team ever left Dulwich for Swindon.

The Dulwich members were hardly to know that within two years the brash 20-year-old would return to England, not as an allrounder to Dulwich, but to Lord's and The

Oval as a Test batsman. Nor could the Yorkshire ground staff, who ejected Lew and Hookesy from the 1975 Leeds Test match for boisterous behaviour, hardly have imagined that the next time they saw Hookesy at Headingley he would be bolstering Australia's middle-order batting.

On his return to West Torrens he resumed his interrupted friendship with Roxanne; he was chosen in the South Australian Sheffield Shield squad for the 1975-76 season; he made his first-class debut against Clive Lloyd's touring West Indians on 31st October. He scored an impressive 55, and remained in the first-class side for the rest of the season, but this was not the only cause for celebration in his cricket domain. On the 9th of December 1976, he was appointed captain of the West Torrens A grade side, when Ian Edgley prematurely relinquished the position. He was 21 years old, one of the youngest Eagles players to be granted the honour. When "Edge" went it concerned the committee and the selectors, but they put aside any reservations about Hookesy's youth and anointed him.

This is how Brian Flaherty, the club coach at the time, recalled the situation, and the atmosphere, in the rooms before the match, which was against Port Adelaide at Thebarton Oval: "Hookesy indicated that he wished to have a chat to the players before the game. He first expressed his pride in assuming the leadership role, and then calmly discussed the opposition. He knew every one of their players, their strengths and their weaknesses, what their temperaments were like and how he wanted each of his team mates to play. I felt that the kid knew more at 21 than I did at 42. Hookesy showed that he had the skills to gain the respect of his team, most of whom were older than he was. I knew then that the club had made the right decision."

Always self-confident, the new captain was able to handle all situations that confronted him on the field. On one memorable occasion he confronted Ken "KG" Cunningham, then the veteran State allrounder; later KG would co-host with Hookesy on the radio 5AA sport-talk program. KG was renowned for his backchat on the field. It was a match against Sturt at Unley Oval and after Hookesy had hit KG to the boundary the veteran explained to the youth, quite colourfully, that this was a man's game and, that with his technique he wouldn't be out there very long. Hookesy retorted that if KG would care to bowl the next ball in the same spot it would go over the fence, not into it.

At the beginning of the 1976 scholastic year, Hookesy finally decided, with Roxanne's encouragement, that he must matriculate. Back in 1972, the separation of his parents and cricket had compromised his study, and he had been forced to repeat matriculation. The second attempt was no more successful than the first, a failing he put down to the demands of cricket and "watching Roxanne study". This time, when Hookesy enrolled at the Marryatville High School Adult Education Centre, he was successful enough in his endeavours to be accepted into the Diploma in Physical Education at Adelaide Teachers College for 1977.

Kerry Packer, an organ recipient himself, and Robyn Hookes at the launch of
The David Hookes Foundation. Robyn remembers: "David had passionate views on
the donor program and, as a family, we had discussed it many times. He thought
it was such an incredible waste not to donate your organs. For us, there was no
decision to be made – of course, we would donate his organs."

The very young David Hookes.
The school uniform could have
signalled the early stages of
a regimented lifestyle, but
the bare feet, the hairstyle and
the glint in the eye forewarned us
that there were sure to be more
expansive moments in the offing.

Three stages in
a developing career.
Clockwise from below,
Colts selection February
1974; chosen as twelfth
man in the Sheffield Shield
against Queensland,
December 1974;
after making 185 and
105 against Queensland in
the Sheffield Shield,
February 1977.

The house in Torrensville where the young
David Hookes grew up.

DENIS BRIEN/KRISTOFER GELLMAN

The South Australian Under 19 Kookaburra Shield winning team in 1974. Hookes is front row, third from right. On his left is the coach, Chester Bennett, and Rick Darling, who played first-class cricket with Hookes, is middle row, first left. Bennett, respected as a coach of young people, tutored Ian, Greg and Trevor Chappell throughout their secondary school years at Prince Alfred College.

ACP

Breakfast for a budding champion. Pat Hookes and her young son celebrate his selection in a South Australian XI to play the touring West Indians in 1975.

Hookes's batting style was all flair, sometimes wondrously cross-legged, sometimes a cross-your-fingers job. But five centuries in six innings prompted the selectors to name him for the Centenary Test team in March 1977, and by then a beer was more of a photographic opportunity than breakfast with his mum.

"Baggy green" call-up, 1977.

In the Centenary Test, Hookes used an old, battered bat. "I went four long years with the same bat," he said – and it looked like it! But, once he signed for the breakaway World Series Cricket, and swapped the baggy green for the wattle yellow, he was able to afford a new bat, and much more.

In Australia's second innings in the Centenary Test, Hookes blitzed the bowling of the England captain Tony Greig. Here, in the 46th over of the innings, he offers Greig a taste of what was to come. This pull shot went for three runs, and impressed the umpire, Tom Brooks.

Historians, statisticians and trivia buffs remember that the famous over, when the two faced off, was the 57th. Hookes hit five fours in a row from Greig's off spinners. It was always going to be some feat to live up to.

Of course, nobody remembers Hookes's first innings in the Centenary Test when, capless and looking young enough to still be at school he made 17 before being caught in the slips – by Greig.

The late Bill O'Reilly said this about Hookes's famous innings: "He times the ball so well that it streaks through the off side field with an effortlessness that makes field placing appear a lost art."

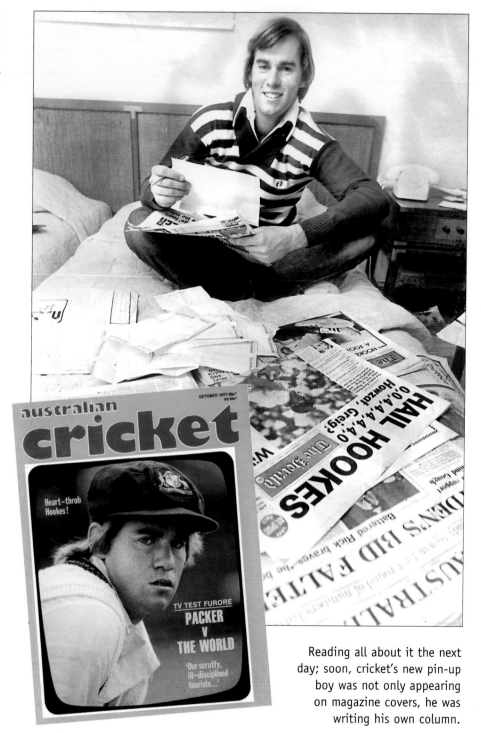

OCTOBER 1977 80c*
$2 90c*

australian
cricket

Heart-throb
Hookes!

TV TEST FURORE
PACKER
V
THE WORLD

'Our scruffy,
ill-disciplined
tourists...'

HAIL HOOKES

0,0,4,4,4,0
Howzat! Greig?

Reading all about it the next
day; soon, cricket's new pin-up
boy was not only appearing
on magazine covers, he was
writing his own column.

Well rugged up on his first Ashes tour, 1977. He said: "I could have done better. My technique, which isn't all that perfect, meant I needed a lot of cricket and the stop-start nature of the tour ... in the beginning it hardly stopped raining for seven weeks ... didn't help."

If the Centenary Test was a heady moment, more head-spinning times were ahead; when Hookes signed for World Series Cricket, sponsored by Kerry Packer (and Ronald McDonald), he found himself in the grand company of most of the champions of the game.

WSC, which pioneered cricket under lights, white balls and drop-in pitches, also introduced the batting bunker; Hookes with Ian David, who had played with him in the Centenary Test.

"New culture" shock. In WSC's first season players battled it out in front of sparse crowds; Hookes sweeps at VFL Park, watched by the wicketkeeper, the West Indian Deryck Murray.

Due to his matriculation exams he missed the three Sheffield Shield matches of the eastern states tour, but still compiled 788 runs in the five first-class matches that he played for South Australia. Matches for South Australia and the Centenary Test during term one of the 1977 academic year, and then selection in the Australian team to tour England meant that he attended only nine days of lectures. He therefore deferred his studies. World Series Cricket then changed Hookesy's life, radically. He withdrew from tertiary studies completely and never returned. Financially secure, he married Roxanne in October 1977.

By then, the lovable barefoot larrikin from working-class Torrensville had reached his goal of playing first-class cricket and had been made captain of his beloved West Torrens Eagles. And, he had achieved three more long-coveted goals, a century against Victoria, the right to wear a baggy green cap and had toured England with an Australian team. The world was at his feet. His friends, peers and club mates watched with approbation, interest and keen curiosity, to see how his life would evolve.

CHAPTER
II

David Hookes had his jaw smashed by a bumper during
Kerry Packer's World Series Cricket. When the ambulance
didn't arrive immediately, a concerned Packer came down
from where he was watching and announced that he would
drive the distressed and bloodied Hookes to hospital himself.

Magic,
and Mayhem

IAN CHAPPELL

David Hookes was playing a blinder at the old Sydney Showground in 1977-78. In the second World Series Cricket (WSC) Super Test he'd scored 81 and in partnership with Rod Marsh had helped right a WSC Australia innings that was in danger of being scuttled by the WSC West Indies pace quartet.

With the WSC Australians in trouble at five for 89 Hookes launched a counter-attack against the West Indies pace men. He hit 17 off one over from Joel Garner and 22, including 20 in boundaries, from Michael Holding. That is why it came as a shock when David suddenly missed an attempted hook shot from the bowling of Andy Roberts and crumpled in a heap, spitting out blood and broken teeth.

It must have been immediately obvious to those in the middle that Hookes was in trouble. Viv Richards, having rushed to his aid, quickly gestured to the pavilion for medical assistance and when Marsh, who'd trotted anxiously from the non-striker's end, saw the carnage he had a look of concern on his face. No cricketer likes to see a fellow player hurt in the line of duty; it's a nasty reminder how close we all are to suffering a serious injury.

Our physiotherapist, David "Doc" McErlane, assisted Hookesy off the ground, and I'd moved down from my vantage point in the grandstand to check his condition. "Sorry mate," Hookes mumbled through the blood in his mouth and the towel that was being used to catch the mess, much as a baby's napkin snares the food that doesn't fit in the aperture.

"You don't need to apologise," I said, probably stuck for anything sensible or sensitive to say. It's a situation captains don't prepare for because you hope it never happens on your watch. Now, when I think about that day, probably I should have been apologising to Hookesy.

You see I'd helped convince David it would be good for his cricket to join WSC. Not surprisingly Hookes was wrestling with his conscience over abandoning a career that had begun so brilliantly in Test cricket to opt for a bigger pay cheque. It must have been a traumatic time for Hookes, as he oscillated between taking the money and sticking with the traditional game. It was during this period he visited me a couple of times and was on the phone asking for advice. The decision would have been made more difficult for Hookes because he grew up following cricket closely and was well versed in the history and traditions of the game.

David used to love to talk about games he'd watched at the Adelaide Oval, and would often ask about some of his favourite players. He also used to remind me of the first time we met on the field. At the time, Hookes was a 17-year-old playing for West Torrens in a match against Glenelg at Thebarton Oval. Ironically, it was because West Torrens genuinely tried to get David a game in the lead up to WSC (when everyone else was banning players who'd signed with Kerry Packer) that I swapped clubs in my final season, 1979-80, and played with Hookesy.

However, when we were opponents back in 1972-73 David says he had me dropped in his first over. I vaguely recalled facing a young Hookes bowling his left-arm "chinaman" deliveries, but not much more. The way Hookesy told the story he deceived me in flight and I hit a straight forward, low catch to his skipper Ian Edgley at extra cover. "Edge" has a slightly different version; he admits it was a catch in that the ball reached him on the full, but he says only because he was such an agile fielder (a Talbot Smith fielding award winner) and that he dived full length to get a finger-tip on something he reckoned sounded like a cricket ball, but he couldn't be sure because he only heard it go whistling by!

The next time we met David was in the nets at State practice, and that is where I first became aware of this chance I'd given off his bowling a season or so before. After that he reminded me regularly. However, I did get my own back years later when we played together at West Torrens.

We were playing Teachers Colleges at Adelaide No.2 ground and, with Edgley away on business, I was skipper. Teachers had batted the first Saturday and made a score well over 300 as West Torrens toiled hard on a good pitch. We'd bowled our overs within the allotted time and even though it was a huge score to chase, Torrens had a batting line-up that contained two Test players (Hookes and me) and one Shield player who would later play for New Zealand (Jeff Crowe). So, we were confident that if it didn't rain on Friday night we'd overhaul the target.

It didn't rain but Teachers obviously had a theory that the West Torrens batsmen were a little impatient. Consequently they bowled their overs slowly and had a bit to say on the field that was audible to the batsmen. I duly took note of their tardiness, and the comments, and when we'd passed their score West Torrens had a lot of wickets in hand and Teachers still had plenty of overs to bowl.

I had to attend a South Australian selection meeting that was conveniently being held in the Adelaide Oval dressing room, so I could see what was happening outside on the No.2. As I left for the meeting it was just on six o'clock, the normal finishing time, but I informed Hookesy, whom I left in charge, "These so-and-so's think they're smarter than us so we'll show them how clever it is to bowl their overs slowly. Don't even think about declaring – make them complete the overs. Oh, and by the way," I added, "I'll be able to see everything from the Oval dressing room."

By the time I arrived back at the No.2 ground dressing room for a drink it was about 7.15pm and the opposition hadn't joined the West Torrens players, who were only a sip or two into their first beer. "Everything go okay?" I asked Hookesy. I thought David was going to explode: "It's all right for you. I was the one who copped all the abuse from the Teachers mob, you pillock," he said.

That was Hookesy's style, even at a young age; he was confident but most of the time was also respectful. He wasn't overawed by anyone's reputation, but he was aware of what people had achieved and used that success as motivation in setting his own goals. Just after he made the South Australian side, when he went to England to play with Dulwich, he reportedly acquired the nickname "The bumptious brat from Dulwich". I could see how in England's structured society he would have appeared brash but he was very quickly accepted and liked in the South Australian side.

From memory, David had the rare distinction of only being included in the State practice squad after his selection in the South Australian team for a game against the 1975-76 West Indies touring side. The selectors were making a habit of blooding young players against touring teams; the season before they'd plucked Wayne "Fang" Prior from the Salisbury side and he'd made a favourable impression against Mike Denness's MCC touring party.

By the time Hookes arrived on the scene Prior, a strong and lively fast bowler, was leading our attack and, along with a number of other younger players, contributed greatly to South Australia's Sheffield Shield win in the 1975-76 season. Even at that early stage of his career Hookes wasn't one to let the grass grow under his feet. He survived the withering pace of a Michael Holding onslaught in the game against the tourists, then he withstood the furious pace of Jeff Thomson to make a half-century in South Australia's second Shield match against Queensland. It was following this innings played at a vital time that I felt Hookes was going to make it at first-class level. The first couple of games had been a stern trial for a young player but those were only minor ordeals compared with what was occurring off the field.

Following a highly competitive opening contest against New South Wales, six players were reported, five of them South Australians. I happened to be one of the offenders but my report was for referring to Kerry O'Keeffe's penchant for not outs, rather than as most people thought, for bowling a protest over of deliveries that bypassed the batsman and landed in the wicketkeeper's gloves. I was annoyed that under the bonus points system, if the captain batting first declared when the points concluded (when the second new ball became due) he had no protection if the skipper batting second continued to build a lead, even though he couldn't gain any more bonus points.

So, I finished up bowling two overs of deliveries that flew over the batsman's head and landed in the wicketkeeper's gloves – because my first over of lobs caused O'Keeffe so much consternation that New South Wales had lost a wicket at the other end. My ploy went beyond a protest and became a tactic!

Anyway the South Australian Cricket Association administrators were so worried about the number of players reported they decided the team should meet with three officials to explain the on-field shenanigans. The SACA decreed that all 12 players, even though only five were reported, should meet individually with the chosen officials of whom president Phil Ridings, who like Hookes was from West Torrens, was one.

We claimed that was unfair because many of the players (Hookes, Rick Darling, Rick Drewer and Geoff Attenborough) were all playing their first season, while Prior was only in his second and Gary Cosier, ex-Victoria, and Denis Yagmich, ex-Western Australia, had only just transferred from interstate. The senior members of the side were worried the officials would harass the young players if they were on their own, and get them to say the older players were a bad influence.

The senior players proposed that all 12 members of the team go in together to be grilled. The eventual compromise allowed for at least one senior player to join each group. Hookesy wasn't in my group but I recall his answer when I asked him how his meeting went. He said: "Well, it lost a bit of credibility when 'Pancho' Ridings called me Russell, my father's name."

Later that season, relations between some SACA officials and me had deteriorated to the point where I decided not to go on the eastern tour to Sydney and Brisbane. I'd become extremely disillusioned about what I perceived were some poor selection decisions and, miserly player payments. Terry Jenner and Ashley Mallett then decided they weren't going if I wasn't and that resulted in a secret vote to determine whether we pulled out en masse.

After a second vote it was unanimous; the players weren't going if I wasn't the captain. Barry Curtin, a perennial source of wit in the side, had just fought his way back into the team and he managed to lighten an otherwise tense situation. He'd scored a half-century in our just completed crucial victory over Victoria and dryly observed, "Jeez, I finally get back in the team after 18 months and I've just voted myself out again."

After the vote there were a few young players, Hookes among them, wondering what on earth they'd done, but eventually sanity prevailed and we all went on tour. It was at that point that I said publicly, "I am no longer playing for the SACA, only for my fellow players." In the first match after that dispute, which was widely publicised as a strike, I stepped onto the SCG following the fall of the first wicket wearing a bright red South Australian cap. As I went from the asphalt onto the SCG grass a wag on The Hill stood up and shouted, "One out, all out."

It was in this acrimonious atmosphere that David began his first-class career. So you see why, roughly two years later when he had his jaw broken after missing a shot his name suggests he would normally hit, it probably should have been me doing the apologising. Following the blow to Hookes's jaw Dr Brian Corrigan did a quick examination and decided the best place for David was hospital. When the ambulance didn't arrive immediately Kerry Packer, who was in the stand watching the game, decided he would drive Hookes to hospital. David was made comfortable on the back seat of Kerry's car and the television magnate then sped off in a cloud of dust.

A few of the WSC Australian players visited David in hospital the next morning and Kerry was there when we arrived. One of the players asked Hookesy, "How was the trip to the hospital – comfortable?"

"You must be bloody joking," mumbled Hookes through clenched teeth that were wired together. "We did 100 miles an hour all the way, passed everything on the road and didn't even slow down for a red light or a stop sign. I was frightened stiff."

"Well that was the idea," Kerry piped up. "To take your mind off the pain of the broken jaw." Hookes made a spectacular return from that broken jaw. His second game back was at the same Sydney Showground and it was the One-day International final against the WSC West Indies. Cricketers have this analogy about coming back quickly after a hit in the head and Hookes was the classic example of "jumping straight back on the horse after a fall".

The only difference on this occasion was that Hookes, just like a jockey, was wearing a helmet, one of those bloody awful motorbike jobs that pre-empted the modern day head protection gear. It wasn't long before Roberts was recalled to the attack and predictably a bouncer followed. David lived up to his name this time and slightly off-balance hooked it over the square-leg boundary. Roberts followed with another bouncer and this time David hit it right in the middle and the ball soared over the rope to bring the cheering crowd to their feet.

That's why cricket crowds remembered David Hookes so fondly; he was always likely to produce a burst of spectacular shot-making that left the fans with a wonderful memory to take home. He was the type of player that fans thought, "I'd better go to the ground today, because it might be the day where Hookesy produces some magic."

While Hookes had a good year in 1975-76 and contributed to a memorable season by helping South Australia win the Shield after coming last the previous two campaigns, he didn't cap off his good work with a century.

The following season, 1976-77, I had retired and was working as a television commentator and I had the good fortune to be there when Hookes scored his debut first-class hundred that sparked an amazing sequence of centuries in Shield cricket. In just six innings at the Adelaide Oval, Hookes scored 750 runs. We televised most of those knocks and Hookesy certainly produced a lot of magic in that period, hammering the fence on both sides of the ground from backward point to extra cover. Using minimal footwork, but generating tremendous power through exquisite timing, he reminded me, and others, of the great South African left-hander Graeme Pollock who used to rocket the ball through the offside with seemingly little effort, and that is exactly what Hookes did regularly at the Adelaide Oval. The pickets must have longed for the days when advertising hoardings would come to the rescue and protect them from such a battering.

It was a heady time for a 21-year-old. That sequence of bowler bashing led to Centenary Test selection and the bombing of Tony Greig, his inclusion in the 1977 Ashes touring side and, finally, the invitation to join WSC. It all happened so quickly, and at such a critical time in his development, that it was understandable he had such a traumatic time making up his mind whether to accept the WSC offer or stick with the Australian Cricket Board.

Throughout the decision-making process we met on occasions and I convinced Hookes it would be good for his cricket to join WSC. I have no doubt it was the right decision at the time, but I can understand if David felt that because of the plethora of fast bowlers signed by Packer his education in playing spinners was neglected a little. In the end a poor tour of Pakistan in 1979-80, where he struggled against the spinners, probably dented his confidence a little and left him vulnerable, particularly to the ball turning away from his bat.

Nevertheless David was happy with his decision once he signed with WSC and we trained together regularly, and often played golf. Most of our training runs would start and finish back at the Adelaide University gymnasium. This involved a 15-minute run along the banks of the Torrens River. Hookesy had this habit of always pulling up when he reached the nearest corner of the extremely long gymnasium building, rather than at the entrance doorway. I used to chide him about this; that he would never beat an "old man" (almost 12 years age difference) as long as he refused to complete the course.

He did finally beat me, and that was in the annual City to Bay fun run where he went across the finish line about a second ahead of me and immediately threw up in the shoe of the runner who finished just in front of him. We used to laugh about that poor bloke getting the shock of his life at the finish line but we couldn't find any humour in being passed by a guy in a wheelchair. In those days it was rare to see a "wheelie" in such an event, so it was a severe blow to our egos when this wheelchair athlete easily passed us just as we were winding up for a sprint down Anzac Highway.

Like training, the golf matches were pretty competitive, usually played at The Grange where Hookesy was a member. Quite often we were joined by Banga Flaherty of West Torrens fame. In those days Banga worked with the 3M company, nowadays he lives on the Gold Coast and is a sports psychiatrist. I reckon he probably decided on that vocation after playing golf with Hookesy and me;

at the very least those matches would have convinced him that sportsmen need help.

Hookesy was just starting to play golf then and was a fairly erratic 16 marker. Being on single figures I could usually beat him, even if it required a bit of gamesmanship. But it was a different story on the tennis court, predictable given the amount of time he spent as a kid under the tutelage of his State champion half-brother Terry Cranage. So when I commenced wielding a racquet at the end of my cricket career I made sure he was my partner.

We had one memorable match at the Bellevue Hill, Adelaide home of famous Australian Rules identity Neil "Knuckles" Kerley. This was more than just a tennis match between friends; this was cricketers versus footballers, which meant a lot of pride was at stake. Former Port Adelaide player and coach John "Jack" Cahill, who just happens to be the father of former Australia Davis Cup player Darren, partnered Knuckles. Fortunately for us Darren must have got his tennis ability from his mother.

The first two sets of this best-of-five encounter went according to the book, Hookes and Chappell leading. However, my partner must have decided it was all too easy and he started to lairise. Very quickly the match was level at two sets all. In the crossover before the deciding set I gave my partner a piece of my mind. "Listen, you pillock, you're the most talented player on the court," I gently reminded Hookes, "but not when you're pissing about. This is cricketers versus footballers and we've got to win, so start playing seriously."

I was pretty sure this would have the desired affect on Hookesy but just in case my character assessment was astray I added another string to our bow. Just before Hookesy commenced serving in the final set I said to no one in particular on the other side of the net, "Tennis is a skill game therefore you footballers have got no chance against a couple of cricketers." When that didn't get much of a response I added, "The only way you pair could win this match is if you jumped the net and whacked us."

I realised I'd gone a bit too far when Knuckles, who was nearest the net, took a couple of paces forward. Just at that moment Hookesy served and, fortunately, Jack hit a good return so Knuckles' competitive instincts took over and he desperately tried to win the point. I refrained from passing any more comments about our opponents and restricted myself to congratulating Hookesy on the many good shots he played as we rolled to a comfortable victory in the fifth set.

Over the years we had a lot of other good victories as doubles partners, all of them gained without me lecturing or him lairising. Probably our most famous win was over an ex-Davis Cupper, Asif Karim of Kenya. Karim had been playing international tennis for about 20 years at the time and we generously "gave" him as a partner – some might say "gifted" – Paul Allott, the ex-England fast bowler, but these are facts easily overlooked when you're recounting a tale at the bar.

In the intervening period between my retirement and Hookesy becoming a commentator for Fox Sports, I used to hear from him fairly regularly. It would mostly be by phone as I was living in Sydney and it was usually to tell me about a young player who he thought had exciting prospects. I recall how excited he was when Darren "Boof" Lehmann first joined the South Australian team which was then under Hookesy's leadership. He would always emphasise that Lehmann was a left-hander, just as he would always point out that (at the time) the last three world record run scorers were molly-dukers, Sir Garfield Sobers, Brian Lara and Matthew Hayden, and then he would enthuse about Boof's stroke play.

He recounted one story about Lehmann when he first made the South Australian side that told me a lot about the young man. David had won the toss in a Shield match and inserted the opposition. When he arrived back in the dressing room Lehmann asked, "What are we doing?" Hookes replied, "We're in the field."

"So you lost the toss?" responded Lehman.

"No," replied Hookes, "actually, I won it."

"Lehmann charged forward," said Hookes, recounting the episode, "and grabbed me by the shirt."

"Why aren't we batting then? I drove to the ground this morning expecting to bat," railed Lehmann.

Hookes was impressed that a 19-year-old would think that way; that on the drive to the ground he was mentally preparing himself to bat because he would be at his freshest on the first morning and the Adelaide Oval had a reputation for being a good pitch. After hearing that story I always followed Darren's career with added interest and was delighted that his perseverance paid off and he experienced success at the international level late in his career. It was also one of the reasons why I invited Darren to join with a few of Hookesy's other cricketing mates in the SACA dressing room at the Adelaide Oval following the memorial service after his tragic death.

Being a current player Lehmann knew the staff well at Adelaide Oval and he arranged for a few jugs of beer to be delivered to the dressing room during the course of our final farewell to Hookesy. This was a part of the game Hookesy loved; sitting around the dressing room over a few beers, in his creams, discussing the game, handing out advice or just dropping the odd "hand grenade" to liven up the discussion. He was never short of an idea or a theory, either on how the game could be improved or how the opposition could be thwarted.

Apart from Lehmann, in that group telling Hookesy stories and reminiscing were Greg Blewett, Wayne Phillips, Tim Nielsen, Ian Edgley and Paul Nobes. Nobes was another player Hookesy was fond of because of his passion for the game and for the fact that he made the most of his ability. In addition to playing with David in the South Australian side, Nobes had also been in the West and East Torrens district sides under his captaincy and he recounted some amusing stories about Hookes the club player. Hookesy would have chuckled had he been there – in fact, I'm not sure I didn't hear one of his evil laughs when "Nobesy" was bringing the house down.

The Eagle
Has Landed

IAN EDGLEY

When David Hookes was promoted to the West Torrens A grade side in 1972 he established firm friendships with many of his regular team mates of whom I was one. This was strengthened when I became his captain during his third season. When Victorian selector Bill Jacobs approached him in 1983 to be captain-coach of Victoria, I began a long-term association as his lawyer and adviser and eventually had the honour of being best man at his marriage to Robyn.

Right from David's A grade debut he showed enormous potential and, although he only scored 134 runs in his first season, he always exuded confidence. In one of those games, Denis "Rocka" Brien, his mentor during the two previous seasons in B grade, was recalled to the A grade side for a match against Teachers Colleges at Thebarton. At one stage Rocka, batting with the 17-year-old, pushed a ball to midwicket and called for a quick, if suicidal, single.

David was sitting on his bat and slow to respond. The fieldsman, eyes agape at seeing an unprotected wicket and David a metre or so short, threw wildly and widely at the stumps, resulting in an overthrow to third man. Rocka apologised to David for the close call. The youth simply leaned on his bat, threw back his blonde mane, laughed and exclaimed, "Nice judgement of a run, Rocka. You just turned a half into two." Already, he could talk the talk.

Still a little wet behind the ears early in his senior career, he was subject to some good-natured ridicule from his more senior team mates. In a match against Salisbury the brains trust suggested that in a second innings, on which there was nothing riding, he be given the chance to open the batting to gain more experience. The real reason was that someone had upset Wayne Prior. "Fang" was at his peak and bowled at the kid with all the fire and venom that he could muster, while team mates, safe beyond the boundary, chuckled. David won out and remained unconquered at stumps.

The next time he visited Salisbury I gave him the opportunity to bowl his slows. A deep field was set for the straight hits and he was encouraged to give the ball some air. An adventurous batsman advanced down the pitch and drove furiously at a ball of full length, lofting it, but only managed to get the ball on the toe of the bat. As the ball passed overhead David had eyes only for the batsman, giving him a long, triumphal look that said, "I've sucked you in." David thought the ball would be easily caught in the deep, until there was a thud … as the ball dropped two metres behind the bowler! Had David watched the ball there was a simple catch-and-bowl chance on offer. The crimson-faced youth took a few seasons to live down the incident. However, to his credit he retained his confidence, laughed it off and, above all, learned about the lighter side of cricket life. There were to be many recipients on the end of some Hookes's tongue-in-cheek badgering in the future.

David's contribution to West Torrens club cricket was enormous. One of the early highlights of his first-grade career was a swashbuckling innings in the South Australian Cricket Association limited-overs competition, the Gillette Cup, against Sturt at their Hawthorn home ground. The Hawthorn curator had put little effort into the preparation of the centre strip. A large bare and disintegrating area presented itself on a good length, while kikuyu runners advancing across the pitch held other bare patches together. Sturt won the toss and unwisely invited West Torrens to bat. The wicket was only going to deteriorate further.

The Eagles openers were dismissed for little return. David, then 19 years old, entered the arena as the number three and soon lost his next partner. I moved into the number five slot and was privileged to witness a magnificent, but savage attack on a helpless Sturt attack. I chipped him that I had batted behind him but beaten him to the half century. This needled him into a blitz of power and smite in which David moved from 50 to his century while I scored two.

He hit nine fours and four sixes, three from one over of leg spinner Derek Grove, and included one which cleared the club house and crashed into the wall of the nearby Church of Christ as worshippers were leaving the building. The last 50 of the partnership was posted in 13 minutes, almost all from David's bat. He then proceeded to demolish the Sturt batting line up by taking six for 41.

A further highlight of his performances in the SACA district limited-overs competition came in an outstanding win in the West End Cup final against Sturt in 1988-89. Hookes and Paul Nobes opened the batting. Gordon Schwartz of *The Advertiser* wrote:

"Victor Richardson would have nodded his approval as a sweetly-timed six by David Hookes bounced through the open Adelaide Oval gates that bear Richardson's name. Hookes was at his arrogant best as he reduced the pace attack to cannon fodder."

In the 15th over of the innings, delivered by future Test player Colin Miller, David blasted him for a six, two, three fours and another six, while a wide on the fourth delivery contributed to a total of 27 from the over. At that stage the score was no wicket for 110 and the run rate 7.33 per over. The captain was caught by his mate, Wayne Phillips for 95 from 76 balls, which included two sixes and 14 fours. Nobes had played a subsidiary role, which looked a shadow of his partner's until one analyses it more closely; David's 91 was scored from 122 deliveries in 164 minutes. The Eagles had amassed seven for 277 from the regulation 50 overs, and then the captain ensured that his match performance would not be forgotten by bowling left-arm orthodox slows and "chinamen" to grab five for 40 and a comfortable victory by 43 runs.

In November 1976, I had to relinquish the captaincy and the club appointed David in my place. In his first game as captain he demonstrated that he was prepared to act "outside of the square". In a "dead" second innings I was fielding in the gully and the ball was edged wide of me. I moved to the ball, picked it up and hurled it at the unprotected stumps at the bowler's end with overthrows the result. This upset the skipper, who claimed I was making a farce of the game, and ordered me from the playing arena. It was an extremely hot day so I was able to enjoy the remainder of the afternoon from a comfortable seat on the other side of the pickets. David was strong on team discipline from the first. And, the incident did nothing to dampen our friendship.

His greatest performance with the ball was in November 1981 when, against Glenelg at Adelaide Oval No.2, he opened the bowling and took seven for 46. It devastated Glenelg who made only 93 in the first innings. Barry Curtin and David Cassidy opened for West Torrens and wiped off the required runs in 19 overs. Before stumps David had again overwhelmed the opposition, removing four more batsmen. The carnage continued on the next Saturday; Glenelg made only 85, and David claimed the rest of the wickets except for one run out.

It was a super rout and David, in finishing with match figures of 15 for 81, joined a very elite group of cricketers. Only three other players had taken 15 wickets in a match in the SACA competition: G Sharp (Kent and South Adelaide) in 1881-82, Bill Whitty (East Torrens) 1913-14, Bob McLean (Port Adelaide) 1944-45, and only Sharp's 15 for 61 bettered David's feat.

Many great and quick fire performances came from the bat of David Hookes at West Torrens, but probably his 173 against Glenelg at Adelaide Oval No.2 in 1985, was his most daunting. In a tick under three hours, he hit 20 fours and eight sixes; many of the latter landed in the adjacent Memorial Drive tennis courts, causing players to call for lets as they went scurrying to avoid injury.

David was as well known for his off-field antics at West Torrens as he was for his on-field demolitions. Soon after his marriage to Roxanne, David bought a flashy car, an Alfa Romeo. He was invited to team mate Roger Dugan's 21st birthday celebrations and as Roxanne was away for the weekend, went alone. He imbibed a little too freely but still decided to drive home at the end of the evening. Fortunately he caused no damage to others or to property, and, for his stupidity, was to learn a valuable lesson. On the drive back to West Lakes he began to feel nauseous, so wound the window down to get some fresh air.

It was a chilly night, and the cold breeze blowing off St Vincent's Gulf filled and chilled the car. This merely increased David's discomfort, so he wound the window up again. His nausea not only returned, it worsened and he was ill through what he imagined was the once opened window space. On arriving home he decided to go straight to bed, as he had an early State cricket practice the next day. Next morning, because he was a bit rushed, he ignored the temptation to use a bucket of hot water and detergent to rejuvenate the Alfa and instead decided on an "outside the square" course of action: he would use the nearby automatic car wash to clean the inside of the car.

He had previously noted that soon after entering the wash small spurts of water spat at the car, so his plan was to have the driver's door open to receive just enough of these spurts on the exposed inside of the window to clean it. What he hadn't noted was that the machine, once it was activated, moved over the car on a track. This oversight resulted in the open door of the Alfa suddenly being jammed against the side of the car wash ... and David trying desperately to close it. The machine won. Large geysers of water and suds poured into the Alfa and on to David until the washing time expired. It was three weeks before it dried out, after which it was left with a used car dealer.

South Australia National Football League matches were played at Thebarton Oval from 1921 until 1989. During the 1980s, the West Torrens Cricket Club would fill to capacity on Saturday afternoons in the winter to watch the local West Torrens home games. The prime viewing point for David and many of his mates was the landing at the top of the exterior stairs leading to the clubroom bar.

This spot lent itself to the atmosphere of the crowd. However, the canopy of a young, yet substantial gum tree, whose circumference was about a metre and a half, obscured the view of the northwest forward pocket. This frustrated the lads, as the wind would often push the ball into this pocket.

Every Thursday evening in winter, as part of their off-season fitness program, David, Roger Dugan and Kevin Lewis would play squash at the Cross Road Centre, which David managed. On the way home, David and "Duges" would have a drink at the Rex Hotel. One Thursday, the conversation centred on the tree, one beer led to another and finally, David said, "The tree has got to go." The intrepid duo jumped into David's canary yellow Jaguar and set off to his mother's house, where they rummaged in her shed until they found an axe, then headed for Thebby Oval. They set about the tree with great gusto, taking turns with the axe. Because it was a still, crystal clear night the axe blows echoed for some distance and attracted the interest of soccer players training on nearby Kings Reserve. David explained they were removing the tree with local council approval and it was being done at night so as not to upset environmentalists. The pair had intended leaving the tree in such a precarious situation that the council would have to remove it, but their enthusiasm knew no bounds and the tree fell across the driveway and on to the mound in front of the clubrooms. David confessed a decade later. Controversy and David were fellow travellers.

His game plan came unstuck in the A-grade grand final against Salisbury in the 1987-88 season, although many maintain it was one of the great matches in SACA club history and probably the greatest grand final. David won the toss and West Torrens were two for 224 when he joined Paul Nobes, who was at his belligerent best in making 215 before succumbing to dehydration. The *Sunday Mail* writer Andrew Tobin wrote:

"After tea it was a run feast for Torrens when Hookes strode to the wicket and tossed a six off the first ball he faced. It was off (Peter) Sleep and the leg spinner's State captain gave no quarter as he banged four more sixes and four fours in his short stay. Hookes bludgeoned the Salisbury attack for 87 off only 68 balls."

The next day Salisbury faced the daunting task of scoring 393 to win, at four runs an over; it was a tough assignment, but their first six batsmen had, or would soon play first-class cricket and three would go on to play for Australia. West Torrens, on the other hand, didn't have to dismiss Salisbury to win. Under the by-laws, the declaration the previous evening was compulsory and West Torrens were only required to bowl the 100 overs which they had received. West Torrens began well and soon Salisbury were two for 64. This brought David's attacking nature bubbling to the surface and he decided that he could dismiss the opposition rather than contain them. Darren Lehmann hit the winning run from the first ball of the last over at 6.16pm, eight minutes after official sunset. The bowlers and fielders toiled courageously but many West Torrens observers couldn't understand why David made so little use of Roger Dugan's slows. Whilst not a penetrating bowler, Roger was one of the competition's most accurate left-arm orthodox bowlers. Earlier in his first-class career Roger had bowled 23 overs to a strong New South Wales top order for a mere 21 runs.

West Torrens hadn't won a premiership since 1961-62 so many a critic laid the blame at David's feet – "his tactic should have been to restrict Salisbury, and no bowler was better equipped for that role than Roger," they maintained. It was a disappointing week for David; he led his State and club to final losses on consecutive Sundays – South Australia lost the McDonald's Cup final to New South Wales – and he missed a place in the Australian team to tour Pakistan, despite making 1,149 first-class runs and being named Sheffield Shield Cricketer of the Year.

Of David's many positive attributes, loyalty to friends, to team mates and to working colleagues stood out. He must have sent thousands of postcards to acquaintances when on tour, or working overseas. He never forgot you. In 1997, he was guest speaker at the Melbourne Football Club breakfast before the Crows grand final victory and was to be remunerated in either cash or two tickets to the match. I had a ticket, but my wife Rose and daughter Amy, who were in Melbourne with me, didn't. David took the two tickets as payment and immediately gave them to Rose and Amy.

At the West Torrens Cricket Club Centenary Dinner he and another former player, Ian Chappell, flew to Adelaide as guest speakers and did not charge a fee. In similar circumstances he arrived in Adelaide for a 30-year reunion of the first South Australian team to win the Australian Under 19 Championship and, the Underdale High school reunion of his matriculation year.

Rose and I met him at Wimbledon. David had arranged for tickets to be left at the gate, but when the three of us arrived it transpired that somebody had sold the tickets on the side. David talked his way into the complex and returned with entry for all three of us, admission to the players' bar and a return to our hotel in an official car.

My family had a holiday house at Penneshaw on South Australia's Kangaroo Island. David consented to come to the island, for no fee, to play in a double-wicket cricket match to raise funds for the local cricket club. In the first round, he and his partner met the brothers, "Spic" and "Spec", one of whom bowled right-arm "nothings". David decided that a long hit over long on was the best way to deal with such bowling. But he toed the ball and presented a simple skier to the other brother at mid on, creating the following scoreline: Hookes, ct "Spic" b "Spec" 1. Whenever he visited the Island he never failed to offer coaching sessions to intrigued and infatuated Penneshaw youngsters.

Unlucky Eagle,
No 13

DAVID RAGGATT

David Hookes's brother, Terry, called him the "West Torrens-Thebby Oval Kid". There could not have been a better description of the boy born and bred 400 metres, or four (David Hookes) drop kicks from Thebarton Oval. No matter where "Hook" was he never forgot where he came from. I could be wrong, but I don't think there were too many of his mates from those days who would have met Princess Diana, let alone knocked her back for a dance.

The kid who loved his sport never changed; how lucky was he to have worked as a sports journalist, working in a field that he loved? Hook displayed silky skills at football, whether as the barefoot kid having a kick with his brother in the street, a Thebarton Primary kid, an Underdale High teenager or a West Torrens Under 19 player.

It was during our time in that West Torrens Under 19 team that I got to know Hook. Our coach of the 1973 premiership team, Reg Gibson, recalls many years prior to that a very young David Hookes, probably about 10 or 11 years of age, watching the Reserves team train and always standing behind the goals to kick the footballs back when they went over the fence.

That early training helped Hook become a very handy player. He was a defender, either full-back or half-back, which was surprising because his cricket career was quite the opposite – all attack. The 1973 Under 19s premiership year was a bittersweet one for Hook because, after playing every game for the season, he was omitted from the grand final team. Reg Gibson relates, how every time he saw Hook afterwards, Hook would jokingly call Reg "the little prick" that dropped him from the grand final.

To make it tougher on Hook that grand final was played at Adelaide Oval. Still, he eventually had his day at his favourite ground, whether it was the 462 partnership with Wayne Phillips or the hundred off 34 balls against Victoria, or, any of his other great cricketing triumphs.

Hook remained a staunch Eagles supporter; he would have been particularly pleased with the blue and yellow flowers (Eagles colours) on the coffin.

Over the years, Eagles supporters had little to celebrate; a rare highlight was watching the Eagles beat the mob from Port Adelaide for the 1983 night premiership at Thebarton Oval. You'd have thought we'd won the AFL premiership at the MCG. We watched the game from the top of the stairs to the West Torrens Cricket Club at the northern end of the ground – with an enhanced view of the oval thanks to the pruning done by Hook and "Duges" to that tree which had forever impeded our view.

When Hook was still living in Adelaide there was no questioning his allegiance to the Eagles in South Australia, but we were amazed to find out he was also a fanatical Collingwood supporter in the VFL. He would proudly wear a Collingwood tie and when possible attend their games in Melbourne. The general consensus is he only supported them so he could have a contrary opinion to everyone else on the subject! After all, there was never going to be anyone in South Australia who would side with him in a Collingwood discussion.

Over his adult life, Hook received many approaches to move to Melbourne and when he finally relented I had the pleasure of travelling with him. It was AFL grand final eve 1994 and it was a very funny car trip. I happened to be driving when we crossed the South Australia-Victoria border. At that precise point I stopped talking to him! And, did he get shitty. I finally let go and said, "Don't talk to me, you bloody Victorian."

We laughed for ages because we had shared a lengthy and healthy dislike for everything Victorian to the point of questioning, "Were they on the same side as us in the World Wars?"

Ironically, Hook becoming a Victorian created a new situation. The Adelaide Football Club (the Crows) were competing in the AFL and again, so as to have a different view on things and being a very passionate Croweater, Hook became a mad Adelaide supporter. He assisted the Crows with many functions in Melbourne, and eventually became an official "Crows Ambassador". He was beside himself in 1997 and 1998 when the Crows won back-to-back premierships at the MCG, and he hosted the premiership celebrations on those two very special Saturdays. I'm sure he drove his 3AW listeners crazy with his rantings about "his" team, the Crows.

So many true things have been written and said about David since his tragic death; Reverend Steve Ogden, at David's funeral, said he had "charisma with a common touch" and that he showed "amazing amounts of loyalty to his mates". Neil Mitchell spoke of how David lived by the adage, "Get on the front foot and have a go". Wayne Phillips said, "Maaaaate, the world is a lesser place for us all, now you have gone."

Hook taught us all so much, from the time I first knew him when he was wearing

No 13 in the Eagles Under 19s up until the last time I spoke with him. His advice was not to dwell on things – "Just get on with it," he'd say. And, he believed, that "every man stood on the same playing field".

CHAPTER
III

David Hookes entered "big cricket" at a time of trenchant anti-establishment sentiment and in his initial first-class season was unwittingly embroiled in strike action. He was surrounded by militant, sometimes abrasive men and was dumbfounded by the scale of personal abuse.

Match of a Lifetime

MIKE COWARD

David's achievement in slaying the giant that was the England captain Tony Greig that unforgettable 14th day of March 1977 instantly became a part of the rich lore of the glorious game. Five daring and consecutive shots to the boundary, by a boy on a stage that tested the nerve of older and hard-bitten men, vested David with a new identity.

From that day forth, the name of David Hookes and the regal celebration of a century of Test match cricket have been synonymous. And this is how it will always be. Yet while it is a wonderful tale, which surely will be told down the ages, the story behind the story is just as alluring. Furthermore, it provides an insight into the character of the man who was destined to maintain such a powerful public presence throughout his life.

Come the last week of October 1976, as South Australia prepared for the first Sheffield Shield match of the new season against Western Australia at beautiful Adelaide Oval, David was seriously distracted and mentally unprepared for the imminent confrontation with Dennis Lillee, Mick Malone and Bruce Yardley and their colleagues.

Earlier in the year he had enrolled at Marryatville High school in Adelaide's leafy eastern suburbs to repeat his matriculation in order to enhance his employment prospects beyond cricket. Now, with the suddenness that befalls even adult education students, the final examinations were upon him.

The fact he had turned 21 five months earlier hadn't instantly delivered him wisdom and knowledge and he approached the exams with some trepidation.

A year earlier to the week, he had been given a searching examination of a different kind – by the legendary West Indian fast bowler Andy Roberts and his 21-year-old protégé Michael Holding. And he passed with distinction, second top scoring to Gary Cosier (130) with an invaluable 55 in his first-class debut for South Australia. He was neither intimidated by the moment nor by the reputation of the bowlers and, from number seven, batted for 138 minutes and struck three boundaries in a performance that signalled to the cricket community that a new star had appeared in the firmament.

So for once in his young life, as he so freely admitted, he entered the summer more concerned with the detail of his school textbooks than the cricket books he had read so voraciously since boyhood.

Choosing to swot at times usually devoted to net practice, David was unready when the battle lines were drawn and he was dismissed cheaply as South Australia were overwhelmed by nine wickets by Western Australia.

The examination schedule left David with no option but to withdraw from the annual tour of the eastern states and, while his team mates headed for Brisbane in the second week of November, he repaired to a darkened room to face the music of a very different kind.

Monitoring events from afar he prayed his exam results were infinitely better than were South Australia's. Seemingly bereft of direction and inspiration following the retirement of Ian Chappell after winning the Sheffield Shield the previous year, South Australia lost by an innings and 45 runs to Queensland, by 132 runs to New South Wales and an innings and 83 runs to Victoria.

It was an unsettled time in the annals of South Australian cricket as the captaincy alternated between Ashley Woodcock, Gary Cosier and Bob Blewett. Be that as it may, the selectors had faith that David could make a difference and, as soon as his examinations and Christmas festivities were at an end, he was reinstated for the return match with Western Australia in Perth.

However, the tale of woe continued. South Australia were defeated by an innings and 79 runs in a little more than two days and a session and David was caught at the wicket by captain Rod Marsh from the bowling of earnest paceman and peripheral International Wayne Clark for one and three.

As the international season with Pakistan gained momentum, cricket commentators in Adelaide appealed to the South Australian selectors to overlook David for the rest of the season to allow him to regain form and confidence with his beloved West Torrens club in the district competition. There was no doubting his rich natural talent, they chorused, but he needed more time to develop.

David agreed and fully expected to be omitted from the next team to play Victoria at Adelaide Oval. Nor was it a matter of steeling himself for the decision. It wouldn't have fussed him greatly had he been dropped. In some ways it would have been a relief.

The weekend before the team announcement David batted for West Torrens against Prospect at Thebarton Oval. Still out of sorts after such a disjointed season he was pushing, poking and prodding when, having made just four, he spooned a return catch to Bob May. May dropped a straightforward interception, the reprieved David made plenty and the State selectors, hopeful he had regained his poise, rhythm and confidence, retained him.

Never could they have imagined the significance of their decision. This time under the command of Blewett, South Australia were brushed aside by an innings and 123. There was, however, a shining light. David scored 163 in a total of 290 to reaffirm that indeed there was a new star in the galaxy.

Given his travails earlier in the summer his innings was extraordinary, coming from 208 balls in exactly four hours with 10 fours and seven sixes. The Adelaide media, which had so fretted for him just weeks earlier, rejoiced at his success and trumpeted his ability to honour the South Australian tradition of playing aggressive cricket. Under Les Favell, a long-serving captain and daring opening batsmen and his successor, Ian Chappell, South Australia had established an enviable reputation for making the game supremely entertaining for the paying public.

David suddenly could do no wrong and over the next three weeks scored spectacular hundreds in each innings of matches with Queensland and New South Wales to bring to five his number of centuries in six innings in a fabulous February. So rich was the vein of form he had discovered, the Australian selectors under the chairmanship of Phil Ridings, himself a West Torrens and South Australian cricketer of distinction in his sprightly days, felt compelled to put his name into the mix for the Centenary Test.

Be it known as "Little Detroit," "The City of Churches" or "The Festival City", Adelaide in February can be excruciatingly hot. And so it was in 1977, around about the century in the old Fahrenheit reading for much of the month. Furthermore, the leading bowlers in the land were in New Zealand with the Australian team following the drawn home series with Pakistan. The Victorian attack had been weakened by the absence of Max Walker while NSW had to cope without Gary Gilmour, Doug Walters and Kerry O'Keeffe.

Be that as it may, David was in imperious form and his freshness and youthful daring captured the attention and imagination of people everywhere. He was staggered that the runs "came from nowhere", as he was given to saying, but at the same time could scarcely credit his level of exhilaration. His sense of euphoria was tempered only by the fact South Australia continued to perform poorly although, in this instance, they managed to tie with Queensland and draw with NSW.

The first hundred against Queensland was the highest of the five, a spectacular 185 after arriving at the crease with the innings again in disarray. On this occasion, however, he enlisted the assistance of Blewett, Peter Sleep and wicketkeeper Russell Vincent and finally South Australia had a score of 431 to show for their labors. David faced 228 balls in four hours and 10 minutes and struck 17 fours and two sixes. In the second innings David again set about the Queensland attack taking 105 from them off just 90 balls in 101 minutes with 11 fours and two sixes.

While there was a crowd of only 1,886 on the opening day of the New South Wales match it was nearly twice the first-day attendance of the previous week, and there was an unmistakable optimism that David would continue on his merry way. And so he did, with 135 in 157 minutes with 17 boundaries and a six.

And, to the unbridled delight of somewhat subdued South Australian supporters, he found an ally in opening batsman Tony Handrickan, who in just his second first-class appearance, gathered 113 and helped David add 204 in two hours 14 minutes in an enterprising fourth wicket stand. In the second innings David helped convert a 66-run deficit into an advantage of 268 with a hand of 156 in 17 minutes shy of four hours with 11 fours, one five and two sixes. He was missed at six, 32 and 115 but in the overall scheme of things these lapses counted for little and he was hailed as a prodigy as the first Australian to score a century in each innings of successive first-class matches.

While it seemed improbable the selectors would make any changes to the team that had drawn the first and won the second of just two Tests in New Zealand speculation was rife that David would be a contender for The Ashes tour of 1977.

David had become an instant celebrity and on the day the Centenary Test team was announced he was invited to the studio of a commercial television network at North Adelaide to comment on the teams and analyse the match.

When his name was read out by the reporter alongside him he mumbled, "Oh, shit!" before regaining his poise and telling viewers of his shock, pride and excitement at his promotion.

His selection was the culmination of an extraordinary few weeks in his life and he was numb, and brimful of mixed emotions as he drove home to field countless congratulatory calls. Over the ensuing years, when he spoke of his path to glory, he would invariably include this observation: "I guess it is a story you can tell young kids in this country – it is true, you are only six or seven innings away from playing for Australia from where you are in club cricket. Okay, it's a long time since that has occurred but the ethos and philosophy of Australian club cricket, to first-class cricket to Test cricket is to some extent still there."

Unlike many of his contemporaries, David understood the significance of playing in a match to celebrate the greatness, longevity and sanctity of Test match cricket. For as long as he could remember he had devoured books and magazines on the game and he was as familiar with the names of Woodfull, Kippax, Ryder, Macartney and McCabe as he was with any of the modern stars at home and abroad. He knew Charles Bannerman had faced the first ball in Test cricket and scored a hundred for good measure. Now, 100 years later, he was to have his chance. Century, centenary, hundred: these were the magic words of the moment.

Given he was 13 years younger than his stepbrother, Terry Cranage, David had effectively grown up as an only child and consequently had developed a fierce independence and resourcefulness. As he didn't have a coach or mentor outside the team environment he was given an aggressive and uncompromising education by well-meaning, if often aggressive, men in the dressing rooms at Thebarton and Adelaide Ovals.

He was reared at a time of trenchant anti-establishment sentiment at all levels of the game, and in his initial first-class season in 1975-76 was unwittingly embroiled in the infamous strike action by his guru Ian Chappell. He was surrounded by militant and sometimes abrasive men and was dumbfounded by the scale of the sledging and personal abuse in his first Shield game when six or seven players were placed on report.

Australian cricket in the 1970s was no place for the faint-hearted and, at 21, David was already developing the thick hide that was required to prosper. After all, he had first been sledged at 13 for wearing short pants in C-grade district competition. Later in his life David often expressed regret that there was no one on hand to "dilute the mood", as he put it. He was an impressionable young man and to some extent he was seduced by the swagger of the times.

Certainly he didn't lack confidence when he reached Melbourne for the match of a lifetime, although he soon learned that his cricket education was far from complete. In 1977 the Melbourne Cricket Ground nets were on the sacred turf beneath the old 1937 Southern grandstand and there David, frustrated at his inability to play Dennis Lillee with any sureness, knocked the ball back to Lillee along the ground. Lillee kicked it back to him. This happened two or three times until Greg Chappell called to David from the adjacent net: "If you want him to bowl to you pick it up and throw it back and show him some respect." David was embarrassed that he was brought to heel in such a fashion, as he fully understood net etiquette. He put the lapse down to nervous excitement and hoped Lillee would, too.

It was, however, of some comfort to him to realise he was no more nervous than every other member of the team. Certainly he was awestruck at the passing parade of legendary cricketers, but so too were his team mates. No sooner had he made a special sighting of one than he heard Greg Chappell speak excitedly of seeing Harold Larwood, while Lillee talked of his meeting with Bill Voce and Rod Marsh of his conversation with Godfrey Evans. Not only boys have heroes.

For more than a quarter of a century now much has been said and written about the exchanges between David and the England captain, Tony Greig, both on and off the field at the Centenary Test. Some stories are true, some apocryphal and all seem to have been embroidered and embellished. Indeed, Greig, to this day, has no recall of taunting David during a lavish cocktail party at the MCG in advance of the Test.

Conversely, David had clear recall of the incident and never failed to mention it whenever he was interviewed about the Centenary Test, and often included it in his often humorous public speaking presentations. Upon sighting David at the function Greig chipped: "Not another Australian left-hander who can't bat." David, somewhat taken aback, said he looked about to see if he could see Marsh and Gary Gilmour, but in their absence presumed the remark had been directed at him. He didn't dignify it with a reply but he did not forget it. He reasoned his moment would come. And come it did that glorious afternoon before a crowd of 55,399.

To that point the match had not gone according to the plans devised by the captains and, indeed, the Melbourne Cricket Club which organised the ambitious celebration at the recommendation of then club vice-president Hans Ebeling, a fine cricketer for Victoria who made his solitary Test appearance on the 1934 tour of England. Indeed, following the dire first innings batting of both teams Ebeling and his hard-working committeemen feared the match would not last as long as the hectic schedule of associated events demanded.

Having been sent into bat by the aggressive Greig in conditions bound to assist the pace and seam bowlers, Australia were bundled out for 138 with only Chappell and Marsh managing to score more than 10. Furthermore, Rick McCosker was in the hands of specialists after a bouncer from Bob Willis broke his jaw. Chappell matched wits with Willis, John Lever, Chris Old and Derek Underwood for three minutes shy of four hours for 40 without scoring a boundary, and Marsh 93 minutes for 28 with three fours. To the undisguised anxiety of officials England were one for 29 at stumps on the first day.

However, 24 hours later, at the close of the second day they had an even firmer grip on their worry beads with Australia three for 104 in their second innings, England having been routed for just 95. David always loved to regale crowds with the story that after the first day's play, Greig declared: "This has been one of the great days. If I live to be 95, I'll never forget it." In the end he never forgot the ignominy of a scoreline of 95. Not one England player reached 20 as Lillee (six for 26) and Max Walker (four for 54) provided a master class for the benefit of the biggest crowd for the match – 62,505.

When Ian Davis fell for a characteristically classy 68 – the first half-century of the match – David joined Doug Walters, one of his favourite folk heroes, in the middle.

David loved Dougie's unconventional, even irreverent approach to the game and quirky sense of humour, and was thrilled to have the chance to bat with him. As David ducked inside the line of the opening volley of short deliveries from Willis and company, Walters just winked and smiled. That was all the reassurance he required. At lunch Australia were four for 186, with Walters on 66 and David 20, and with a lead of 229 the pendulum had tilted in Australia's favour. But immediately after the adjournment Walters was caught at the wicket by Alan Knott from Greig's bowling and the match was again very finely balanced. Marsh joined David.

An attacking player by nature, suddenly David asked himself why he was paying such deference to Greig's bowling. Was it because he was the England captain? It certainly couldn't be out of respect for his off-break bowling. Without wanting to seem too cocksure he considered Greig a very ordinary off spinner indeed.

The first two boundaries from the third and fourth deliveries of the over were premeditated. In his mind David resolved to drive Greig back over his head should the ball be given a little more air. And that is exactly what happened.

Experience had taught him that in such circumstances a spinner is likely to respond by whipping in a quicker delivery. His intuitiveness bore fruit and David needed just to help the delivery on its way for another boundary.

To use the vernacular of the dressing room, the fifth ball was "in the slot" and David hammered it to the pickets beyond Derek Randall in the covers. The sixth delivery was over-pitched and David played it with power and grace off his toes through mid-wicket to bring up his half-century, and the crowd to its feet. It was his favourite offering in the sequence. But still he wasn't finished. Since his days in short pants in C-grade district competition he derived a special thrill executing a cover drive and he unleashed another to the seventh delivery. And, had it not been for a desperate lunge by Dennis Amiss, the last ball would have ended up in the gutter as well.

The crowd was still on its feet at the end of the over, whipped into a state of near hysteria by David's command performance. Commentators were brimful of emotion as they described the euphoric scenes and scribes searched for more and more superlatives. Contrary to popular opinion Greig said little to David during the over. Indeed, the loudest voice belonged to Keith Fletcher, who at the end of the over appealed to Greig to be moved away from short leg to Underwood with David in such a mood. However, Greig told him to stand his ground and in the very next over Fletcher tumbled forward to take a good catch to end David's thrilling cameo.

As he left the ground to a memorable reception, Greig hissed: "Piss off."

In his autobiography with his good friend Alan Shiell, the former South Australian batsman, David confessed that he momentarily lost self-control and sledged the England captain. "I half stopped, and turned around and spat the dummy and said: 'At least I'm an Australian playing this game not a f – ing Pommy import.' I shouldn't have said anything, of course," David wrote.

After stumps that night, and in advance of the rest day, Greig came into the dressing room with a long-necked bottle of beer and two glasses and asked David if he could sit and yarn with him. It was a gesture of respect and goodwill that David appreciated and never forgot.

David had only been at the crease for two hours and five minutes yet he had turned the match decisively in Australia's favour and was the toast of one of the greatest sporting towns in the world. Nevertheless, he had to share some of the rest day headlines with McCosker, who had stunned his team mates and the cricket community at large by batting at 10 with his broken jaw swathed in bandages. Like everyone else at the ground that day, David never forgot the high emotion of the crowd singing "Waltzing McCosker" as the badly injured opener made his way to the middle.

Such was McCosker's courage that on the fourth day he held out long enough to shepherd Marsh to his century and in 2004 his score of 25 (in 88 minutes with three boundaries) was rated as the 50th greatest innings played by an Australian in a fascinating poll of former players, selectors, historians, statisticians and commentators.

Marsh, the pugnacious left-hander beloved by the people, batted for three minutes shy of five hours for his undefeated 110 (from 173 balls with 10 boundaries) to become the first Australian wicketkeeper to score a century against England. It was a magnificent accomplishment, and a suitable complement to his achievement in eclipsing Wally Grout's Australian record of 187 dismissals when he dismissed Lever in England's first innings. So bold was the fightback the Australians finally amassed nine for 419 declared and occupied the crease for 620 minutes. In the first innings Australia and England batted for a total of 500 minutes.

For victory England required 463, a score never achieved in a fourth innings. That they made such a valiant attempt to scale their Everest and ensure the game reached the tea adjournment on the final day, when the players were presented to Queen Elizabeth and the Duke of Edinburgh, was due to a remarkable achievement by Derek Randall. An impish, eccentric character, the 26-year-old Randall constructed the innings of his life to defy the Australians for seven hours and 28 minutes for a sparkling 174 that included 21 boundaries. He received significant support from Amiss, Greig, Knott and Mike Brearley, but in the end the target was out of reach and Australia triumphed by 45 runs – coincidentally the exact margin of Australia's victory in the first Test match played from the 15th to 19th March 1877.

Where in 1877 left-arm medium and orthodox slow bowler Thomas Kendall had been the Australian hero with the startling analysis of seven for 55 (off 33.1 overs) in his first-class debut, in 1977 the standard was carried with great pride by the indefatigable Lillee. Renowned as the world's greatest fast bowler Lillee, with characteristic courage and determination, toiled to take five for 139 (off 34.4 overs) and finish with the remarkable match figures of 11 for 165 (off 47.7 overs).

[It was not until 1979-80 that Australia and New Zealand reverted to six ball overs and so fell into line with the rest of the cricket world.]

The achievement of Lillee and his colleagues was seen in a vastly different light two months later when news finally emerged of the formation of the revolutionary World Series Cricket movement by the media magnate Kerry Packer. Lillee, well known for his militancy, had been the first to sign. To the disbelief of the "cricket establishment" and the game's faithful, the contracts were first discreetly placed before the elite Australian players on their brief tour of New Zealand which ended just 11 days before the Centenary Test. More startling was the revelation some contracts were completed and signed in the dressing room during the Centenary Test.

David, of course, had not toured New Zealand and was oblivious to all the clandestine discussions within the dressing room, although it did cross his mind that 400 dollars was a miserly fee for such an important match that had drawn an aggregate crowd of 248,260 and generated gate takings of 418,018 dollars. But, then again, he rationalised that 400 dollars was a significant sum for a student teacher, and remained quiet.

He was not, however, unaware of the extent of the antagonism the players felt toward the establishment generally and officers of the Australian Cricket Board in particular. Immediately following his first innings dismissal for 17 David was approached in the dressing room by Australian Cricket Board chief executive David Richards and told to change his shoes.

David had batted in his favourite Adidas rubber-soled sandshoes that had brought him such good fortune in Adelaide during those blazing hot February days. As a consequence, the canvas was soaked in sweat that caused the three identifying stripes to be more conspicuous than was customarily the case. Richards suggested David had painted the stripes to draw attention to the Adidas brand. In fact, he was guilty only of not cleaning his shoes and immediately whitened them and wore them again for his famous cameo in the second innings.

Certainly Greg Chappell made it clear to Richards that he had the interests of his player and not the ACB at heart. Such was David's impact that prominent television personalities Don Lane and Ernie Sigley immediately approached him with an offer to manage his affairs. Suddenly he was a very marketable young man.

Ian Chappell suggested David delay any decision on personal management until he had spoken with John Cornell, a noted comedian and television identity and close friend of Lillee who had played a significant role in convincing Packer of the merits of forming the radical World Series Cricket movement. David duly signed with World Series – a decision many critics considered unwise at such a tender age and the principal reason for an unfulfilled International career. David was never so certain. Indeed, he always believed the Australian Cricket Board's bizarre decision to overlook the World Series players for the tour of India, which followed the peace settlement in 1979, cost him a priceless education at a critical time in his development as an elite player.

In the end, David played only 23 Tests with a solitary century. Perhaps it would have been different had his introduction to the international arena come in more conventional circumstances. In an interview for the ABC documentary *Cricket in the 70s – The Chappell Era* in November 2001, David was asked specifically to appraise the role of the Centenary Test in his sporting life. After the slightest pause he said: "I'd do it all again, of course, but, as a cricketer, I would rather it had not been as dramatic as that."

Not Another Bradman

JACK FINGLETON

I will always think that this match really came alive in tempo and inspiration on the third day when Hookes came in. Greig so palpably again aimed to get him caught in the slips, and Hookes seemed so avid to tilt with him, that one wondered why such a seasoned campaigner as Walters, at the other end, didn't walk down to Hookes and say, "David, they are trying to get you caught in the slips. Take your time and just watch them go by." But Walters didn't do the obvious and Hookes was left alone to battle on as best he could.

He galvanised the match into action when Greig bowled his slow spinners around the stumps. Like the old soldier that he is, Greig took infinite care in placing the field. A man here, a man just a few paces there and so on, all calculated, I thought, to bemuse and impress the young batsman.

Hookes's reply was to loft Greig high over long off, a brave yet perfectly safe shot. Next he swung him fine for four, next he delivered himself of a superlative cover drive for another four, next he hit him mid-wicket to the on for a beautiful four and the crowd went into rhapsodies of delight and enthusiasm.

It was lovely to watch but Hookes hadn't finished. He hit yet another brilliant cover drive, perfectly placed, for another four, five in succession, and the last ball of the over Hookes flashed to mid-off where Amiss was in the way and stopped another four. The happy crowd agreeably booed Amiss.

Greig took his sweater, pretended to crawl into it, cringing away from the setting, but this, as I saw it, was when the Centenary Test came aflame and never afterwards was

This is an excerpt from Jack Fingleton's Centenary Test report in the *Australian Cricket Yearbook 1977*.

diminished. We owed it all to a young Adelaide student, in his first Test not overawed by anybody, the situation and least of all the English captain.

I hope they don't start to call him a second Woolley, a second Pollock or a second Bradman and so on. He is just himself, David Hookes, of Adelaide, fitted to stand in his own right and not needing anybody else's name to push him along. He will do that himself and again before very long.

He still has a few things to learn. When not to play at the ball and how to use a dead bat in defence so that he doesn't give a close-in fieldsman a catch, as he did immediately after his onslaught on Greig.

Fletcher caught him up close and when the lad waited (as was his right, as the ball was taken behind his back) for the umpire's decision, Greig allegedly snapped a few words at him. Hookes came back, so he appears eminently suited for modern cricket. He showed maturity, also, when the press inquired of him what words passed with Greig. "Oh," said Hookes, "he just said 'well played', and I said 'thanks'."

What We Really Said

Tony Greig

The Australian sporting public treasure their heroes and the great sporting moments involving them. I unfortunately was on the receiving end of one of those moments courtesy of Hookesy. As a result of this, and because I am so intrinsically linked to David's sparkling debut performance in the Centenary Test, when he died people approached me and sympathised with me almost as if I were Hookesy's brother. It was been quite incredible.

The first time I laid eyes on David Hookes was when he appeared on the MCG to play his first innings in the Centenary Test. I knew of his success in the then Sheffield Shield and I'd heard how he'd scored a lot of centuries leading up to that wonderful occasion. When he appeared with Australia in big trouble we were cock-a-hoop. I went straight to silly point, and it wasn't long before I had my first conversation with young Hookes. It was time to indulge in a little sledging, after all the Aussies had taught us all we knew about this delicate art of trying to put the opposition off. I've often been asked what I said to David because it was obvious to all that I had said something. We both refrained from telling the story until just recently when 25 years later the Nine Network persuaded us to re-enact that over and we decided to tell all.

The truth is, whilst John Lever was walking back to his mark, I said to the fresh-faced young Hookes, "Tell me, son, have your testicles dropped yet." As quick as a flash, and almost as if he had expected a bit of a sledge, he responded with a smile on his face, "At least I'm playing for the country I was born in."

It became clear from very early on Hookesy wasn't going to take a backward step. He didn't last long in the first innings, I caught him at second slip off a good delivery from Chris Old. In the second innings, Australia were in another spot of bother when Hookesy arrived. I decided that the way to get Hookesy out was to bowl my spinners from around the wicket into the little bit of rough that had formed. I set a pretty strong offside field and decided to toss it up outside off stump.

My first two deliveries were treated with a fair bit of respect but then the carnage began. The roar that greeted the fourth consecutive boundary, which was a superb shot whipped through mid-wicket, was deafening. I wanted to crawl into a hole. I think it's fair to say I had contributed to making the day for 80,000-plus Aussies. Needless to say I took myself off!

I must have seen the replay a hundred times. All I can say is that a good bloke took me to the cleaners that day and later became a friend with whom I spent many hours, particularly overseas, in commentary boxes.

My other lasting memory of that day is, at the end of the day's play, walking into the Australian dressing room with a beer in my hand for David Hookes and the distinctive, yet mischievous smile on his face and the understated way in which he reacted to my gesture.

Message from the Don

SAM LOXTON

I was an Australian selector in 1976-77 when an act of aggression was taking place in Adelaide. A young man by the name of David William Hookes made 185, 105, 135 and 156 for South Australia in successive first-class games. My disappointment was that I saw not a shot played by the young man, as I was allocated other games to watch by the chairman of selectors Phil Ridings. Phil, a former captain of South Australia, was of course on duty, and saw this incredible performance.

So did someone else, namely Sir Donald Bradman, who wrote to me, saying among other things, "that it had been a long time since he had seen a young player with such timing", and that he felt the youngster "had a bright future". Who would know better than "The Don"? Shortly after this Hookes was selected in the Australian side for the Centenary Test at Melbourne, for my part basically on sight unseen, but with sound credentials, and I believe this was the case with Neil Harvey, our other colleague.

By sheer weight of numbers Hookes had forced us to select him. I remember sitting with Neil Harvey in the Melbourne Cricket Ground committee room directly behind the wicket when he came in at five, and I hoped the lad would have success.

I watched as he tried to come to grips with the situation, realising that he had a technique problem. He was thrusting his right foot up the pitch before the bowler delivered the ball, a no-no if ever there was one in the art of good batting. This may well have been a nervous reaction.

At lunch I mentioned this to Sir Donald Bradman who, I am certain, had observed the fault in his protégé. I can't recall when he ever missed anything going on out in the centre. I am unaware if anything was said, but I do know that a transformed Hookes arrived at the crease in the second innings, with Australia again in trouble. His footwork was copybook and his treatment of Tony Greig was an unbelievable sight.

Tyro Ahead of his Time

LEN PASCOE

On Wednesday June 1, 1977, the headlines in London's *Daily Mirror* screamed:

GROUPIES TEMPT TEST TEAM
David Hookes The Girls' No 1 Pin-up

The paper published a picture of the then 21-year-old player naked from the waist up and gave his vital statistics as six feet tall and 40 inches around the chest. David was quoted as saying, "I came to England last year as an ordinary fellow, not as a Test cricketer. The girls I met then reacted in a different way to the ones I am meeting now. Back then they treated me just like any other fellow. But once you become a cricketer playing for Australia their attitude completely changes."

This old scrapbook clipping gave an insight into David Hookes. He knew where he'd come from, and knew what was real and what was not. He was no fool and did not tolerate them.

The Ashes tour of 1977 was to be the most controversial in the history of the game because more than half the team signed for Kerry Packer's World Series Cricket. It was a time of great secrecy, opportunity and sacrifice and David made that sacrifice. Had he stayed with the so-called cricket establishment he certainly would have been a megastar, a future Test Captain.

As it was, he made history in other ways. David won his spot in the Test side with an exciting style of cricket, hitting deliveries on the rise, hooking, and cutting bowlers all around the paddock, often risky, never boring. When he strode to the wicket one felt that the nerves had the better of him, yet whether he made a few or a lot, it was in quick time.

The New South Wales players had heard of his feats and followed his scores for South Australia, hundred after hundred. Now we were about to face him on his home turf, the Adelaide Oval. Typically the nets out the back did everything, seamed, swung and bounced, just perfect to get me into the right frame of mind to put an end to this superstar's run of success. I couldn't wait.

Well, the centre wicket was playing a bit slow, in fact a lot slow! Steve Rixon stood up to the stumps. That stirred me up. "At least stand back so I can look like a fast bowler," was my shouted response. David, playing half forward, was rapped on the pads. We appealed with gusto for what looked like an open and shut case of leg before wicket. The umpire responded in the negative and David went on to score another hundred. I vowed one day I'd get even but that was never to be.

The WSC years were hard. Our batsmen really copped it from Joel Garner, Michael Holding, Colin Croft, Andy Roberts, Imran Khan, and Mike Procter, all fierce fast bowlers whether by bounce, pace, ball movement or just sheer assault and battery. David's comeback innings after the broken jaw was such inspirational stuff, hooking, pulling and driving the same bowler who did the damage. David enjoyed a challenge. That day he left a legacy for everybody, not just cricketers: overcome adversity, do what is necessary to improve yourself, because great achievements don't come easy. That episode is now part of cricket folklore along with the other Hookes gems.

The West Indies were at their awesome best in the late 1970s when Viv Richards, Clive Lloyd, Gordon Greenidge and Desmond Haynes were shredding bowling attacks. David's batting style was like a West Indian's. He gave the bowler a chance, invited him to take him on, but if he fell short of the mark, David took full toll.

By his own admission he did not reach the heights his ability suggested he might. He had a simple explanation: "I was just not good enough." I find that hard to accept and I say he was ahead of his time, that we did not fully understand the cricket he wished to play. Today we see it as the norm, back then it was reckless, or carefree.

David, it can be said, was controversial, abrasive, a stirrer, incredibly intelligent, a larrikin and a pain in the neck. For all that, he was equally as good a bloke.

Another scrapbook clipping shows David and Joel Garner with broad, cheeky grins, decked out in their South Australian jumpers, waiting to take on the New South Wales "Blue Bags". The article beneath says:

"Although South Australian captain David Hookes says the matter is over, the incident in which the team lost almost certain outright points at the Sydney Cricket Ground last season nevertheless still festers. With two wickets down and needing only 11 runs for outright victory South Australia were forced to quit the field when New South Wales said it didn't want to field in light drizzle."

Over? Unlikely! Knowing David he'd have been just aching to get on top of the Blue Bags and translate the cheeky grin into a message: "That's for last season." He loved to have the last word, David.

CHAPTER
IV

Hookes seemed, from the pavilion anyway, to be in control of the first three balls. Not so the fourth, which was short and climbed and hit him with a tremendous crack on the jaw. His broken jaw was still partly wired when he played in his comeback match six weeks later.

Child of the Revolution

RICHIE BENAUD

Always be there. No matter what might be the sport or the incident, if you have a first hand recollection of what happened, and the effect it might have had on sporting careers or lives, it is better than having 50 angles of video-tape at which you can look. For me, being there with David Hookes at the Adelaide Oval was, and is, one of the most vivid memories ranging over 55 years of moving through the excitement of club cricket, Sheffield Shield, Test matches and a maze of commentary boxes, some resembling tomato sheds, some wildly thrown together cubby-houses, and some plush with their carpeted floors and walls.

David wasn't the star of the Centenary Test, but he has been talked about as much as the result, and the shape and excitement of the game, because of that Tony Greig over which Hookes shredded with sublime stroke-play. After the Centenary Test, and before the tour of England, Hookes signed with World Series Cricket as, at that stage, had many other Australian and some overseas cricketers.

One of the least enjoyable moments of "being there" was when Andy Roberts bowled David that bumper in the World Series Super Test at the old Sydney Showground, a game played on one of the best pitches I have ever seen in my life. The match was the start of the West Indian dominance of opposition teams with their great line-up of fast bowlers. This had all come about because of the shellacking Greg Chappell's team had given Clive Lloyd's team in 1975-76 in Australia. Dennis Lillee, Jeff Thomson, Max Walker and Gary Gilmour were a magnificent group, though they weren't as fast as the combinations West Indies put into the field in the 1980s when they were such a dominating team.

Andy Roberts was pretty much at his peak when he was in WSC in 1977-79 and this day at the Showground, on a "belter" of a batting pitch, he was bowling very well. Hookes was in equally good form, and the contest was something to see with Hookes, partnered by Rod Marsh, only 19 short of a century having faced fewer than 80 balls, and with the tea interval taken.

The West Indies bowling attack in this game consisted of Roberts, Joel Garner, Michael Holding and Wayne Daniel, no slouches in the pace department and they all gained plenty of bounce from the surface, though there was also pace in the pitch to allow the batsmen to play their strokes. When the players walked out to the centre (no cuddly, whispered huddles in those days), Clive Lloyd called over to Roberts, "What do you think?" Andy called back, "I've not got much left in me … " Lloyd: "Okay, just give us three or four good ones!" David was an interested listener from several metres away and, with all the confidence of any 22-year-old, mentally stored away the fact that Andy might not be as quick in the 30 degree heat as had been the case before the cream buns and weak tea.

In fact, Andy was struggling a little and David seemed, from the pavilion anyway, to be in control of the first three balls. Not so the fourth, which was short and climbed at him and hit him with a tremendous crack on the left hand side of his jaw. The jaw was fractured and had to be wired, which meant only liquids for several weeks, a tough style of diet and David lost 14 kilograms in two weeks.

The players said it sounded a terrible noise, and I believe them. His jaw was still partly wired when he played in his comeback match six weeks later and then, when he came up against West Indies again a week later, the bowler he first had to face was … Andy Roberts. It was one of those incidents which are sometimes remembered for the shock effect, and that certainly was one of the feelings I had as an observer because I had once gone through the same thing. By a quirk of timing and fate, I was chosen by the New South Wales selectors in 1948 to make my debut in the Sheffield Shield game against Queensland to start on New Year's Day 1949. At the same time, they named me in the New South Wales Second XI to travel by train to Melbourne two days after the Sheffield Shield game finished.

It was a time in Australian cricket when 18-year-olds, even 16-year-olds like Ian Craig and Bob Simpson, could be chosen to play Sheffield Shield cricket. The Melbourne trip was to give me some experience of playing in a level of cricket higher than that to which I had been accustomed in club matches. It would be nice to say my Shield debut was a rip-roaring success, but it wasn't quite that. The first day was completely washed out, and the match was over in three days with the Queensland batsmen unable to come to grips with the pace attack of Ray Lindwall, Keith Miller and Alan Walker. I fielded at cover and deep fine-leg and received an apology from Arthur Morris, the skipper, because he hadn't been able to fit me into the bowling attack. I had the feeling the Queensland batsmen would have enjoyed seeing me come on rather than spending what must have seemed an eternity fending balls away from their chests on a pitch so green that you could hardly distinguish it from the rest of the square.

The trip to Melbourne was far more eventful. Our skipper was Dr Brian Dwyer, a high-quality club cricketer who might well have gone on to the first-class game had he not decided a medical career was his number one priority. Victoria batted most of the first day and New South Wales had to go in for the last half-hour, and Brian asked me if I would be ready to go in as a night-watchman if a wicket fell. I jumped at the chance because on the batting order pinned behind the dressing room door I was listed to bat at seven. It could be a great opportunity to be not out overnight and start again on the second day, a chance to make runs.

The first part went well, except for the batsman who had been dismissed. The next morning I reached double figures with a couple of firm shots and then Jack "Dasher" Daniel, the Victorian opening bowler, bowled a bumper which I tried to hook, but missed. The ball didn't miss me, though, and you could have put half a cricket ball in the dent in my forehead as they stretchered me off the field and up the steps to the dressing room. The upshot was that after the train journey back to Sydney I was told I couldn't play cricket again until the next season. I had an operation designed to put the bits and pieces of bone back into some sort of fancy arrangement above my eyes. Successful, too, or in theory anyway, and the only reminder these days is a line that looks like a spectacles' impression across the top of my nose.

The next best thing that happened to me was when I faced my first ball in club cricket the following summer. An opening bowler who had been in that New South Wales Second XI team bowled it, and he knew that bit about "getting back on the horse after the accident"! He let me have a bouncer and I hooked it for four past square-leg, by far the best way of erasing a bad memory.

Although we were of different eras and we were different style players, one part of David's career and one part of mine ran along similar lines. There is a thought about Hookesy that he should have played more than 23 Tests and that he should have made more runs at that level. That is something of a harsh judgement because of the circumstances in which he came to Test cricket, the fact that he then was part of WSC which meant he was for two seasons batting against the finest bowlers in the world. There have been a number of players around the cricket world who have laboured under the burden of cricket followers believing they should have done better.

I think David was one of these, and the idea probably had its birth in the matches right at the start of his career when he hit those five centuries in six innings in Adelaide, then played the Centenary Test, toured England with the 1977 Australian side and joined WSC. I am able to claim some authority for the above rating because I saw all this happen. In the 1976-77 season, Channel O Queensland TV, under the chairmanship of former Test allrounder Ron Archer, made a decision to televise some Sheffield Shield cricket. Their second decision was to do the last three home games of the South

Australian season, ranging through the period from 4th to 21st February. The matches were against Victoria, Queensland and New South Wales and Channel O were using them as an admirable boost for the Sheffield Shield and, as well, as a dry run for the Centenary Test for which they had been allowed to buy part-rights from the national broadcaster, the ABC.

The previous two seasons, Channel O had run a series of matches at the 'Gabba in Queensland in which the club teams of the Brisbane competition were each allowed to invite two players from southern states to take part in televised 30-overs-a-side matches. All clubs but one, Valleys, invited the present-day players; Valleys invited Alan Davidson and me, and we won the final. That was our first mistake because we then had to go back the following season and defend the title. We won again, but at the expense of a torn hamstring for me and torn rib ligaments for Alan.

I was also reporting on the Shield matches for News Limited newspapers around the country so it was, as far as I was concerned, likely to be a busy time and hopefully an interesting one. I knew most of the players likely to take part in the three Adelaide matches, though they were out of my timeframe as a Sheffield Shield player, having played my last Shield match against South Australia in 1963-64 at the Adelaide Oval.

In 1976 I had heard of David Hookes as being a promising player, though when the South Australians played their first match that summer in Perth I was more interested in what Dennis Lillee was doing. He took two for 59 and five for 68 and David failed to make an impression.

I thought he had been dropped but, in fact, he was doing exams and wasn't available for selection until late January when he failed twice in Perth against Western Australia. This didn't make a great impact on me because I was preparing to fly to Adelaide for the South Australia versus Victoria match that was scheduled to start on 4th February and was the first of the Channel 0 matches. When the South Australian selectors announced their team for this match Hookes was included but, as he later said, all that proved was that there was a very fine line between success and failure.

As we know, in the club match the previous Saturday he had given the simplest of return catches to Prospect medium-pacer Bob May and was walking off when the bowler dropped what had been a leading edge. Hookes then made 79 – a fine line, indeed! What it also showed was that it is vital to take whatever chances might be offered to you. In David's case it was a matter of having had a very ordinary and fortunate summer, and make your runs when the selectors are searching around for some new talent. At the time the Australian team, under Greg Chappell's captaincy, were playing against New Zealand, in New Zealand.

What he did was show me and the other commentators and writers in his 12th first-class match, the first game of the three in Adelaide, was that he had real talent, was skilful, hard-hitting and versatile, and his performance in this game (163 out of 290, seven sixes) was quite magnificent. I did wince a little in sympathy because four of those sixes came in five balls off a leg spinner, Colin Thwaites. Here suddenly was a young batsman dominating a quite decent Victorian bowling attack and making headlines. However, that was only one innings and he failed the second time around attempting a wild shot off pace bowler Ian Callen as the South Australians were bowled out for only 86, a dispiriting effort on what was still a good pitch.

It confirmed for me that the South Australians were probably a rather ordinary team, going down by an innings and 123 runs in only three days. Having watched that second innings, I was hoping for something better as far as a match was concerned a few days later when the South Australians took on Queensland. Well, as it happened, I only had time to say "welcome to our viewers" and South Australia had lost three for 14 and David Hookes was on his way to the centre. No wonder there was a certain amount of unhappiness in South Australian cricket circles about the batting skills of the locals; at that point, I had watched them lose their last 13 wickets for 100 runs!

Hookes changed all that in the next three hours, making 185 and sharing a splendid partnership with Peter Sleep, to turn around the South Australian fortunes and the match became a real thriller, ending in a tie, only the second in Sheffield Shield history. That suited me with all my media commitments because I had a connection to both, on this occasion as a commentator and with the first as a player. That was at St Kilda Oval in 1956-57 when New South Wales, batting last, tied with Victoria with Test player Jim Burke batting with a broken finger and being caught behind off Ian Meckiff with the scores level. This tie in Adelaide came from nowhere. David Hookes's brilliant second innings (105 out of seven for 171 declared) enabled South Australia to set Queensland 263 to win at something like seven an over (there were eight-ball overs in those times), and brilliant stroke-play from Phil Carlson took them to seven for 261. A single and three run-outs off the fourth, sixth and seventh balls left the scores tied, Carlson, Malcolm Franke and Col Cooke being the ones short of the crease. Hardly believable!

Equally extraordinary was the game against New South Wales where David hit his twin centuries, 135 and 156 in lightning-fast time, and in the press box we were all thumbing through the record books to see if anyone had previously hit centuries in each innings of successive matches at first-class level. All the scrambling around first, naturally, focused on the young Bradman, but the answer was "no". Then we found the one – Surrey batsman Tom Hayward had done it 71 years earlier when he hit, in one week and in successive matches in the County championship, 144 not out and 100 against Nottinghamshire and 143 and 125 against Leicestershire. Certainly a rich vein of form, which was precisely what David had produced in this week in Adelaide.

Now it was a question of what would happen to David when the Australian selectors sat down to choose two teams, the one for the Centenary Test and later the touring side to play for the Ashes in England. The full team returning from New Zealand had as its top eleven, in the two matches in Christchurch and Auckland: Alan Turner,

Ian Davis, Rick McCosker, Greg Chappell, Gary Cosier, Doug Walters, Rod Marsh, Gary Gilmour, Kerry O'Keeffe, Dennis Lillee and Max Walker.

David's problem wasn't really a problem at all. Like any other young cricketer he had aspirations to play for Australia and, because of his success in those three Adelaide matches, he had moved quickly from trying to hold his place in the South Australian team to being talked about as a real chance of making the touring team to England.

Gaining a spot in the Centenary Test twelve was a far more difficult matter because this was a prestige match in which everyone wanted to play, and it wasn't a match where the selectors would be setting out to experiment. There was plenty of time for that later, so the Hookes family was interested in the team announcement but not overly confident. There was unrestrained joy when the announcement came that the Centenary Test team would be the 11 players from the Auckland Test ... plus David Hookes! Almost all those players returning from New Zealand had already signed for WSC. I knew nothing about that because I was preparing for the Centenary game, but I would at a later stage. David knew nothing about WSC either. He was now thinking of the fact that he might well be carrying the drinks and that the selectors might have brought him into the twelve for experience. It turned out though that the selectors had other ideas and, in fact, Alan Turner, the opening batsman, was named 12th man on the morning of the game and the captain, Greg Chappell, was obliged to shuffle the batting order to put Rick McCosker in first with Ian Davis. David came in at five with Doug Walters at six.

It was in that batting spot that he made 17 but, in the second innings, Greg Chappell put Walters in at five ahead of David, a good decision influenced by the injury to Rick McCosker, which had him going in at 10 after having his jaw fractured by a Bob Willis bouncer. The innings Hookes played was part of the batting resurgence in the Test after Australia and England had been bowled out cheaply. The fact that runs were now being made certainly made life easier for the players making them – and also for television commentators and journalists covering the match.

There was another effect as well. It had been such a spectacular knock from Hookes that he was approached by WSC and signed. I knew nothing of that either. I was preparing to leave for England where I would be covering the Australian tour for the BBC, something I had been doing over the previous 14 years since BBC had contracted me to do the England versus West Indies series in 1963.

I was to find out much more about it in March when my firm, Benaud and Associates, accepted a consultancy position with WSC on the same basis as the players, a retainer fee and confidentiality concerning the fact that there would be many of the world's leading cricketers taking part in matches outside the existing structure of Test cricket. When the news broke in England it was one of the biggest stories in the history of cricket, or any other sport for that matter.

The Cricket Boards of all countries and the International Cricket Council started by banning the WSC players, and any staging of matches on traditional cricket grounds.

This meant the WSC players had to play on grounds not normally used for cricket and it was through this that some of the far-reaching benefits for cricket materialised. Now, in 2004, drop-in pitches are commonplace; in 1977 they were not only unheard of but were ridiculed by the traditional authorities. There has never been a better pitch-maker, groundsman or curator than John Maley, who was retained by WSC to make pitches on which the best players in the world could play in this competition involving Australia, West Indies and a World team. He did a brilliant job. He was the one who devised the drop-in idea, and many other things, which meant the players would play on the best possible surfaces, though not on the usual grounds.

There was no doubting the animosity from the traditional cricket authorities and this ranged from the banning of players, refusal to allow grounds to be shared and attempts to persuade players who had signed for WSC to break their contracts.

The latter aspect brought about one of the more famous cases in the High Court of London where Mr Justice Slade presided over the hearing of Greig v Insole, the two protagonists representing WSC and The Test and County Cricket Board, as it was then known. World Series Cricket was represented by Mr Robert Alexander QC, and Mr Andrew Morritt QC, each a brilliant barrister. Mr Alexander later became Lord Alexander and President of the Marylebone Cricket Club. Had anyone suggested in 1977 Bob Alexander would become President of MCC, he would have been thought to be slightly off his rocker.

This court case was started towards the end of that 1977 English summer, at a time when the Australian team players, including David Hookes, and most of them with WSC, were on their way back to Australia preparing for their next style of cricket which would be quite different from anything they had experienced before. Drop-in pitches, playing under lights, in coloured clothing, and in country areas and all kind of things they had never before experienced. I was in the High Court for almost a month and my wife Daphne had flown back to Sydney to start working on the consultancy retainer we had accepted. I was staying with friends in Knightsbridge and, at the end of each day in court, I would take the transcripts of the court proceedings home with me and study them carefully for the meetings we had every morning at the Dorchester before going again to the High Court.

The court case itself, Greig v Insole, was on the basis of WSC claiming that the traditional cricket authorities had indulged in Restraint of Trade and Unlawful Contract Interference. We were asking for declarations and injunctions and, after the month-long hearing, Mr Justice Slade said he would be delivering his judgement early in 1978. Before that judgement was handed down there was plenty going on with Australian Cricket Board (ACB) representatives endeavouring to persuade some WSC players to break their contracts.

David was one they targeted. It was a case of being offered business positions, cash contracts, some of them very tempting, and it came to the stage where David and an accountant flew to Sydney around the start of the 1977-78 summer and put it to Mr Packer that the pressure from the ACB had been so great that he would like to pull out of his WSC contract. The general gist of the meeting was that David was shown the series of television commercials just about to be featured right around Australia and that Mr Packer would take a poor view of any of his players who had signed contracts stepping away from them. David's accountant gathered up his papers and indicated to David that he would thoroughly enjoy playing WSC. The injury at the Showground made it far less enjoyable for David and he did suffer some after-effects from the broken jaw.

The first year of WSC was a mixture – a lot of successful aspects, some not so successful – but there was no doubt in our minds that the limited-overs matches under lights held the key to real success. Every possible effort had to be made to gain access to the Sydney Cricket Ground and to have lights installed. The New South Wales Cricket Association (NSWCA) and the ACB fought every hard yard to bar us from playing there. It was just as important to stop the lights being installed. The SCG Trust officials told us there were legal obligations that would force them to give preference to the NSWCA, although this sounded a little hollow because there were no match-scheduling conflicts. These delaying legal manoeuvres kept us at the Sydney Showground for the first season of WSC.

However, planning started immediately to gain access to the SCG for the second summer, install lights and play the first major WSC match at that ground. The first important thing was that the State Labor Government, led by Neville Wran, changed the structure of the SCG Trust and Channel Nine's Bruce Robertson was put in charge of lighting the ground for cricket matches and, in years to come, all sports fixtures. We had seen that the lights at Football Park, WSC's venue in Melbourne, were passable, but could be made better. They were not necessarily ideal for facing the fastest bowlers in the world, although the batsmen said once they were in for a couple of overs their eyes quickly adjusted.

Bruce Robertson and his staff eventually recommended Siemens to take on the installation of the six lighting towers which, when installed, provided light equivalent to a sunny day without cloud. The cricket authorities reasoned initially, and correctly, that lighting at the SCG might well be the beginning of other advantages allowed to WSC, and all that came to fruition with the first day-night match played between West Indies and Australia at the SCG on 28th November 1978.

I was there two-and-a-half hours before the scheduled start, and even then there were people in the ground. The curiosity factor was very much in evidence as we checked reports of traffic build-ups. The fast-growing impression we all had in the WSC office facility on site was that there was likely to be a very good crowd even for the start of the match, though normally a lot of spectators would come to the ground once they had finished work in the city. An hour from the scheduled start we were certain we were going to have a great crowd, and half an hour later there were long queues.

Mr Packer asked the SCG authorities to have more people manning the entrance gates and then, when it became clear there would be a capacity crowd for the match, he announced that he wanted the gates opened with free admission for all latecomers. We estimated 52,000 spectators saw that match and the television ratings were outstanding on Channel Nine. David made only four in the Australian innings, run out when batting with Ian Davis, but the memory of that game never left him, nor any of the other participants either.

It had been a good game of cricket, even though a low scoring one, Australia making five for 129 to West Indies 128. It was spectacular in its setting and for WSC it was a crucial happening. For Daphne and me it was a brilliant night. At the close of play she was in the NSWCA executive room (it was WSC's for 24 hours!) and I joined her there after I had dictated my newspaper column to the Sydney *Daily Mirror* and other News Limited papers. I picked up a chardonnay on the way and walked over to the side of the room where Kerry Packer was standing. He had a mineral water in his hand and we raised glasses. There was no need to say anything.

Justice Slade's judgement handed down in favour of World Series Cricket in the Greig v Insole case in the High Court in London was no great surprise to anyone who had studied Restraint of Trade and Unlawful Contract Interference decisions over the years in Edward Grayson's excellent book, *Sport and the Law*. These went back into the 1950s with soccer football examples; George Eastham v Newcastle United was the most important precedent. Also Florence Nagle, who trained racehorses for many years in England, had won a famous victory over the Jockey Club in 1966; this, too, was in the matter of Restraint of Trade and The Right to Work. There were others as well, but they were two of the most important when looking at the case.

When the news came through of the legal victory, there were a few glasses raised in WSC circles, but there was still much to be done because, although the law case had been won, there was a WSC tour of the West Indies to contemplate and there was still no coming together of the two factions, the ACB and WSC. The match under lights at the SCG with the huge crowd present, and then the Slade judgment, both added a great deal to the pressure on cricket's establishment, so, too, the fact players from India and Pakistan were lining up to ascertain if contracts were available and how soon they could see and sign them. This made it clear that official administrators around the world, and particularly those in Australia, needed to think carefully about how the game would be organised in future years.

The catalyst to the agreement between the ACB and WSC came with the meeting of Sir Donald Bradman and Mr Packer on 13th February 1979; Mr Packer told me about it a few days later in Kingston, Jamaica, at a reception the evening before an Australia versus West Indies WSC match. The agreement between the ACB and WSC produced fury in England, mostly calm agreement in other areas and, since that time, Channel Nine in Australia have always been the television arm of Australian cricket, now run by Cricket Australia.

David Hookes pointed out, in talking about his two years of WSC, that he felt an important part of cricket history. He said, "I was proud to be involved, particularly as I felt something of a trail-blazer for the dramatic changes to the game with day-night matches, coloured clothes, white balls and many other things. There's no doubt that the financial lives of cricketers improved immeasurably because of the stance we took. World Series Cricket pioneered a much better, far more realistic financial deal for cricketers around the world."

That WSC tour of West Indies was the one where crowd disturbances posed problems, and the game in Guyana finished in a wholesale riot when the ground authorities decided the game would start on the scheduled first day despite most of the ground being a sea of mud after two days' rain. The mayhem that followed produced the only occasion when cricketers wore their helmets in the pavilion as a safety measure, with rum-influenced and tomahawk-wielding spectators splitting doors open in their search for the umpires and cricket officials. They told David and the other team members they weren't interested in bothering the players!

David's career after WSC spanned 15 years up to his retirement in 1991-92 and it included some wonderful performances as well as some low times, including his sacking as South Australia's captain and being dropped from the Test team in the 1985-86 season in Australia.

He will be much missed for his cricketing skills of the past, his forthright nature where he often spoke as he batted on the attack in constructive fashion. Just as much, too, in the area of coaching where he lifted Victoria to a wonderful final summer until tragedy overtook him.

Too Much, Too Soon

GREG CHAPPELL

Unfortunately, David's first Test, the Centenary Test, was probably the highlight of an international career that never reached the heights his second innings performance in that match promised. David made a successful tour of England a few months later in a young and inexperienced team. He was forced to take on more responsibility in the batting line-up than should have been the case on his first tour, but with scores of 42, 50 and 85 in the series he came home with his reputation enhanced.

World Series Cricket probably came a season or so too soon for some of the younger Australian players, especially David. Had he had another season or two of experience he may have coped better against the might of the West Indian and Rest of the World bowling. It seemed that David was much more subdued from that point. That broken jaw from the Andy Roberts bouncer may have had a bigger impact than was first realised.

David dominated first-class attacks for the remainder of his career but never seemed as capable of playing through the more difficult periods that were more prevalent in Test cricket. The crash-or-crash-through tactic that served him so well in State matches often let him down at the higher level.

David was a tough opponent who hated to lose – he didn't want to give up the bragging rights that went with winning! As a captain he was a tough taskmaster but never demanded more of his players than he was prepared to give himself. His captaincy was creative and instinctive, and a shrewd cricket brain was often in evidence whether when opening the bowling with one of his spinners, or when taking deliberate short runs to keep the strike when batting with the tail in a tight run chase.

His aggressive attitude sometimes had an edge of cynicism that detracted from his general good humour and natural cheekiness, but even if he had overstepped the mark on the field you could be sure he would be the first one through the dressing room door at the end of the day with a beer in his hand and his trademark grin to settle any differences. His simple, evangelical approach to coaching was proving very popular with the Victorian Bushrangers.

David was a complex character in many ways and yet he had a simple approach to his cricket that carried over into his life. If he upset you it was hard to stay mad at him for long for his genuine warmth was hard to deny. He attracted people to him with the power of his personality and he kept them with his generous spirit. David collected friends like others collect antiques.

In Case of Emergency …

ROD MARSH

To say David Hookes loved a bit of excitement is an understatement. One only had to watch him bat and it was patently obvious he was there for a good time, and not necessarily a long time. If David enjoyed something he did it in a whole-hearted manner and didn't really think about the possibility of there being a downside to what he was enjoying.

This was never more evident than during our World Series Cricket tour of the West Indies in 1979. In that turbulent time in world cricket our World Series group was perceived as the bad guys, and it was very important our public image was squeaky clean. So, in order to police any poor behaviour the players agreed to a self-regulated code of behaviour. This addressed such things as swearing in a public place and generally anything that would give the public any cause for complaint. If anybody did break the code of conduct they were brought before the fines committee (which was made up of a good cross section of the touring party) and if found guilty, given the fine which best suited the crime. From memory, the minimum fine was 10 dollars and the maximum was 100 dollars.

Our first playing venue in the West Indies was Jamaica. Jamaica in 1979 was not a very safe place and we had been advised not to venture out of the hotel, unless we went in sizeable groups. The hotel had a pool and a bar, but believe me there was little else to do. Cricketers love to get out of the hotel and do a bit of shopping, or more particularly get to a decent golf course. After a week of solid training, there had been very little activity outside the confines of the hotel. The lads were getting restless!

To set the scene it is necessary to mention that the hotel in which we stayed was completely full, literally teeming with people. The majority of these were Cuban nationals who constantly moved in swarms, hell bent on getting from point A to point B in the shortest possible time via the shortest possible route. We Australian cricketers soon learned that to get between any of these Cubans and an opening lift door or the breakfast bar was to risk being trampled to death. There was never an "excuse me" or any form of apology when they near knocked you off your feet while you were trying to order a Red Stripe beer from the bar. The boys were not only getting restless, they were getting very pissed off with these Cubans.

But everyone was very mindful of the code of behaviour. Maybe we didn't want to be fined. Maybe we took our personal accountability right on board. We were angelic! The ugly Australians had become the gentlemen of world cricket. Yeah right! Something had to happen, someone had to snap. It wasn't going to be me; I wasn't going to be the first. Mind you I could have gladly whacked one of those rude bloody Cubans!

It all happened around one o'clock in the morning. I don't recall which day but I do recall the loudest fire alarm I have ever heard. We all filed out of the hotel in some sort of order except for those Cubans. They tried to knock us down and trample us in their haste to avoid the possible danger. It was quite funny to see them all panic and it became pretty obvious that one of our team saw more humour in the moment than most.

When we did eventually get back to our floor a few of the boys discovered some broken glass from a fire alarm, which just happened to be adjacent to the room of David Hookes. In the morning it was decided David should be called up before the fines committee to see what he would say if accused of causing the mass evacuation of the hotel. He was duly accused and, to everyone's amazement, pleaded guilty without any hesitation. He did so with a smile on his face, and explained his act as one of retribution against all the rude Cubans who had pushed their way past our players for the past week. There was no option but to fine him and, what's more, he copped the maximum. David left the fines meeting a poorer, but satisfied cricketer.

Around one the next morning the shrill sounds of the fire alarm were once again waking everyone from their slumber. The Cubans were panicking again and again we watched with great mirth as they knocked each other over in their haste to vacate the hotel. We took our time getting downstairs; I think everyone had the thought in the back of his mind that there might not really be a fire, but rather one of the team was up to a little more mischief. But I don't think anyone really thought David had been silly enough to do it again.

But sure enough the same fire alarm had been broken. And, what's more, David said not to bother with the fines committee; he just handed over the maximum to the treasurer. When he was quizzed about the second incident he simply stated he had got so much enjoyment from watching the Cubans panic the night before that he wanted to see it again. David was smart enough not to try for the hat-trick. He had made his point to the Cubans (he hoped) and he had certainly had his fun. He didn't really care about the fines, as money was not important to him. Fun was important, excitement was important and basically every day had to be lived to the fullest. Thankfully it was.

CHAPTER
V

In 1980, David Hookes was chosen for Australia's tour to Pakistan, never an easy tour. A hamstring injury and flawed footwork conspired to trip him up. Rod Marsh considered Hookes's tour batting average of 1.66 then said it would have equalled his breath-test reading after a party!

Cellar to Penthouse

PHIL WILKINS

It is a natural phenomenon, rarely seen and never forgotten. Political leaders sometimes have it, occasionally entertainers, more often athletes and sportsmen and exotic women. Julius Caesar must have had it, and men like Alexander the Great, Napoleon Bonaparte and John F Kennedy. The Beatles conquered the world with personality and song; Cleopatra and Marilyn Monroe graced it with rare beauty; Muhammad Ali ruled the sporting universe with fists and charisma.

A quarter of a century ago, a crowd a thousand strong swarming through Miami International Airport stopped in their tracks at the spectacle of a man striding through the terminal. He was a black man, hooked of nose, gleaming of face, dressed in an electric blue suit. He radiated vitality and personality, exuding an aura almost superhuman. The crowd stood and stared as he came through the terminal. Most of them had never heard of him and, being American and baseball and gridiron disciples, they failed to recognise him.

But, without identification or explanation, they sensed he was a man apart, a champion by any other name. In fact, although he was from just across the water, from the tiny Caribbean island of Antigua, he was a potentate from another realm, from the kingdom of cricket. He came and went and most of them never saw Isaac Vivian Alexander Richards again. But they never forgot him. "Vivi" was that sort of man.

It was similar to seeing Keith Miller coming through the arches from the Nursery end at Lord's, black mane "Brylcreem-ed" back on his head, as if he had just shrugged off his RAAF pilot's suit and parachute and was going to the visitors' dressing room to change into his creams. There was no cricket that day at headquarters, but the spectacle lived forever. "Nugget" Miller was irresistible to people. Like Hookesy. He was the first to profess he was no champion, but David Hookes was a man spectacular of personality, an irresistible character, a wonderful cricketer, and he bore an aura. He glowed in a crowd.

"Ah," he would have observed at such an expansive eulogy, "you're having a lend of me." He and his devilish grin attracted people, won them over. He had good, constructive thoughts and strong opinions, expressed them and pursued them, a man who wanted his convictions accepted and adopted. But, underneath that intensity, somehow you got the impression he never took himself too seriously. As a cricketer, as a true, great, shining champion, we will always wonder about David Hookes. We will wonder and we will never know.

For all his thousands of runs, his centuries and successes, memory serves to suggest he came to depend less and less on footwork, and without footwork, he could never be a true champion. Inevitably, he would be brought down. The game is ruthless and it is like that. Certainly, he was no dancing man at the wicket late in his career, no batsman as nimble in footwork as Neil Harvey. Dennis Lillee remarked after he bowled to Hookes in 1987-88 that he believed he had become "very lead-footed".

Perhaps while less physically imposing than Graeme Pollock, Hookes was a batsman of eagle eye with a hand as heavy as a wrecker's ball, who could stand on the popping crease and smash a ball to shred the six stitches, when at times he considered footwork superfluous. It worked on true pitches. Whenever a judgement is passed about David Hookes, the consideration jars to a halt at that day at the old Sydney Showground where the young International began to hook Andy Roberts, discovered fractionally too late that it was the West Indian fast bowler's "other" bumper – he had several of different pace according to those in the know – and was struck that dreadful blow.

In that initial season of World Series Cricket, some media organisations pretended that the best cricketers in the world would eventually pack up their kitbags and go away, or at least return to the sanitised, under-paid security blanket of the International Cricket Council and its organisations. I was pursuing the traditionalists' Test program that day, the first day of the Second Test in distant Perth between the born-again Bob Simpson's under-strength Australians and Bishan Bedi's Indians, in what proved one of the most enjoyable series I ever witnessed, won eventually by Simpson's XI, three Tests to two.

The news filtered into the WACA Ground press box that Hookes had been hit a fearful blow by Roberts and had been driven by Kerry Packer himself to hospital. Later we heard how he had asked his more senior batting partner Rodney Marsh: "I can say f – – , can't I?" and was led from the field, spitting blood and bone chips into the towel in which the physiotherapist wrapped his head. The doctor who examined him at the wicket said: "Hookesy, this is going to take you five years to get over." Maybe it took forever. Maybe that day at the Showground drained some of the mercury from his batting soul, removed that exquisitely fine edge of the master batsman.

Is this the moment that forever changed David Hookes's cricket career path? His jaw has been broken by a bumper from the West Indian Andy Roberts.

NEWS LTD/ACP

Player assistance arrived first, and then later, to avoid such traumatic scenes in the future, the traditional cap was replaced by more substantial head protection. WSC World XI players Barry Richards, Dennis Amiss and Tony Greig, right, promoted the helmet brigade, unattractive then, but the way of the future.

Hookes at Brisbane's famous 'Gabba, post-WSC. This sweep against England in 1982-83 promised so much ... as did his baggy green comeback innings there against the West Indies in 1979-80, until he carelessly miscued a hook off Colin Croft. Hookes's response to his critics confirmed his determination: "Okay, it wasn't my best shot but the hook has been a good friend to me over the years and there's no way I'm going to cut it from my repertoire."

Master and pupil. Hookes was a confessed fan of Ian Chappell; Greg Chappell was a fan of Hookesy's barbecuing skills.

In the early 1980s, beards and cricketers went together. Hookesy obliged.

Hookes often sharpened reflexes, spoke about hand-eye co-ordination, but his time with WSC would usher in a tougher attitude to the physical side of the game. "During the break between the first and second year of World Series the players put a lot of work into both the fitness and basic skills of cricket in a determined bid to prove to the sceptics we could successfully stand on our own two feet," he said.

ACP

Hookes hooks at the MCG. The bowler is England's Norman Cowans and the Test the fourth in the 1982-83 season. Australia lost by three runs. Hookes made 53 and 68 and later said: "I let myself down, and Australia, by playing two poor shots to get out. If I had been a Test selector, I would have asked myself: 'How come Hookes isn't getting a Test hundred when he's in the best form of his career?'"

Hookes was a prolific run scorer for South Australia, for whom he hit 26 centuries. What wasn't always acknowledged was his potential at the bowling crease.

The fastest century in the making, off 34 balls against Victoria. "Let's have a go and see what happens," he told his opening partner Rick Darling.

Cricket writer Phil Wilkins: "The spectacular rise of South Australia from cellar dwellers to penthouse gentry in Hookes's first year of captaincy made the 1981-82 season one of the most enthralling in Sheffield Shield history."

A few summers on, Hookesy was in the record books again, partnering best mate Wayne Phillips in a stand of 462 against Tasmania. Phillips: "We started to have a look at the record books to see what might be. One record immediately grabbed our attention – the stand of 308 between Ian Chappell and Barry Richards."

Hookesy and Robyn were married at Lancelot Castle in 1989. Robyn: "It was the most amazing wedding, an incredible party. We didn't have to do it, we were already a family, so getting married was more a celebration of us."

In 1985, a very social cricket match was played between Rod Marsh's XVIII (that is 18!) and Colin Cowdrey's XVIII to celebrate the opening of the Yulara complex at Uluru. Not too many players, Hookesy included, got to bed before four o'clock on the first morning, and yet had to be up at six to be driven out to Ayers Rock, which some brave types duly climbed. Hookesy was late starting the climb, so he jogged all the way up and met most of the struggling climbers on the way down.

Less exciting was his participation in a testimonial match at the 'Gabba.

The great South African batsman Graeme Pollock, at slip, watches Hookes in the Bradman XI versus World XI match at the SCG in 1994-95. Some judges thought their styles were similar.

Hookes slogs in the World Series, and snares a catch.

Australia celebrates winning the World Series Cup against New Zealand in 1982-83.

A rough moment. Victory in this McDonald's Cup was sweet, but Hookes's politically incorrect comments about Tasmanians in a pre-match interview got him into trouble.

A magic moment. Hookes leaving the field with Simon O'Donnell after his steady, unbeaten 32 had helped shepherd Australia to a rare Test victory in the mid-1980s. Australia beat New Zealand by four wickets in the Second Test at the SCG.

It certainly impaired his confidence for some time and, for all his run mountains, he was never quite the same supreme batsman again. We will always wonder but we will never know.

It was, of course, a time when batsmen were liberally peppered with bouncers, when the unwritten law of three bouncers an over was policed infrequently. It also coincided with the time when the thought processes of Clive Lloyd and Deryck Murray were combining to produce the four-act fast bowling theory, a policy that for some years dispensed with the need for a specialist spinner in a cricket team. Consequently, to avoid the obvious consequences of an all-pace attack and to prevent injury, cricket belatedly followed baseball and began experimenting with equipment to counter the headline attack of Roberts, Holding, Wayne Daniel and Joel Garner, the attack of that particular day, and the fast bowlers who followed by the express trainload.

One of the first helmets I saw was that freighted out to the West Indies some months later by the Queensland batsman, David Ogilvie, on Australia's 1978 tour of the West Indies. By then it was too late for Hookes. Many refinements have been made to helmets, but it is fair to say, had the equipment been as sophisticated as it is nowadays, Hookes's injury would almost certainly not have been as serious as occurred at the Showground.

The second season of WSC dragged on for Hookes, criss-crossing the nation, travelling from Perth to Sydney, from Maitland to Melbourne, from Lismore to Traralgon, spreading the WSC gospel. At last, he began turning his game around, making 116 and 56 in the Third Super Test at VFL Park at Waverley. In the Fifth Super Test at the Sydney Cricket Ground against Tony Greig's World XI, Hookes top-scored in a losing side with 96 against an attack comprising Imran Khan, Mike Procter, Garth Le Roux, Clive Rice and Derek Underwood. Kerry Packer introduced floodlights to the SCG that season and the public voted in its acceptance of day-night Internationals with its feet.

Facing bankruptcy, the Australian Cricket Board eventually accepted it could not defeat World Series Cricket and settled for a one-sided truce, television rights included. Prior to the warring parties burying the hatchet, Ian Chappell led his so-called team of rebels to the West Indies. It was to be the last cricket for the WSC team. For Hookes, it only prolonged the agony.

Fourteen games in the Caribbean produced not a single century from the young batsman who had established his reputation as a prolific century-maker. At every turn, he kept facing Roberts and Holding and Garner, and now Malcolm Marshall. There was no avoiding the issue. It was cricket on the front line all the time. The Australians drew a marvellously gruelling series, with Greg Chappell and Dennis Lillee reconfirming their greatness and the team escaping the riot of the Bourda Ground in Guyana after donning cricket helmets, barricading themselves in their dressing room and arming themselves with stumps.

Hookes was glad to get home in one piece with precious little to show for the tour. Ian Chappell had kept blind faith in him, retaining him for the five Super Tests despite the left-hander having a top-score of 28 for the series.

Hookes avowed then, and maintained later, that his WSC days were the most combative of his career, a period he conceded when he never felt in control. And to think they have never accorded two years of Super Tests first-class status. The blues of Oxford and Cambridge should never bewail their privileged plight. In the run-up to the 1979-80 season, the reunion season, Kim Hughes led the Australian Cricket Board's team to India for 10 weeks in a six-Test series, a tour Hookes realised later would have benefited him enormously in how to cope with, and overcome, spin bowling.

Hookes began his new "official" cricketing life encouragingly enough for South Australia, despite straining a hamstring muscle, only to make a duck batting at number six in the first limited-overs International in Sydney – against the West Indies, naturally! When the Australian team for the First Test to play the West Indies was announced, Hookes was among eight former WSC players selected with Allan Border, Kim Hughes and Rodney Hogg, the trio from the other side of the fence. Then, fielding as twelfth man in a limited-overs game against England, Hookes lunged for a catch and tore the hamstring off the bone.

Hookes was chosen on trust for the Australian team's tour of Pakistan under the captaincy of Greg Chappell early in 1980. Never an easy tour, Hookes found this one the tour to end all tours. Now, we can accept he was on Mission Impossible. It was not simply the fact that invariably Pakistan's pitches were doctored to suit the whim of the captain of the time, then Javed Miandad, but it's fair to think that Hookes very probably kept looking along the pitch at the world-class attack of pacemen Imran Khan and Sarfraz Nawaz and spinners Iqbal Qasim and Tauseef Ahmed – but seeing the face of Andy Roberts.

It was a tour on which the pitches suited the spin bowlers, in a land where batsmen had to be dancers to counter spinners. Hookes's hamstring injury and his flawed footwork conspired to trip him up. That and his continuing nightmare.

Hookes made five and three in the first game against a President's XI in Rawalpindi and then registered a pair of ducks in the First Test in Karachi. He was dropped for the Victorian opening batsman, Julien Wiener. When chosen to bat at number three against a Governor's XI in Multan, he accumulated two and nought.

Confidence shot to pieces, he was ignored for the final Test, his aggregate in three games from the five-game tour a woeful 10 runs. All this from a player with the game at his feet in 1977. Rodney Marsh considered Hookes's tour batting average of 1.66 and suggested it would have equalled his breath-test reading after a party.

Dennis Lillee was having almost as exasperating a tour. Wicketless in his first two Tests, he wrote home to wife Helen, declaring: "I finally got a wicket today – my first in Pakistan. But it was only in the nets, and it was only Hookesy." Hookes returned to

Adelaide, and things got worse. Once a celebrity of the Centenary Test in Melbourne now, as a failure, he was bypassed for the Centenary Test in London in August 1980.

Five appearances for South Australia failed to yield a half-century, including a duck against the touring Indians at his beloved Adelaide Oval, the ground neighbouring the sandstone and bluestone colossus of St Peter's Cathedral, which had trembled before his previous century assaults. By now, he was muffing catches, symptomatic of a cricketer whose confidence is skulking around his boot studs.

His catching provided so many additional runs for rival batsmen that Mike Coward enquired: "Who is David Hookes playing for this summer, South Australia or the opposition?" Hookes was omitted not simply from the Test side, but also from the South Australian team for three Sheffield Shield matches. It was like putting an injured animal out of its misery. A member of the Test side in Pakistan in February 1980, he was back playing club cricket by December.

Hookes drove to Bailey Reserve for West Torrens's club match against Adelaide in a wretched state, knowing there was a Sheffield Shield match taking place at the Adelaide Oval. And still the runs did not flow, although there were some consoling moments as a bowler. Hookes sat out Australia's traditional representative period of Christmas and the New Year and after a frustrating, enforced five-week lay-off, he returned for the Croweaters as a quasi-allrounder, batting at number seven against Western Australia in Adelaide for innings of 33 and 67, including clobbering leg spinner Tony Mann to the top of the Members Stand.

Retained for the remainder of the season, Hookes was party to South Australia finishing bottom of the pile in the Sheffield Shield. Times were tough for the golden boy and his State. Not a single century did he register for State or Australia that summer. As Hookes told Alan Shiell, his biographer and once a double century-maker for South Australia, looking back into the most desolate crevasse of his career: "If only I could delete the summers of 1979-80 and 1980-81 from my career, and have them all over again." He might also have mentioned 1978-79, the season when the misery began.

Hookes received a phone call in the winter of 1981 from John Inverarity, his South Australian captain. "Invers", the tall, angular former Test allrounder from Perth, a much-regarded intellectual and by then deputy headmaster at Pembroke School in Adelaide, asked Hookes to have dinner with him and his wife.

They enjoyed the meal and invaded Inverarity's wine cellar, and eventually the elder statesman enquired of the young international: "How would you like to captain South Australia next season?" Inverarity told Hookes that in his 38th year he considered the moment opportune for him to step down and said he believed Hookes had the necessary leadership qualities and strength of character to carry the burden of captaincy.

Hookes discovered how great the burden when he enquired if South Australia, wooden-spooners of the Sheffield Shield in 1980-81, were about to lose any players. Inverarity casually informed him that the Test pair, off spinner Ashley Mallett and paceman Jeff Hammond, were both about to retire as well as the State's trusty new ball bowler, Geoff "Scatters" Attenborough. Hookes swallowed hard and rang Ian Chappell, who in his blunt-as-an-axe manner, enquired what Hookes had to lose; after all, South Australia had just finished last in the competition.

And, unsuspected though it was at the time, Rodney Hogg, one of the most formidable fast bowlers of his era, and then overseas with the Australian team, was later to withdraw from domestic cricket with a back condition. The spectacular rise of South Australia from cellar dwellers to penthouse gentry in Hookes's first year of captaincy made the 1981-82 season one of the most enthralling in Sheffield Shield history.

South Australia selected a quartet of pace men for their first game in Perth – Ross McLellan, Andrew Sincock, Graham Winter and Dean Sayers, none of them express, which seemed as inoffensive as any attack assembled. For spin, they had the allrounder Peter Sleep. Predictably, they were beaten by a Western Australian side containing nine players with Test experience, seven of whom were to accompany the 13-man Australian team on its tour of New Zealand.

South Australia drew their next three games and appeared to be running on empty. From little acorns mighty oak trees grow. At home in Adelaide, there were encouraging signs against New South Wales, however, with Hookes cracking a century, as did a square-shouldered, young batsman from New Zealand named Jeff Crowe. In Sydney, with Crowe enjoying another unbeaten hundred and South Australia only 11 runs from outright victory, rain began falling.

The New South Wales players fled to the dressing room. Hookes sat stubbornly on the roller until the weather really turned foul, ending the game as a draw. Hookes was charged with dissent and fined his match fee, 130 dollars. South Australia's blood was up and so was their captain's, and the Croweaters were on their way to glory.

In Brisbane, with Inverarity compiling his 21st first-class century, South Australia headed Queensland on the first innings for their first points and began the ascent. When the Maroons came to Adelaide, Wayne "Flipper" Phillips hammered 260 in his inimitable way and Hookes drilled four sixes in a row from leg spinner Dennis Lillie in South Australia's outright win by an innings. They led Victoria on the first innings and began the home run, three consecutive games, all of which they won outright for maximum points, a period in which opener Rick Darling continued the scintillating batting which won him Test honours.

South Australia downed Tasmania in Launceston by five wickets; Western Australia in Adelaide by nine wickets; and then, with 8,000 spectators streaming into the Adelaide Oval on the last afternoon, they overcame Victoria for a nine-wicket triumph, which provided the State's 12th Sheffield Shield success since the competition's inception in 1892-93.

For Hookes, captaincy honours aside, it was his most enjoyable season. He led a harmonious team essentially of his own vintage, Invers excepted; players like Darling,

Crowe, Phillips, Sleep, Winter, Sam Parkinson, his vice-captain and wicketkeeper Kevin Wright, Kim Harris, Malcolm Dolman, Kevin Lewis and Brian Vincent. In the process, Hookes buried the myth that bowlers win matches and, by natural progression, competitions. Obviously, he took a leaf from the Bradman "Book of Invincibles" and their 1948 tour of England.

"We proved that batsmen, as well as bowlers, really can win matches if they score consistently enough and, more to the point, quickly enough to give their bowlers sufficient time in which to dismiss opposing teams," Hookes said. "Inverarity and Sleep aside, we had an inexperienced bowling attack, yet we dismissed opponents, often with hours to spare, because our batsmen had helped create that time by hammering totals of 400 and 500 in four sessions."

Despite an encouraging summer, a Test recall was still some way off for Hookes. He made a solitary century against New South Wales, inevitably, in Adelaide. Later that year, 1982, the Australian team, without Hookes, returned groggily from Pakistan, having lost all three Tests – chiefly to the wiles of leg spinner Abdul Qadir – and two limited-over Internationals; the third was abandoned in a riot. To cap off the most inglorious of tours their three first-class games were drawn.

Less than six weeks after he struck a magnificent Test century in Faisalabad, Greg Ritchie returned to find himself bypassed for Hookes for the First Test against England, Hookes having hit twin centuries against Victoria. One was that fastest hundred in Australian first-class history, from just 34 balls with three sixes and 17 fours in just 43 minutes. Significantly, the centuries were made on the Adelaide Oval, ever-lovin' Adelaide, the ground with the truest pitch in the world, where he had erupted into international cricket in 1977.

When Hookes made 74 and 39 in the State match against the touring Englishmen, the selectors decided it was time for his reinstatement. It was his first Test in 32 months but, for all his superlative form, Hookes returned to the side as nervous as a kitten, and Ian Botham did not fail to notice it.

The champion allrounder took one glance at Hookes's name in the Test team and, later at the crease, and determined he would do his level best to resurrect the Andy Roberts phobia. He began plying Hookes with bouncers. Hookes considered he received two poor umpiring judgments in the series, but he was also astute enough to recognise that he, and he alone, had failed to cash in on resolute starts of 53 and 68 in the Melbourne Test. Conspicuous hundreds would have done more for the longevity of his Test career.

"Those two half-centuries in Melbourne really should have been converted into centuries," he wrote later in his autobiography, *Hookesy*, of the wonderful Test which England eventually won by three runs. "If I had been a Test selector, I would have asked myself: 'How come Hookes isn't getting a Test hundred when he's in the best form of his career?'

"I let myself down, and Australia, by playing two poor shots to get out. I really was annoyed with myself for wasting two 'free' opportunities to score centuries. Two others had come in 1977 when I got 56 in the second innings of the Centenary Test and 85 in our only innings of the Fifth Test at the Oval. At the time I didn't appreciate the importance of either opportunity. But I did during 1982-83, and I started to pile the pressure on myself."

Hookes recalled a thought of Greg Chappell from his testimonial magazine: "It was a shame Hookes didn't get a century in that series against England because it might well have opened the floodgates for him and he probably would have gone on to become a regular member of the Australian team for years."

Hookes considered his productivity of 344 runs at 49.14 from the series against England, took a large, dispassionate step backwards and summarised his standing for Australia with the utmost objectivity when he wrote: "I enjoyed my busiest, most successful season in 1982-83. Yet, my failure to score a century in any of the five Tests was, I suspect, the beginning of the end of my days as a Test player." It takes a good man to assess his own career with as much clarity as David Hookes.

Those observations alone, by Hookes and by Chappell, finally put anchors and chains on any claim he had to greatness. For all the runs he made, Hookes never made a first-class century on the Sydney Cricket Ground. Perhaps the proximity of the Sydney Showground and the shadow it cast over his career had some influence. More probably, it was the inadequacy of his footwork against spin which hampered him, just as it did on shifting pitches in England.

But, invariably, he scored big hundreds against Victoria and after three in as many innings against them in 1982-83, it came as no major surprise when he was approached to join them with the temptation of becoming State captain-coach for the next three seasons. Hookes almost moved to Victoria and it required the intervention of then South Australian premier, John Bannon, to keep him in Adelaide.

Later, he wondered, with far deeper relevance than he could ever have imagined: "Even now, there are times when I wonder what different paths my career and life would have taken if I had accepted that first opportunity to become a 'Vic'."

Hookes went to Sri Lanka on the Australians' initial tour of the "Teardrop Isle" in April 1983, as vice-captain to Greg Chappell, scoring 100 runs between lunch and tea on the second day of the Test in Kandy for an unbeaten 143. It was to be his only century in 23 Test appearances. Midway through 1983, Hookes was again chosen as Australian vice-captain, this time to Kim Hughes, for the World Cup, leading them in their last qualifying game against India at Chelmsford with Hughes injured.

The Indians won comfortably, moving into the semi-final, defeating England at Old Trafford and ultimately coming to Lord's to down the highly-fancied West Indies in the final by 43 runs. On the evening of Australia's elimination, Hookes and Allan Border were in the bar at the Waldorf Hotel in London when Hughes walked in, wearing his

Australian blazer and tie. To their amazement, Hughes told them he was flying back to Australia that night.

Hughes had sent out a message through Kepler Wessels during the Indian game ordering Hookes to change his fielding strategy of two players back for the last two balls of each over. Wicketkeeper Rodney Marsh responded to Wessels' direction with: "You go and tell f – – g Kim Hughes that if he wants to captain the side, f – – g play." Hookes was well aware of the tension between Hughes and Marsh and Dennis Lillee, which had simmered since World Series Cricket days, and probably before.

When Hookes proffered his opinion to Ken "KG" Cunningham on radio about the issue, he observed: "I guess I'm echoing a lot of players' thoughts in that I believe Rod Marsh would be an excellent captain of Australia."

Hookes emphasised that he was not advocating Hughes be dumped as captain, merely suggesting he become vice-captain for two years, or even have Marsh as Hughes's vice-captain. Hughes replied from Perth: "It's nice to know the Australian captain is getting the support of his vice-captain." In the furore, Hookes was required to fly to Sydney charged with breaching his tour contract. To his amazement, he was fined 1,200 dollars of his 5,000 dollars World Cup fee.

Hookes wondered later if his comments about Hughes led to his omission from the Australian team soon after for the First Test against Pakistan. He watched the game from his hospital bed with viral pneumonia, eventually returning for the limited-over series only to tear a cruciate ligament striving to catch Clive Lloyd. The 1984 tour of the Caribbean was predictably gruelling, the West Indian fast bowlers battering the Australian batsmen from pillar to post with Allan Border, now vice-captain to Hughes, the gallant exception, the bravest of the brave.

Like all other batsmen, Hookes had a mediocre tour, having a top-score of 51 in five Tests. Hookes's career was in decline and, although chosen for four Tests in 1985-86 after missing the 1985 tour of England, his International career was "history", as he acknowledged. By the time he was 30, he was finished as a Test player; so much promised and so much unfulfilled.

He continued playing, of course, until 1991-92, still prolific at first-class level in the Sheffield Shield competition: scoring 1,000 runs in the seasons of 1985-86 and 1987-88; making 306 not out against Tasmania in Adelaide in 1986-87; passing John Inverarity's Shield aggregate record.

But his volatility and unpredictability – once making opening bowler, Sam Parkinson, captain for a session – did not impress the State selectors and they sacked him in 1990.

For all that, Hookes was the player every journalist and media man, candidly and privately, wanted as Australian captain, as permanently as any cricketer could be, for his quick wit and spontaneity, for his aggressive leadership, tactical knowledge and simply for his vibrant personality. Who else but Hookesy would have gone to Tasmania for the

McDonald's Cup final and responded to the television interviewer when told there would be a capacity 12,000-strong crowd at North Hobart Oval: "That'll be great – 24,000 heads!"

He walked out on to the field the next day and read a sign: "Two heads are better than half a brain, you f – -wit!" You still get a laugh from it. And South Australia went home with the Cup. There were two fateful, terrible days in the 48 years of the life of the boy from Mile End. The first led to consequences that echoed throughout his career and changed the course of a path surely bound for the crystal peaks where the great cricketers walk. The second ghastly event ended a wonderful life. The game of cricket was enhanced with him in its ranks and followers of the game were the better for knowing him.

Crash, Bang, Wallop!

RICK DARLING

For a young boy of 15 from Waikerie, a Riverland town 170 kilometres north-east of Adelaide, coming down to the "big smoke" to trial for, and then play in underage representative teams, was quite a daunting prospect. That's how I came to meet Hookesy. It was 1973, and we were playing in a South Australian Combined Secondary schools trial for Under 19s. I made 50-odd and can't remember what Hookesy made.

But what remains etched in my memory is the sight of a brash 17-year-old, full of confidence, who thrived on being the centre of attention. We both made the team and so began a friendship that flourished over 30 years.

We played South Australian Colts together. Hookesy's first first-class game for South Australia was in October 1975, mine in December. We won the Sheffield Shield that year under Ian Chappell, our idol when we were kids playing in our backyards, and even then I could see Hookesy thought that moulding himself on Chappelli was the way to go.

We were team mates for the next 14 seasons. I was overwhelmed playing with, and going on tour with greats like the Chappells, Terry Jenner and Ashley Mallett, but Hookesy took it all in his stride. Off the field we shared a unit for a while and I joined him at the West Torrens Cricket Club, where he was captain. And it was under the captaincy of Hookesy that we next won the Shield, in 1981-82. I wish I'd played a Test or two with Hookesy but he joined World Series Cricket; I did, however, enjoy his company in a few One-day Internationals.

His death sharpens the memories, from the seemingly trivial – helping him off the plane in Adelaide after he badly did a leg while taking a catch against the West Indies – to the most stunningly brilliant, that record fastest century off 34 balls in only 43 minutes in the Sheffield Shield match against Victoria.

I was lucky enough to be the batsman at the other end. It was the 1982-83 season and in the ensuing years everyone, from television and radio commentator to reporters to people in the street, has had a friendly dig at me (whose preference was to always try to go after the bowling) for being such a slow coach!

Hookesy was all fired up after a verbal confrontation with the Victorian captain Graham Yallop, after Yallop had set us 272 in a session, or about 30 overs, to win the match. Some commentators called it a "safe" declaration, Hookesy called it "ludicrous". Hookesy's philosophy demanded that the game should be played in the right spirit.

Hookesy promoted himself to open the batting, a message to Yallop that shouted, "I'm dirty and I'm coming to get you." My usual opening partner Andrew Hilditch, a batsman with a more sedate approach than Hookesy, was dropped down the order to act as a rear guard if things got wobbly. When I walked out with Hookesy there was no hard and fast plan on how we might pull off an improbable win, only Hookesy's short and sharp message, "Let's have a go and see what happens". They were the words often favoured by two great South Australian captains who had preceded him, Ian Chappell and the just as aggressive Les Favell.

Yallop could never have imagined what was about to unfold. His tactic with the new ball was "business as usual" – Rod McCurdy bowling to four slips, two gullies and a short leg. I pushed a single then all hell broke loose. Hookesy slammed 18, a six and three fours, off the first over from a bloke named Peter King. From his two overs King conceded 38 runs. Yallop got into a flap and sent his slips cordon and the short leg to protect the boundaries! I could see the fire in Hookesy's eyes. I said to him, "I'll push the singles and you go for it." Then I pretty much only had to lean on my bat and enjoy the ride. What a ride!

I hadn't even reached double figures (I was nine) when Hookesy hit a three to go from 99 to 102! Can you believe that? I was scoring at a run a ball, but Hookesy was scoring at three runs a ball. It was one of those magic cricketing moments that inspire commentators to beg people to leave work and come down to the Adelaide Oval to witness something special. They'd have had to be quick!

For the record, in Hookesy's 107 off 40 balls he hit three sixes, 18 fours, two threes, three twos, five singles and faced six "dot" balls. He was 50 runs after 17 minutes, I was four. He had 83 runs off six overs, I had seven. When Hookesy got out South Australia were one for 122. By then we were optimistic about getting the runs, but the wheels fell off. I was out for 11 (off a dozen balls) and we slumped from two for 128 after 10 overs to seven for 207 when bad light stopped play with six overs remaining. Andrew Hilditch was nought not out.

I was lucky, too, to bat with Hookesy in the Sheffield Shield matches leading up to his memorable Centenary Test appearance. Over that incredible three-week period when he scored all those centuries, it sticks in my mind how much more purposeful and controlled he was then than when he set that fastest century record. He knew that the

Centenary Test was coming up followed by a tour to England so he was out to impress the selectors Phil Ridings, Sam Loxton and Neil Harvey. They had all played the game in a similar way to Hookesy so must have loved watching him. During that three-week period he faced 914 deliveries and hit 14 sixes and 67 fours. It was his springboard to the next level. He grabbed the imagination of the Australian cricketing public.

We drifted apart when he left to live in Melbourne, but the memories are good – the laughs and good times we had when we roomed together early in our careers, to the reunions celebrating past achievements, is something I cherish. And, because Hookesy was born on the 3rd of May and I was born on the 1st of May, we used to celebrate our birthdays together, usually at the West Torrens club rooms (now demolished) where we'd be watching a local footy game. Hookesy loved his Eagles and loved being with his mates.

I remember Bob Simpson saying to me on my first tour of the West Indies in 1978 that when you look back on your career it probably won't be the on-field experiences that you remember as much as the off-field camaraderie with your mates. Hookesy certainly gave me both. He had such a wide knowledge on most subjects and to me it seemed there weren't enough hours in the day to do all the things he wanted to do in life. Whether he was telling a joke at a bar or a barbecue, addressing the players as captain, giving an after-dinner speech or meeting royalty, he loved being the centre of attention and loved doing whatever he was doing.

True to his Word

PAUL NOBES

Club cricket is not always high on the priority list of first-class cricketers, particularly in these modern times when the itineraries for International games are so full on. Back in the late 1980s I was the opening batsman for West Torrens and David Hookes was both my club and State captain.

David and I took club cricket very seriously and were looking forward to the grand final, West Torrens against Salisbury, which was to be played at the Adelaide Oval. As outlined by Ian Edgley, a great number of West Torrens supporters still think this was "the one that got away".

A couple of our name players were Tim Nielsen, who became South Australian wicketkeeper and Andrew Sincock, who had a stint as coach. Well-known Salisbury players were a very young Darren Lehmann, Glenn Bishop and Peter Sleep, the leg spinning allrounder who played for Australia.

The week leading up to the match coincided with the winding down of State practice and Hookesy spent all of it baiting "Sounda", the squad's affectionate nickname for Sleep. Hookesy's verbal barrage went something along these lines, and always in the hearing of plenty of bystanders: "Sounda, I'm going to slog the hell out of you in the final."

Hookesy, a left-hander, had a theory about leg spinners; there was no such thing as a "good one", simply because the ball would always be coming into him and he could slog it away on the leg side, regularly. He liked to try to prove the point as often as he could when facing leg spinners in the nets. As the week went on Hookesy had got bolder: "Sounda, I'm going to hit the first ball you bowl me for six," he'd say. Often.

On the first day of the final I was batting at the other end when Hookesy came in ... to face ... Sleep! I don't think the thought had crossed Hookesy's mind during all the sledging pre-match that he might be confronted with that possibility. And, even though West Torrens were coasting at two for plenty, I didn't think he would have the balls to try to pull off what he had been threatening all week.

How wrong I was. Sounda bowled a regulation leg spinner, not a bad ball at all, Hookesy swung as hard as he could and "toed" it. I'd like to say the ball sailed over the Victor Richardson gates, the perfect climax. But it just dropped over the fence at forward square leg. Hookesy looked down the pitch at me and smirked. How could I have doubted him?

A Partnership Broken ...

WAYNE PHILLIPS

Yeah, yeah ... partnerships are made to be broken. That may be the case for the majority, but I never thought it would be the case for this one. Hookesy and I enjoyed a tremendous amount of recognition (totally justified, of course!) as a result of that day and a bit in March 1987. The partnership of 462, unbroken, against Tasmania used to be regularly recalled until those Waugh twins, Stephen and Mark, broke it for New South Wales against Western Australia in the 1990-91 season.

But I am happier to reflect on our little performance before I give deserved recognition to the Waughs. David captained South Australia with firm direction and one of his strengths was to ensure all players were aware of their roles in the team, and therefore the game. He generally saw your role as getting your team into the best possible position to win the game of cricket and then, when you were in that position, with the support of your team mates push hard to secure victory.

This was a method of play instilled into David by Ian Chappell when Ian captained South Australia. David enjoyed the opportunity to pass many of the "Chappelli" traits on to his players along with a few of his own well developed thoughts and ideas on how the game should be played.

There was little hinging on the result of South Australia's game against the "Apple Islanders" late in the Sheffield Shield season of 1986-87, but it was a game of cricket there to be won, played at our home ground Adelaide Oval and with maximum points a great way to finish the season. We expected a good pitch for batting in Adelaide and, as the summer conditions imposed themselves, we got exactly that.

Tasmanian captain David Boon won the toss and was keen to have first use of this pretty good strip. History will show that whilst a few of the Tasmanian batsmen got starts South Australia were able to wrap up the Tasmania first innings for 240, with Tim

May claiming the figures of five for 60 from his 20.2 overs. Our innings started late in the evening of day one and at the close of play South Australia had progressed to no wicket for five, Glenn Bishop on two and Andrew "Digger" Hilditch three. I can only think Digger had most of the strike during that brief time!

The South Australian room was well satisfied at the conclusion of play and we were eagerly looking forward to a big day with the bat during day two, and maybe beyond. Day two of the game was one of the better days offered up for cricket – clear blue skies, cool with little or no breeze.

We enjoyed a couple of sound partnerships, 51 between Hilditch and Don O'Connor followed by a stand of 103 between Hilditch and Hookes for the third wicket and, at the fall of Digger's wicket, South Australia were well placed at three for 181 shortly before lunch. Hilditch was, and still is, one of the more astute judges of cricket and, even though I did not hear his comment when he returned to the rooms following his dismissal, it has since been replayed many a time in cricket and social circumstances.

"I've missed the bloody picnic," was his call and, as history will show, he might well have been right.

Hookesy and I pushed the score along with no real record-partnership breaking intent. We wanted to set ourselves for a big first innings with a view to batting once and then bowling our visitors out in their second innings. Our aim was to put our team into the best possible position to win the game.

We kept the scoring rate moving along nicely with very few dramas on day two and, at the close South Australia were … well … still well placed at three for 462. The partnership at that stage was 281 and, with David having taken his score to 230, I felt as though I had played little more than a supporting role with my 110.

It was only whilst enjoying a beer after stumps, and with the game progressing so well for us that we started to have a look at the record books to see what might be, if we could maintain the momentum.

One record immediately grabbed our attention – the stand of 308 between Ian Chappell and Barry Richards for South Australia against Western Australia in Perth during the summer of 1970-71. It was the then highest partnership for any wicket in South Australian Sheffield Shield history. We were both big fans of Ian and Barry and had enormous respect for their playing records and importantly the style and method of their respective games. But, to sneak past their record looked pretty attractive; if we could grab it, it would certainly be worth coaxing a beer from them when next we crossed paths!

The name Bradman always presents itself when Australian and South Australian batting records are discussed. The great man featured in a partnership of 356 with Ron Hamence for South Australia against Tasmania at the Adelaide Oval in 1935-36. That stood as South Australia's highest partnership for any wicket in first-class cricket (now we were really starting to take an interest in cricket history!).

Day three of the match was another "pearler". The Tasmanian attack was under pressure and Hookesy and I felt we had a real chance to snuff out any sort of challenge they might have mounted.

We quickly went past the Chappell-Richards stand. The ground announcer broadcast regular updates which clearly grated on the Tasmanian fielders. David and I were never big on talking to each other at the completion of an over, but this was different because of the large enjoyment factor attached to it. And, we even started to engage in a bit of chat with some of the visitors.

And, as the partnership went past 400 and the game was looking safer and safer for South Australia we really started to enjoy our work. So did the announcer. Updates on the records being eclipsed became more regular: "And, the next target is ... 300 for David Hookes". And, so on.

As Hookesy went past that milestone and our combination passed 450 the game was approaching lunch on day three and the visitors were on their knees. The Tasmanian wicketkeeper Richard Soule tried to lift his ailing mates by calling for "one more effort" before the adjournment. "C'mon, boys let's get a wicket before lunch," he yelled. The response from his skipper Boon was rather terse: "That's what you said yesterday, you dickhead." Amidst the laughter we headed for lunch and declared the innings closed.

Importantly, from a South Australian perspective, we went on to win the game comfortably but it was not until we had captured the final Tasmanian second innings wicket that we started to fully enjoy what had occurred over the previous couple of days.

The record has since been broken, as mentioned, and is still held by that wonderful duo, the recently retired Stephen and Mark Waugh. I had spoken to David about our record going and while there was a bit of disappointment (actually quite a lot on my behalf) we were both delighted it is now held by two great players, who have both provided so much entertainment to so many people around the cricketing world.

The Waughs played their cricket in a positive fashion and sought a draw only when all options of securing a victory had been explored. They also understood the history of the great game and embraced not only the laws, but the spirit of cricket as well. There is no better way to play.

It's hard to believe the partnership has gone ... but so much harder to believe that Hookesy has as well. I am still coming to terms with that.

Plan for 'Deano'

BARRY GIBBS

If anything, Hookesy's sharp cricketing brain pushed the boundaries more than his bat. A classic example of this occurred in a South Australia versus Victoria Sheffield Shield match at Adelaide Oval in October, 1988. Dean Jones was making a meal of the South Australian attack, as he often did, helping himself to runs almost at will.

Hookes noticed that "Deano" was batting about a metre outside the crease, which explained in part why he was getting so many half volleys and so few balls were getting past his bat.

David, who was standing at first slip, hatched a plan to counter the advantage, risky as it was, that Jones was taking. He had a quiet word to wicketkeeper Peter Anderson and the bowler, Andrew Zesers, and instructed "Zes" to bowl the ball so wide of off stump that Deano would not be able to reach it.

Anderson's job was not to make any attempt to take the wide delivery and, instead, allow it to go through to the waiting Hookes in the slips.

Everything worked like clockwork. Zesers bowled the ball so wide that the umpire called "wide", Jones offered no stroke, Anderson didn't move, Hookesy took the ball cleanly in his preferred left hand, then threw the stumps down with a very surprised Jones well out of his crease. The square-leg umpire had no option other than to give Deano out, run out.

It was a brilliantly conceived and executed manoeuvre that surprised just about everyone, especially the hapless Jones, who headed off to the dressing room with smoke coming out of his ears. When Deano had cooled down a bit later, while having a quiet beer, he was asked for his thoughts about Hookesy's tactics. "Technically brilliant, but morally lousy," he said, a bit grudgingly.

CHAPTER
VI

When Hookes started out in One-day cricket Australia tended to play for fun and save the serious stuff for the Test arena. That changed in 1987 when Australia, with a game plan, won the World Cup. Hindsight suggests Hookes, given free rein, would have been brilliant opening, like Adam Gilchrist.

Now, this
is the Plan …

ALLAN BORDER

D avid Hookes was one of my best mates. Our careers intertwined for the best part of 30 years. He epitomised what Australian cricket is all about, in fact what the Australian character is all about: play it hard and fair and to win, but always in the right spirit. In many ways he was unique. He was always scheming. It was a trait that had more than a thread of mischief running through it. For Hookes, this could have been a typical cricket day:

Wake up with a conniving thought;

Get to ground late (missing warm-ups);

Have a few throw downs and a couple of catches;

Get "Nugget" Rees[1] up on table to give the boys a rev up before start of play;

Take chairs away so Nugget can't get down from table (you need to know Nugget);

Make sure game progresses at a rollicking pace, conjuring something controversial
to spring on the opposition;

Have several verbal stoushes with the opposition (especially dumb fast bowlers);

After day's play do press conference giving 20 provocative quotes, taking particular
aim at selectors;

---

[1] Barry "Nugget" Rees has been an integral part of the home dressing room, be it for South Australia or Australia, since he was first introduced to the Adelaide Oval by former Australian Test captain Barry Jarman. "Nug" is afflicted with a mild case of chromosomal abnormality which effects his ability to deal with heights as easily as most. It does not effect his passion, enthusiasm and loyalty for those he supports.

Be the first into opposition rooms carrying icy cold slab of beer;

Moan incessantly about umpiring decisions or how "arsey" someone was if his side lost;

Gloat unmercifully about everything if his side won;

Be last to leave dressing rooms;

Go to pub with team mates and opposition and continue to tell bullshit stories;

Look like you are drinking one-to-one with everyone but skillfully pour half the contents into a nearby pot plant;

Towards the end of the night tell everyone that you are going to the toilet, but instead sneak out (generally this is known as "doing a runner" but in cricket it's "doing a Hookesy");

Get back to hotel and get key to own room and someone else's;

Order 5.30am wake up call for unsuspecting team mate;

Use someone else's key and ransack room putting every piece of furniture, clothes bed, TV, etc on balcony;

Go to own room, bolt door and take phone off hook;

Go to bed with conniving thought for tomorrow.

I first came across Hookes during an Under 19 Australian schoolboy championship played in Melbourne in 1973. I was playing for New South Wales and Hookes for South Australia. Hookes was one of those kids that people naturally gravitated towards, such was his personality. All the talk at that carnival was that he was the next big thing.

Our next meeting was a few years later during the 1976-77 season, the time when Hookes was belting Sheffield Shield attacks to all parts, and he put together his amazing five centuries from six bats. Our NSW attack was no match for Hookes, who scored twin centuries. What sticks with me about those hundreds is not so much the sheer accumulation of runs, but how he scored them.

He was a thrashing machine, and no bowler could rein him in such was his total domination. The older members of the NSW side, players like Graeme Watson, reckoned he reminded them of Graeme Pollock, which I subsequently discovered was a pretty big wrap.

Watson should have known because he was on Australia's 1966-67 tour to South Africa and, at Cape Town, he saw Pollock smash a Test century off 139 balls, then turn it into 209. Back in those days in Sheffield Shield, it was customary for the sides to get together for a few beers and a chat after the day's play. It was during these sessions that my friendship with Hookes really started to blossom.

That run feast nailed him a spot in the Australian side for arguably the biggest Test match ever played, the Centenary Test – typical of Hookes to snare the biggest stage of all to make a start to an International career!

As a result of that match, and a certain five consecutive boundaries off a certain England captain's bowling, David Hookes became a household name. In my mind, I'm not so sure that as the years went by Hookes was altogether happy with that. I believe that he felt unsatisfied with his career overall, and the constant reminder of the Centenary Test heroics rammed home this lack of fulfilment.

But we shouldn't let such reservations get in the way of the truth: Hookes was a fantastic player and, in the right mood, absolutely devastating. There is little doubt that Hookes could have played a lot more Test cricket if he had been willing to make certain sacrifices, like practising with more intensity or changing his game so he was more calculating in the way he accumulated his runs.

However, in saying that, there will be thousands among the followers of the game who would concede more power to him for not going down that path, and instead staying true to the way he wanted to play the game. He would always take the attacking option, both as a captain and player. He couldn't stand the game just drifting along.

As a One-day player, Hookes should have been a sensation. He had all the right ammunition; he could hit all the big shots to the different zones, and he could play the finesse glides and nudges that are also very important. On top of that, his fielding was top class, and he had a strong throwing arm. His left-arm finger spinners could be handy as well. So why isn't he rated in the top echelon of One-day players?

I tend to think it's because when Hookes was starting out in One-day cricket we players didn't take that form of the game as seriously as it is taken these days. We still managed to go all right, but we tended to play just for the fun of it and the serious stuff was saved for the Test match arena. We never really looked closely at any specific tactics as far as batting and bowling line-ups were concerned, and it really wasn't until we won the World Cup in 1987 that we had any sort of a game plan.

In hindsight, I should have been a lot more proactive in working out the best way to use Hookes. For example, I think that I could have used him at the top of the order in a very similar role to the one played today by Adam Gilchrist. Hookes would have been brilliant given a free rein to play his shots and improvise. Ah, the benefit of hindsight!

Nor would his scheming mind have been out of place in the One-day game, where captains and players are forever devising ways to eke out another run or prevent opponents from scoring one. This story about Hookes might offer some insight into that theory.

One particular day Hookes found himself batting with the tail. The opposing captain was placing all the fielders on the boundary, trying to entice Hookes to take a single. As well as cutting off Hookes's options to score fours, they wanted to try to get the tail-ender on strike. As you might imagine these tactics irritated Hookes, who hatched "The Plan".

At the fall of a wicket, Sam Parkinson, a great mate of Hookes's and also up for anything mischievous, joined him at the wicket. The same tactics in the field were employed. Hookes decided it was time to unleash The Plan. What unfolded was pure theatre. As the bowler was about to deliver the ball to Hookes, Parkinson would take off running. Hookes would knock the ball into the outfield but only take a few steps down the pitch. Parkinson would run past Hookes, make his ground at the striker's end, and then charge back to complete a second run before the deep fielders could return the ball from the outfield. Hookes would simply turn around and walk back to the striker's end.

There was much confusion and mass protest and arm-waving from the fielding team, but the umpire could only call "one short"; one run would be added to the total and Hookes would retain the strike. Brilliant! Of course, it hardly passed the unfair play rule but Hookes would have pointed out the fielding tactic wasn't necessarily in the spirit of the game, either. Still, only Hookes could dream up such a tactic. His other dream was to accept a contract to play World Series Cricket.

I'm not sure whether anyone will agree with me but I believe his time with WSC had a detrimental effect on his batting. Consider this: at 21 David Hookes was the brightest batting prospect in Australian cricket, if not world cricket. For the two years of WSC, Hookes played against, day in and day out, some of the best fast bowlers the game has ever seen. Some might say that this should be good for your game but I maintain, whilst that may be true in small doses, a relentless barrage over two years is not so beneficial, especially at such a young age and when you have just started your Test career.

I suggest that this period in his career had a long-term effect on the rest of his time in the game. He still had precocious talent but the footwork and the mindset had been damaged. If Hookes's talent had been nurtured under the normal circumstances of home-and-away Test series against all the different competing countries I personally think that Hookes could have been one of the best. That's just supposition, of course. And anyway, what we got from Hookes was exceptional and I count myself fortunate to have witnessed some of his best.

I batted with him for most of his one and only Test century. We were playing the very first Test between Australia and Sri Lanka in Kandy. It was a typical sub-continent wicket, very good to bat on but taking more and more spin as the game progressed. We were lucky enough to win the toss and batted first. I have little recollection of how the game progressed in the initial stages; my memories are of batting with Hookes between lunch and tea on the second day. In that period, I scored around 40 runs (I thought I smoked them!).

At the other end Hookes was on fire, belting the Sri Lankans to all parts to make a century in a session and finish on 140 not out! It was breathtaking stuff, and rammed home the talent that Hookes had at his disposal.

A tour of the sub-continent is a test of character as well as cricket technique; a squad needs a few characters to get through, those who can lighten the load of constant playing, travelling and practising. Hookes could. In Sri Lanka fireworks could still be bought, a practice outlawed in Australia. Do I need to say any more!

Fireworks and Hookes were a dangerous combination. His "war games" wreaked havoc around the hotel grounds. I deserted and Hookes, wondering where I'd got to, found me lying on my bed reading. He was disgusted that I had left the battlefield and protested when I refused to rejoin. But eventually he said, "Fair enough," and left, quietly. A rat, I should have smelt!

I'd just returned to my book when a penny bunger lobbed into the room and on to the bed, scaring the proverbial out of me and leaving a scorch mark that dismayed the hotel management and ensured Hookes had to face justice from his peers.

On a tour to Pakistan, Hookes and I were room mates and that further strengthened our friendship. The team received an invitation from Majid Khan, the great Pakistani opening batsman, to go on an early morning pheasant shoot on a property just outside Lahore. I was young and naïve, otherwise my warning sensors would have been on high alert because the hunting party included Hookes, Mick Malone, Rod Marsh and Dennis Lillee. If there has been a more dangerous social quartet in any sport I'm yet to meet them, especially as this occasion involved shotguns! I can distinctly remember driving out through the countryside and Malone chanting, "When do we get the guns, when do we get the guns?" It was shades of the movie classic *Police Academy*.

On reaching our destination there was high excitement among the quartet, but trepidation seized the rest of us when, during the rundown on the dos and don'ts, Malone started to chip in with, "Yeah, yeah, mate, but when do we get the guns?" Basically, we were to form a straight line, about three metres apart and walk in formation through the grass while the dogs scurried about trying to flush out the unsuspecting pheasants. Of course, the quartet rushed off eager to shoot anything that moved, while the rest of us moved along at a less than enthusiastic pace.

Shortly, the hunters were scattered in all directions. As luck would have it, a pheasant flew out of the long grass right next to me. That scared me, but the sight of eight shotguns pointing in my direction about to blast away certainly got the juices flowing. I hit the deck as bursts of gunfire exploded all around. The bird escaped. It turned out to be a fun day (we all survived!), and a particularly good one for the pheasants (so did they!). I don't think any of our blokes are going to challenge Michael Diamond for a place on the Olympic Shoot Team!

After cricket, my strong friendship with Hookes continued at Fox Sports on the show "Inside Cricket". He had made the transition from cricketer to cricket commentator with consummate ease. He was a joy to work with, always pushing the boundaries and making thought-provoking comments.

Most discussions started on cricket, but such were Hookes's argumentative skills he could quite easily move on to any other topic, especially if he thought he could get you riled.

His role as Victorian coach was totally fulfilling his passion for the game. He was really enjoying the hands-on role of working with young cricketers and was making a huge difference to those players in his charge.

He was a great mate and confidant, at times controversial but always a straight shooter. His passing hit everyone who knew him hard, and I can't help but think of a line from the Joni Mitchell classic "Big Yellow Taxi" that goes: "Don't it always seem to go that, you don't know what you've got till it's gone". For me, that's what it feels like.

Wipeout
at Waikiki

GREG RITCHIE

David Hookes was never a guy to shirk a challenge, whether it be wearing his favourite South Australian cap or wearing the baggy green for Australia. In 1984, having completed a very arduous tour of the West Indies where Australia were comprehensively beaten, Hookes and others who batted in the top order, Ritchie, Wayne Phillips, Dean Jones and Roger Woolley, had a little stopover in a place called Hawaii.

We all had units for a week on the 17th floor of The Outrigger Resort on Waikiki Beach. There were many surfers out on the famous Waikiki break enjoying what was a perfect break day after day. Mind you, the surf looked rather innocuous from 17 floors up; in fact it only looked about two to three feet.

David had seen me ride a surfboard in the West Indies on a couple of occasions and it really got up his nose that I – aka "Fat Cat" – could do it and he couldn't. So, the suggestion was made one evening over a few beers that the next day we should all try and ride the famous Waikiki beach break, or reef break, on the grounds that if Fat Cat could do it they could all do it!

Well, Jones, Phillips and Woolley all pulled out pretty quickly but Hookes said, "Nah, I'm going to be able to do this if Fat Cat can do it." It was agreed that at nine o'clock in the morning we would go down and hire two surfboards and I would take Hookes out to the reef break and we'd ride the boards.

In the morning the surf had picked up a little bit, but still looked rather innocuous from 17 floors up. We went to get the boards. Hookes was wearing stubby shorts not board shorts; he wasn't bald, but the only thing that made him look like a surfer was the fact that he had a little bit of blonde hair.

"Can you guys surf?" was the call from the guy hiring the boards. What else were we going to say but, "Course we can," and we made our way out through the famous Waikiki boat channel to where the waves were breaking and about 30 guys were enjoying what was a perfect little right-hander.

I told Hookes that this probably wasn't going to be as easy as he thought. The reef was only about four feet deep where six-foot waves were breaking. It was going to be a rather precarious thing for both of us to do, but I'd surfed since I was eight and was somewhat experienced. Hookes was a novice who had never surfed before.

"Bullshit," was the call from Hookes. "If you can do it, Cat, so can I; just show me and I'll watch from here for a while and we'll see how it goes." So we sat off to the side of the break for a while. It's a pretty mean wave at Waikiki ... well, maybe five foot isn't big for the Hawaiians, but this thing was barrelling a little bit and it was certainly sucking up too.

In some sections it was exposing the coral, and I just thought to myself, "This is probably not the best wave for a novice to catch, and it's certainly going to keep my mind on the job as well."

So I waited a while, but soon I could wait no longer – it was such a pure wave and such clean conditions. I said to Hookes, "Mate, you sit here. I'm gonna catch a wave and you can have a watch and hope I don't kill myself." He said, "Yeah, righto."

I picked the smallest waves in the sets, waited until I got an opportunity and caught a wave. After a nice little ride of about 50 to 60 metres I went off into the channel, coming off the wave not too far away from Hookes, who had a big smile on his face. He said, "That didn't look that hard to me, Fat Cat. My turn."

"Okay," I said, "but before we do let's have a look at a couple of other guys, the way they do it, and I can explain some of the finer points to you." So, we went through the basics of catching a wave ... not too far up the front of the board ... let the tail rise ... let the wave pick you up. I said, "It's probably not a good idea to try and stand the first time, Hook; why don't you sort of just lie down?" He thought that was okay and wanted me to show him how all that would pan out.

So I paddled out again and showed him how to catch a wave and just lie on the board, showed him how to steer it and came back in again. Then we both paddled out and I got him into a pretty good position right over as close to the channel and the deep water as I could, where he wasn't going to hit any exposed reef.

I said, "Okay, Hookes, here comes your wave." It was one of the smaller ones in the set, probably about three to four foot. I could see the expression on his face. He had a big smile, which turned to a look of excited anticipation when the back of the board lifted and he could feel that he was on the wave. Then came the look of "Holy smoke, what am I doing?" as, instead of turning, Hookes pointed the board straight down the wave and, sure enough, that's where he went, straight down to the base of the wave.

The board bounced straight off the bottom, Hookes didn't, which was lucky. He came up in the channel, but the board went careering through the white water, heading for the rocks at Waikiki because Hookes had dismantled the leg rope that should have been attached; the thought of being attached to a runaway surfboard hadn't appealed to him.

He shouted to me, "Give me your board and you go get mine." I said, "No way, you're on your own." He said, "I'll swim in."

He did, and got hit by a couple of waves and even by a surfboard; he also cut a foot pretty badly on some coral. To see him come out of the surf and up the beach with so much "claret" coming out of him provoked a lot of humour among Jones, Phillips, Mrs Ritchie and Mrs Phillips and certainly Robyn Hookes.

Hookes's pride was hurt, so he made sure he didn't make much of his plight, and he didn't pay too much attention to dressing the wound for the first couple of days only to find that by day three the foot was so red it looked like he had the worse case of gout you've ever seen in your life. He had a serious coral infection.

Worse still, I reckon every time we went to a restaurant some imbecile trod on it. He spent the last two days on crutches.

He made us promise that none of us would never ever say anything to his team mates back home; three hours later Wayne Phillips had phoned half the South Australian team. I don't think Hookes ever rode a surfboard after that, but if anyone ever asked him if he had surfed he'd have responded with a very laid back, "Oh, yeah, Waikiki … surfed the reef at Waikiki." He was a wonderful human being.

A Tad Headstrong

DENNIS LILLEE

There is always one thing I will remember about David Hookes. Out of the blue, and just as exciting as the arrival of Doug Walters, emerged this tremendously confident young lad who always had an opinion. But you couldn't help but like him because there was always a smile or a laugh attached to his comments. Some people took him the wrong way but he certainly didn't rub me the wrong way.

If people didn't like what he said then he simply didn't care. That's the way he was and to be like that at a young age is pretty different. I think the fact that he was appreciated by a guy like Ian Chappell, who was respected by all cricketers, had a bit to do with it. You tended to give a guy in that position a bit more of a chance to express himself, whereas the other guys who were a bit bombastic were more likely to get the "who the hell do you think you are?" treatment. And make no mistake, there were a few bombastic cricketers around you simply couldn't warm to. Those were my first impressions of Hookesy.

Now to the Centenary Test, which some said was the most significant match in the history of the game. Because of Hookesy's attitude to life, an event like the Centenary Test wouldn't faze him; for me, it was a daunting prospect. Hookesy proved he was not fazed by taking on, verbally and physically, an equally brash opponent in Tony Greig, who was known for his confrontational attitude to life. It was Hookes one, Greig nil, a score line made in heaven!

Although he did well during World Series Cricket against some of the best players on the planet, it was strange that his Test career didn't go on and reach the same dizzy heights. Yet, he continued on his merry way in the Sheffield Shield as a player, coach and mentor, much along the lines of Ian Chappell, his hero basically. Maybe this is a clue to why Hookesy's Test career didn't set the world on fire: he probably didn't try to adapt to Test cricket like most other players simply knew they had to.

When you reach that level you've got to change your style. It doesn't have to be a major step, but it has to be done. But a bloke like Hookesy, whose style was outright attack, would have found it difficult to play more defensively. It seemed Hookesy wanted to make a statement every time he went out to bat.

The 1984 tour of the West Indies was one that didn't go well for Hookesy, or for most of Kim Hughes's team against Clive Lloyd's awesome outfit. Rain paved the way for a draw in Georgetown, and Allan Border's heroics provided the same result in Port-of-Spain before the home side romped to wins by 10 wickets, an innings and 36 runs, and 10 wickets in Bridgetown, St John's and Kingston. Press reports were not glowing.

Guests at the team hotel in Kingston had been advised it was too dangerous to go out jogging around the streets and Jim Woodward, who was covering the tour for Sydney's *Daily Telegraph,* copped the tip and stuck to the running track that wound its way around the hotel and inside the security fence. Woodward was plodding around the track one morning when he felt an object strike him on the head, followed by several other direct hits. The missiles turned out to be rolls of toilet paper launched from the balcony of an obviously peeved Australian left-hand middle-order batsman. Hookesy had his own special way of venting his animosity.

The Puerto Rican Fade

JEFF CROWE

Nice mobile home," were the words shouted at the traffic lights from the sleek new silver Alfa Romeo GTV purring away next to my chugg'n' green VW station wagon around the Adelaide suburb of Grange one afternoon in 1977. Just Hook making a play as we were idling at an intersection, that's all. Damn funny, though, when you think about it!

My parents had just arrived in town to check out my adopted home and soon learned the wit of my great team mate and captain. From there the Hookes and the Crowes formed a terrific, warm relationship. My father Dave, also with first names David William, died in May 2000 and just adored Hook, the way he played and the way he joked.

There are a million stories that all involve Hook. One of the classics for me happened when we were in a bar (funny that) late in the evening, when I was touring with New Zealand and catching up on old times. Just as I had bought the next round, David said to me, "Going to the blokes for a 'hit 'n miss', see you in 'five'." He was nearly right. About six months later I saw him again – and had learnt a valuable lesson: never stay longer than you should, just go quietly without any drama or fanfare. I think he called it the "Puerto Rican fade"!

He was so much fun off the field but definitely more on it, and any chance to catch up with him to have a feed or lubricant was simply automatic. It was his actions and demeanour on the park that I watched with wonderment. I guess a lot of it was inspired by Chappelli, Ian Chappell. Hook's complete passion for the game and its values was impressive.

No one, especially New South Wales, will forget the Sheffield Shield match at the SCG when South Australia were 11 runs from victory when the local umpires pulled the plug due to bad light and storms rolling in. Hook wouldn't leave the ground because as far as he was concerned it was still playable, and leant on the roller for what seemed like hours suggesting, "Let's finish," until lightning threatened to cook him. He couldn't believe the premature end to the game; he thought it had been manipulated and let everyone involved know about it.

How could I forget my return, as a Kiwi, to the Adelaide Oval against my former South Australian team mates. Right from the word go, Hook made me feel as uncomfortable as possible. I can only imagine what it was like for anyone playing against him for the first time. When he came on to bowl with brother Martin tearing the Croweaters apart, he used a brilliant tactic on me, his mate, to deliver the ball before I had even looked up from the batting crease.

It was only because Wayne Phillips from behind the stumps warned me he was bowling that I had time to squeeze the ball out. The look on his face was of a pure competitive nature; it was his clear cut message to me that I was now the opposition and "anything goes, pal".

Hook was a true leader, and I followed his every word and course. He led by example in his own flamboyant and unique way. I respected his sharpness and ability to seize the moment that only few can do. I will miss him ringing me at some ungodly hour, when I am living on the other side of the world, just to say he's eating a "cop the lot" hamburger from Fast Eddies in Perth, one of his favourite spots after a few pints. I miss him because I just loved being with him.

Window of Opportunity

RODNEY HOGG

There were many sides to David Hookes. Apart from often thinking outside the square, another intriguing aspect to Hookesy was his idolisation of the great Ian Chappell. He simply loved the bloke, I'm sure modelled himself on him. If "Chappelli" was to take up smoking cigars, Hookesy would too.

It seemed to be part of some sort of fraternity in South Australian cricket. The great Les Favell, who was a captain and father figure back in the 1960s, started it all. Chappell learnt much of his cricket from Les. Chappelli passed this on to Hookesy and then Hookesy did exactly the same thing for Darren "Boof" Lehmann. I know Boof idolised Hookesy, and he did have a lot to thank him for as far as the development of his game went, and his attitude.

Chappelli and Hookesy were both walking, talking cricketing encyclopaedias. Chappell would never forget anything; without batting an eye, he could remember in detail what happened on the third day of a Test match at Trent Bridge 10 years ago. For some odd reason Hookesy had the same talent, but with a twist; he could also recall the most insignificant facts from the history of the game, or of matches he had played.

The two were also fiercely competitive; their style was to attack and only defend in the direst of circumstances; they hated the thought of a draw and they were pretty good at giving verbal sprays to the opposition; they both loved to play the hook shot, which when you think about it is the most aggressive counter play in the game of cricket. Batsmen who play the hook shot have what might be called "attitude".

When I first saw David Hookes I noticed he had a presence, an aura of confidence about him. I wondered to myself, "Who in the hell is this young pup?" It was 1975 and my team Woodville was playing against Hookesy's beloved West Torrens. The captain-coach of Woodville was a pretty fair trundler named John Nason, and Hookesy was facing.

There was nothing wrong with the first ball bowled, but Hookesy got inside it and flipped it over the grandstand and out of the ground for six. I thought, "Christ, how in the hell did he do that?"

What most people wouldn't know about Hookesy is that at grade level he bowled a pretty useful bouncer. Again I go to an encounter between Woodville and West Torrens. Hookesy, bowling his bouncers, picked up four quick wickets and had us in trouble. Michael Clingly, now a tycoon on the Gold Coast, and whose father played State football for South Australia, and Hookesy were having a bit to say to each other.

Hookesy, off his long run, bowled to Clingly who played forward, dropped the ball just about dead, then set off for a single. Hookesy kept coming and ran straight through Clingly, knocking him to the ground.

Things were totally out of control even though former Test umpire Max O'Connell and experienced umpire Mike Gandy were standing. In the finish the players sorted it out.

Hookesy, could get a bee in his bonnet. A mate of mine, Woodville's David Kelly, was selected to play for South Australia as wicketkeeper. Three games passed with Kelly wicketkeeping and skipper Hookes standing at first slip. In the entire three games, Hookesy didn't speak one word to David Kelly. Why?

I've got no bloody idea, but I did think it odd. Maybe he thought that Kelly had been selected ahead of somebody Hookesy preferred, but who would know?

Personally, I wouldn't have reacted too kindly to that sort of treatment. Kelly was at David's funeral so there remained a friendship and respect between the two.

In another match a young quick named Brian Vincent was bowling so well to Hookesy that he decided on the intimidation trick. For about four balls, Hookesy walked all the way back to the bowler's mark with Vincent before walking all the way back to his crease to take strike. Needless to say the bowler lost his concentration, line and length. The umpire should have nailed Hookesy after his first go.

Another memory of Hookesy is going to stick with me as long as I drive a car. One day Hookesy was in the front seat next to me and I was trying to reverse park into a pretty tight spot. After four unsuccessful attempts I spat the dummy.

Hookesy piped up: "Listen, maaaaate, why don't you wake up to yourself and look to your left next time you try?"

I looked to my left. There was a tinted glass window and in the window was the reflection of my car. Looking in the window I could see how far back I could go and how far forward.

Windows aren't always available when you are trying to park your car, but when they are I always think of my mate. Many of the friends Hookesy had never saw enough of him. I am one of those.

Victim of the Sting

JIM MAXWELL AND PAUL NOBES

Maxwell: David Hookes relished a challenge. And, he respected opponents who would go with him to keep fading contests alive with a surprise declaration, and a fourth innings run chase. Sometimes the tactic misfired, but Hookesy's only regret would be the failure of his bowlers to do their job, or some stupid shot selection that wrecked the pursuit of a target.

On 11th February 1989, the third day of a Sheffield Shield match at the SCG, New South Wales were labouring in their first innings reply to South Australia's 356. John Dyson and Mark Taylor had made a slow start against the persistency of Joe Scuderi, Peter Gladigau, Tim May and Andrew Zesers, and with little momentum from the middle order of the Waugh twins and Steve Smith, the match appeared destined for first innings points. During lunch Hookes spoke to the NSW captain Geoff Lawson.

Nobes: Because NSW were struggling to get to our first innings score Hookesy and "Henry" (Lawson) agreed that we would give NSW some easy runs so they could declare 50 runs behind our score, therefore sacrificing first innings points to us, but allowing us to set them a target on the last day. The plan was we would bowl some crap with aggressive fields and NSW would score quickly.

M: South Australia had to bowl their spinners and keep the field up, which they did. Lawson told Hookes "he'd see how it goes for half an hour", which Hookes read as a commitment from NSW that they would declare. With Greg Matthews and Peter Taylor thrashing the bowling, particularly Peter Sleep's leg spin, the score ran rapidly past the anticipated total for a declaration.

N: When NSW got to within 50 runs Hookesy actually started to walk towards the rooms but Henry was nowhere to be seen; obviously he was about to renege on the deal. Hookesy was ropeable.

M: All of a sudden NSW were rushing towards a first innings lead and Hookes's demeanour quickly changed from cheerful expectation to blood red fury. Hookes was wicketkeeping at the time, temporarily subbing for the injured Peter Anderson.

N: The expletives were very loud and very much directed towards Henry, who must have been hiding somewhere in the rooms. Barry Richards, the South Australian coach, had quickly drawn up a plan on a piece of paper which was passed on to Hookesy: "Get Scuderi and the other bowler to bowl two and a half feet down leg side." The idea was to make it almost impossible for NSW to score runs.

M: A small, but stunned and stirred crowd booed Hookes's tactics, and broke into mock applause when one of the leg side missiles went through Hookes's gloves for four byes. Matthews and Taylor added 143 in an hour and a half, and Lawson declared as soon as the first innings points had been secured. Hookes's bad language drew a rebuke from the crowd, and he would have copped a serious penalty under the current code of conduct.

N: Hookesy was livid, clearly upset by what had happened and, as I was batting at three there was enough time for him to explain to me his side of the story. I'll never forget going out to bat in the second innings; I was totally pumped and not thinking too clearly. Everyone on both sides had become pretty emotional. I remember standing at the non-striker's end and having words with Henry.

M: Lawson, who subsequently claimed that there had been a "misunderstanding", had the last laugh on Hookes when he trapped him leg before for one.

N: I then had to face the pace of Mike Whitney, who I proceeded to hit for a number of boundaries. There was a lot of sledging between balls, both ways. He then ran in and bowled a "beamer", straight at my head, which was totally out of character for "Roy" (Whitney), and just illustrated how fired up we'd all become.

Mark Taylor and Steve Waugh were quick to apologise and when Mike was half way back to his bowling mark he turned and held up his hand in an apologetic gesture. "Sorry, mate," he shouted back down to me, "that was for your captain Hookes." I replied: "You missed him by a mile." Hookesy could certainly stir emotions.

M: Far from setting up a finish, South Australia were struggling at three for 46, but an Andrew Hilditch century in a rescue partnership with Darren Lehmann ensured the match fizzled out on the final day. On that fourth afternoon, a Sunday, I did a lengthy interview with Hookes, questioning him on the way he had behaved, why he had reacted so tempestuously, shifting the blame towards NSW for failing to enter into the spirit of the game, pointing out that quite a few people had called the ABC, enraged about the language in the field.

They'd had children there, they said, where was the value system, what was the game coming to, that sort of thing. David sought appeasement and very articulately defended his tactical position, if not the team's behaviour. He was careful to avoid a charge of collusion, because the appointed match referee, former Test umpire Ted Wykes, was empowered to investigate any shenanigans.

Hookes's on-air performance inspired a series of letters from listeners, some of whom were still upset by the appalling example he set for youngsters within earshot of his expletives, and others who reckoned Hookes had a career as a barrister or a politician, following his defence under cross examination from the ABC commentary team. I thought then that he might have a future as a cricket commentator, as an analyser of events.

Looking back, the events that took place were wonderful theatre, keeping in mind that none of the commentators or spectators had any idea about what the captains had been up to during the lunch break. It was the sharp-minded, uncompromising future Australian captain, Steve Waugh, who coined the most appropriate description of the day's events as the players filtered into the dressing rooms for the usual end of play beers: "Mate, that was the best sting I've ever seen."

Hot, Cold, and Cut

IAN MCDONALD

D avid Hookes was such a high profile cricket personality, that it comes as a surprise to many people that he actually only had a short span as an Australian player. It has always been an intriguing selection mystery as to why he played only 23 Tests between his blazing debut in the 1977 Centenary Test at the MCG, and his final Test nine seasons later on India's 1985-1986 tour of Australia.

There are reasons, of course, but no satisfactory explanations, because he was too entertaining a batsman not to have played more Tests. Reasons such as the World Series Cricket revolution, which rocked the cricket world in the months following the Centenary Test, and a dismal 1977 tour of England when Australia lost the Ashes three-one. Hookes scored 283 in nine Test innings on that tour, with 85 in the Fifth Test his highest score, to average 31.44. He was one of 13 players on the tour who had secretly signed up with Kerry Packer and how his career would have developed had he remained in official ranks with Allan Border is open to conjecture; you can't rewrite history.

When peace was signed between the Australian Cricket Board and World Series Cricket in the 1979-80 season, he suffered a severe hamstring injury in an early season Shield game, and was to have recurring trouble with the injury, playing in only the First Test against the West Indies.

All told he missed the last five Tests of the summer and the last four World Series Cup One-day Internationals, but he was still on the selectors' list when he recovered and was chosen for the 1980 tour of Pakistan. In hindsight, he was later to admit that because of the hamstring trouble he wasn't fit enough and struggled with his footwork against the Pakistani spinners.

Four weeks later, when the squad was named to go to England for the Centenary Test at Lord's, he wasn't in the touring party and he was even dropped from the South Australian team. He remained in the wilderness, missing out on the 1980-81 New Zealand tour of Australia, the Indian tour of Australia in the same season, the 1981 tour of England, and the 1981-82 West Indies tour of Australia. That's a lot of International cricket to miss out on.

Hookesy, however, never lacked determination or courage. His confidence, and undoubted talent returned and the runs started flowing again in Shield cricket, and eventually he fought his way back into the Australian team for a successful 1982-83 season, followed by the one-off inaugural Test against Sri Lanka at Kandy where he scored his only Test century. Perhaps that is one of the answers; he scored eight Test fifties, including four in the 1982-83 summer against England, which was proof of his good form, but he was unable to go on and build centuries. If he had, they may never have got him out of the team.

Instead, he ended up in hospital with viral pneumonia and missed the 1983-84 Test series against Pakistan. Then he tore a cruciate ligament in his right knee in a One-day International against the West Indies at the MCG in January 1984, and history repeated itself – he wasn't fully fit when he went on the 1984 tour of the West Indies, which the home side won three-nil. With an average of 24.80 it was again a disappointing tour.

Even Hookesy thought it was the end. He was ignored by the selectors for 18 months, until the 1985-86 season when he was surprised by a recall for the Second Test against New Zealand in Sydney and elevated to vice-captain because Allan Border's deputy, Andrew Hilditch, had been dropped.

It was a modest return; he faced three balls and was run out batting with Greg Ritchie. When he strode back into the dressing room he was surprisingly calm, didn't hurl his bat at a locker or yell at himself. It was a heartbreaking way to get out in his comeback and he summed it up later in the day saying, "I'm older and wiser now."

In the second innings he figured in fighting stands with Greg Matthews and Simon O'Donnell to score 38 not out and help steer Australia to victory. The series moved to the Third, and final Test at Perth where he did himself no favours. Playing without discipline he swung across the line of flight trying to hoist Jeremy Coney over mid-wicket and was caught for 14, and then was bowled for seven in the second innings at a time Australia desperately needed him to make a stand, and Australia lost the Test and the series.

Another three-Test series in Australia followed against India. The First Test was on his home ground at Adelaide and his many supporters were baffled as he pottered around for an uncharacteristically slow 34, before being bowled in the last over before lunch pushing forward over the top of a half volley.

There's no doubt the selectors would not have been happy with his efforts in Perth and Adelaide, but in the Second Test in Melbourne he batted reasonably well for

42 before deciding to step down the pitch against spinner Ravi Shastri, only to miss the ball and be bowled. Luck wasn't with him in the second innings when he was given out for a duck, caught bat-pad again to Shastri. When he came off the ground he was adamant he hadn't hit the ball, saying, "I didn't even play a shot at it."

Hookesy's disappointment became even more acute when he was made twelfth man for the Third, and final Test at Sydney. That duck proved to be his final appearance for Australia; he was never selected for another Test and he was also dumped from the One-day squad and one can't help wondering why, after ignoring him for 18 months before bringing him into the team, the selectors had showed such a lack of patience by allowing him just four Tests.

It always rankled him that he was never given a final chance in Sydney because he felt he was close to hitting form, something he proved five days later when he blazed 243, with 10 sixes and 26 fours, for South Australia. However, it was too late. Injury, illness, clashes with officialdom and a tendency to "do it his way", all contributed, but this colourful and entertaining batsman really had the ability to deserve a longer career playing for Australia.

CHAPTER
VII

Mateship is the quintessential characteristic of the Australian male. Only those who have been a Test cricketer would understand the bond that is forged between team mates. David Hookes's cricketing days were over, but his life as a touring commentator extended those glory days.

Career Metamorphosis

Graham Cornes

There was no early indication that David Hookes was destined for a significant career in the media. There are those who are blessed at a young age with the vision of their life's expectations and pursue it relentlessly, and methodically. Then there are those whose substantial station in life is arrived at via that bewildering fusion of talent, opportunity, fate and an ability to discern the choices that will enhance a life rather than diminish it.

That David Hookes was born with, and further enhanced a prodigious sporting talent, was obvious. What was not quite so obvious was his instinctive feel for the career opportunities that were presented to him. Intuition, rather than any hard-nosed business aptitudes, guided him. His media star rose and rose, and was still in its ascendancy when his life was tragically cut short.

As an inner-suburban urchin, like so many of his era, Hookes's sporting interests were seasonal; summer was cricket season, winter was footy season, Australian rules football. He dreamed of playing both at the highest level; he confessed much later in life that one of the great disappointments of his sporting career was being omitted from that Under 19 West Torrens rules team that played in the 1973 grand final.

It is well documented that Thebarton Oval, a typically ugly suburban sports ground, was his shrine to both sports. David Hookes would rather have been there than anywhere else. The oval was affectionately known to all as "The Pug-hole". It teetered on the rim of a huge excavation from which was dug the clay that supplied the adjacent brickworks. The chimneystack from the brickworks dominated the suburban landscape, and in winter cast its long shadow over the playing field.

In the time of Hookesy's childhood the local football ground was a meeting place for the urban tribes that lived their lives vicariously through the exploits of the local footy stars. If you couldn't get to the ground, or couldn't afford to go, which was a reality for many of the working class families, you listened to it on the wireless.

That wasn't entirely free either, but at least the cost of a wireless licence wasn't prohibitive, particularly when the wireless was the working class family's entire entertainment centre. Most of the local radio stations broadcast the football. The odd one even presented the football teams on selection night, which was Thursday.

The commentators, whilst well known in football circles, were not instantly recognisable in the street. Of course, there was the obligatory selection of past champions, but often they were radiomen, who gravitated to the commentating game by accident. The great Victor York Richardson, South Australia's greatest all round sportsman, (he represented Australia in cricket and baseball, and won the Magarey Medal, South Australia's highest football honour) was one of those past champions who commentated through those years of Hookesy's childhood. Hookes hung on his words of sporting wisdom, unaware at the time how fate would eventually link him to Richardson through his own cricketing exploits and Hookes's venerated mentor, Ian Chappell, Richardson's grandson.

There are other famous radio names that flow back through the mists of memory of those years: Bert Day, Ken Aplin, the AFL Hall of Fame Umpire, John Mehaffey, Murray Tippett, Eldon Crouch, Gordon Shwartz, and ex-footy stars Pat Hall, and Tom Warhurst. The latter, a debonair tennis star, who played football so elegantly for Norwood, was later the South Australian representative for Adidas sporting goods, which supplied Hookes with much of his sporting clothing and footwear.

Television was the new exciting medium, but the full impact of sporting telecasts was yet to be felt. The American shows dominated television programming, however local football replays, the Saturday evening reviews of the matches, and the Sunday football shows became mandatory viewing for all South Australian footy fans.

These locally produced programs were outrageously parochial, and made local heroes of the footballers. They also made celebrities of the presenters, some of whom, as in radio, were professional broadcasters. Others were star players of the past and present. Several were umpires, including one Kenneth George ("KG") Cunningham, also a South Australian first-class cricketer of considerable talent, who was to play an enormous role in Hookes's transformation from cricket star to multi-media personality.

As a boy, however, Hookes knew none of this; neither could he have guessed. Radio and television were grand mysteries to him, and the stars of the electronic media were as glamorous, distant and exciting as those idols of his who played Test cricket for Australia.

Adelaide is a unique city, a model of town planning through the genius and foresight of Colonel William Light, a heroic, but ultimately hapless veteran of the Napoleonic Wars; it is by far the easiest of Australia's capital cities in which to live. Colonised in 1836 by free settlers, as distinct from those of the "convict stain", Adelaide over the ensuing centuries developed its own personality and psychology. It wasn't always pleasant, nor was it loved or appreciated by those from outside. Conservatism and resistance to change often suppress initiative, and render Adelaide excluded from progress.

Charles Landry, the internationally renowned consultant on urban cultures, city futures, cultural planning, heritage, and strategic policy development completed his tenure as an "Adelaide Thinker in Residence", with a not altogether glowing, and, in part, contradictory analysis of the city:

> *"There's a sense of high-mindedness, a self-conception that it is caring, ethical, reasonable, and a view that in the end, Adelaide is really better than all those other upstart cities that have sacrificed a good quality of life in order to chase gaudy ambitions ... It is a place where the 'tall poppy' syndrome appears worse than it should be ... It is a place that always thinks it is smaller than somewhere else and has an inferiority complex which some say makes the city feel suffocating rather than liberating."*
> [RETHINKING ADELAIDE "CAPTURING IMAGINATION" CHARLES LANDRY.
> DEPARTMENT OF THE PREMIER AND CABINET]

Nevertheless, South Australia has produced more than its share of sporting champions. The driving force of a collective inferiority complex should never be underestimated. In this fertile sporting environment, David Hookes flourished. From prodigy to precocious young talent playing Test cricket for Australia, through the turmoil and excitement of the World Series Cricket revolution, through the frustration of Test demotion, to the stellar proportions of his South Australian captaincy, Hookes became a South Australian sporting icon. With it came the first flicker of a career in the sporting media.

Throughout his playing career Hookes had flirted with the media, but it was always in the role of the subject rather than the commentator. With maturity as a man and status as an international sportsman, came the confidence to front the camera and speak into the microphone. But he was always the guest.

Hookes's first opportunity to venture into a more active role in the media was the inspiration of "KG" Cunningham. By the mid-1980s, Cunningham had developed a surprisingly unique sporting programme on radio station 5DN. Surprising it was, because the self-deprecating Cunningham was the most unlikely radio host.

He had been forced to leave school at 13 years of age, because of a stuttering problem. And, the programme was unique because few radio stations in Australia would have taken a risk with an all-sport programme at "drive-time". It was a stunning success, a South Australian phenomenon, which at times rated an unbelievable 26 per cent of the local market.

Sport had saved Cunningham. Despite his speech impediment and a painful shyness, he was an outstanding young cricketer, and a more than handy footballer. His cricket career developed to the stage where he was a wonderful contributor in the great South Australian Sheffield Shield teams of the 1960s, and he toured New Zealand as a member of Australia's B team.

He stopped playing football but took up umpiring and, for several years, was the elite umpire of the South Australian National Football League. His sporting life gradually restored a confidence and self-esteem that was lacking as a child, and whilst he could never be described as an eloquent speaker, he could convey his passion in a captivating manner, without the slightest hint of his former impediment.

He had only two loves, and two interests in life: family and sport. As bewildering as it might have seemed to any interstate visitor who happened upon his programme, he was a South Australian institution. Just as incredibly he hosted the Saturday evening football show on Channel Nine, a wrap-up of the day's local football action. It could only have happened in Adelaide.

Cunningham recognised that the charismatic Hookes, with his international reputation, and as the captain of the South Australian cricket team, could only enhance his programme. Consequently 5DN contracted Hookes to appear regularly on Cunningham's drive programme. He reported on the day's cricket proceedings, often live, in the studio which was conveniently located close to Adelaide Oval; appeared on a Saturday morning sporting panel, and occasionally appeared as a panelist on Cunningham's television show.

He was still first and foremost a cricketer, but his media savvy and his exposure (if he indeed needed it) were improving constantly. He had no aspirations for a fulltime radio career, but fate was about to intervene.

Radio station 5DN had no serious competitors in the news-talk-sport format in Adelaide. On the other side of town, radio station 5AA had been plugging along with a similar format, but because the station was owned by the TAB, the totalisator board, their format was heavily interrupted by race calls from all over the country. It was known as "the racing station", and made little impact in the marketplace.

Nevertheless, there was a competitor of sorts to the unassailable KG. Ian Aitken, an affable, extroverted ex-Perth footballer, who had made his name locally as a local television football commentator, hosted the drive programme at 5AA. Given the requirement of the owners of the station to broadcast the races, Aitken's programme was cruising along professionally enough, but with no real expectations. The ground was about to shift beneath him.

Neville Roberts was one of David Hookes's close friends. Like Hookes, Roberts had grown up at Thebarton Oval. A star footballer from an early age, he had expanded his career into the Victorian Football League, before returning to Adelaide and playing again for West Torrens and Norwood. He and Hookes had shared several business projects, the most notable of which was a gymnasium and fitness centre. Roberts had that entrepreneurial drive that generated enthusiasm and opportunity. Unfortunately, not all of his ventures were successful, and understandably, there was occasionally some residual resentment when they failed. Roberts had a proposal that he was keen to spin to the management of 5AA – he and David Hookes would host a drive-time sporting programme in direct opposition to KG Cunningham.

He was able to secure a lunchtime appointment with 5AA's general manager, Stan Barrett, and programme director, Nigel Cocks. Roberts did most of the talking, with Hookes providing tacit support.

Stan Barrett was something of an enigma in South Australian radio circles. An American from South Virginia, he had served with the US Navy attached to a marine unit, before pursuing a career in radio which took him from the National Academy of Broadcasting in Columbus, Georgia, to radio stations as far afield as Canada and Puerto Rico. In what he said was the smartest move he ever made, he settled in Australia.

Barrett was an autocratic senior executive. It was a strength, but in a corporate world that was beset by a new order, it was paradoxically also one of his weaknesses. His other strengths were that he knew radio, and he certainly could identify talent. While Neville Roberts dominated the discussion and the presentation, and Hookes played his cameo role, both Barrett and Cocks came to the same conclusion: David Hookes was the man that they really wanted at 5AA.

Not long after the meeting, they offered him the job as a fulltime, on-air partner to Ian Aitken. Despite the fact that he still had a year of his contract to run at 5DN, and had never given any indication that he wanted to work full-time in radio, Hookes went to Cunningham and told him he was leaving … to work in opposition to him. It was a bitter blow to Cunningham, who cherished loyalty and felt that having given Hookes an opportunity he could have been given the chance to find an enhanced role at 5DN for him.

Never a confident individual, despite his now substantial status in Adelaide, Cunningham's insecurities were also aroused at the thought of Hookes working in direct opposition. There were terse words, and the threat that 5DN would hold Hookes to his contract, but he left, and by the following Monday was working on air at 5AA. Neither Hookes nor Cunningham could know at that stage how good the move was to be for both of them.

For the first nine months of 1990, life in Adelaide's radio world continued as you would expect it to in Adelaide – comfortably familiar and with little change. The FM music stations by now had the major share of the market, but 5DN and Cunningham dominated the news-talk-sport audience. At 5AA, Hookes and Aitken were making small, but insignificant inroads into the market.

Hookes was the State cricket captain, and as such often had to leave the studio by 5.30pm, but with careful programming and recorded interviews, they were able to maintain the impression he was in the studio for most of the four-to-seven o'clock shift.

What was obvious in those early days, was Hookes's breadth of sporting knowledge, and the affinity he shared with his guests. He was a very good radio interviewer, who would not hesitate to ask the tough, interesting questions. He definitely had the respect of those people whom he was interviewing, and, of course, like most sportsmen he had a wicked sense of humour.

The year 1990 was a good one for sports radio, as controversy abounded. Port Adelaide, for over a century the dominant South Australian football team, attempted to break away and join the expanding Victorian Football League. It was seen as the ultimate act of football treachery, and provoked a savage reaction and a raft of legal injunctions from the other nine South Australian teams.

It was the most volatile moment in South Australian football history, and as Port Adelaide were beaten back to their suburban haven a hastily formed Adelaide Football Club rose to join the newly named Australian Football League (AFL).

Cunningham's programme drove football opinion, and the controversy was grist for his radio mill. He will tell you it was one of the most trying but exciting times in his radio career, as he was abused, threatened and even assaulted while covering Port Adelaide games.

The world of the media can move in strange and different ways, and Australia's laws of media ownership restrict the access that any one organisation can have in a specific market. In late 1990, in a sudden, unexpected strategic shift, radio station 5DN, for so many decades the voice of conservative commercial radio in Adelaide, acquired a coveted FM licence, and overnight became 102FM.

Ken Cunningham's world came crashing down around him. He was one of Adelaide's highest paid media identities, and he still had a contract, but a middle-aged sporting commentator who saw the world through the perspective of family, cricket and football was never going to back-announce the music tracks on an FM drive show. In a half-hearted gesture to fulfil their contractual obligations, the management of 102FM moved him to breakfast, but he was desperately unhappy and, after one survey only, he and the radio station agreed to part company.

In a cruel twist, over the course of that one survey, David Hookes and Ian Aitken inherited a fair proportion of Cunningham's audience. Where else could they go?

Possibly the ABC could have benefited but generally the national broadcaster had never been a threat to commercial stations, and the ABC's audience share only ever really spiked during the cricket season.

While Cunningham sat at home in a deep, morose depression, Aitken and Hookes celebrated unprecedented ratings success. For Aitken, it was to be short-lived.

Commercial radio can be cutthroat. It is all about ratings and advertising revenue. Hookes was marketable, but not yet established; Aitken, despite a professional and entertaining programme, and now respectable ratings, was not easily marketed. Stan Barrett, 5AA's general manager, was about to make a tough decision.

Barrett knew Cunningham was available, and would attract far greater advertising revenues than Aitken, but Aitken along with Hookes had just had his best survey result. Barrett made the call. He convinced Cunningham that if he didn't accept this opportunity, another high profile South Australian would. Within a day, Cunningham was Hookes's new on-air partner and Aitken had been unceremoniously dumped.

Cunningham recalls clearly the day he reunited and reconciled with Hookes. It was in the 5AA boardroom, and the atmosphere was a little strained. Hookes was definite that his programme was now relevant in the marketplace, and just because Cunningham was joining him, didn't mean that he needed to do anything differently.

Was he being arrogant? Disrespectful perhaps? Some would think so, but more likely it was just a manifestation of an inferiority complex generated by his lack of experience in this new medium. He need not have worried. The two combined beautifully and, over the next four years, the "KG and Hookesy" sports show consolidated further its drive time status. It became even more popular when 5AA became "racing free", the TAB having obtained a narrowcast licence to broadcast the racing on another frequency.

There is no doubt the four years Hookes spent with Cunningham shaped his broadcasting persona and prepared him for greater opportunities. He acquired the whole range of skills necessary for a diverse career in sports broadcasting. He hosted, interviewed, fielded talkback callers, and he commentated on football and cricket matches. At the same time his stellar first-class cricket career slowly came to an end. When it did, he realised more than ever, he was a cricketer first, and a media commentator second.

He was vulnerable to any approach that allowed him to maintain even a tenuous connection to his wondrous days of touring and the dressing room camaraderie. Such an opportunity came in the form of a brand new medium. Pay television.

Subscription television did not come quickly to Australia. In 1994, it was still a phenomenon that was viewed enviously by those who could see it when they ventured overseas. Australia, historically quick to embrace most new technology, was ripe for this viewing revolution.

Rick Jemison, a South Australian whose professional life had started as a journalist at Rupert Murdoch's *Adelaide News*, was about to offer David Hookes an opportunity that he had been dreaming of since he had finished playing cricket.

Jemison had moved from the print media to television, working at both the Seven and Nine networks. By 1990, he was working in London for Murdoch's subscription network B Sky B, and then moved to Hong Kong when Murdoch established his Asian platform, Sky TV. But Hong Kong was too claustrophobic and when the opportunity arose to return to Australia to develop Galaxy, pay television's pioneering network in this country, he took it. One of the channels on Galaxy was to be a sports channel, Prime Sports, a product of the Prime Network in America; Jemison had to assemble a team that could cover Australian sports, predominately cricket. He knew exactly what he wanted: a new breed of cricket commentators.

Australia had Bill Lawry, Tony Greig, and Richie Benaud, but he wanted a different type of commentator to complement and interpret the new technology that Prime was bringing to cricket telecasts. Prime innovations were "Spin Cam", and "Ultra slo-mo", now common to the commercial telecasts. He wanted his commentators to read the game, predict the game, and to not state the obvious.

Jemison met with Hookes in September 1994, and offered him a job working in the new medium. There was no haggling over salary. Jemison had a budget, and that was it, but Hookes would have accepted anyway. It was simply too good an opportunity to turn down. Hookes was particularly keen to reside in Adelaide, so Jemison agreed that when he wasn't on tour, he would fly to Melbourne once a week to record Prime's magazine-style panel and chat show.

Prime's first cricket series was the 1995 Australian tour to the West Indies. Under Australia's important anti-siphoning laws the commercial networks had first rights to the tour, but declined to telecast the series and Prime secured the rights. Hookes, Dean Jones, Mike Whitney, and the eminent, former Adelaide journalist, Mike Coward, formed the fledgling commentary team.

The West Indies is never an easy place to tour. The transportation difficulties are immense. Hoping to circumvent the unreliability of the commercial services, Prime had chartered an ageing Russian cargo plane to transport the team and its equipment. It was truly a travelling circus, with the ride rough and safety uncertain.

Hookes revelled in the adversity. His commentary was respected, and several of the magazine pieces he did on location were superb. Jemison was delighted. His television protégé had taken to the new role like the proverbial duck to water. When the tour was completed, Hookes returned to Adelaide and the routine of commuting to Melbourne for his weekly panel show. Again, opportunity was about to knock.

Men of destiny are not hard to identify in our society. The beam of opportunity shines on them, illuminating their talents. David Hookes was a man of destiny, whether it was his cricket or his media career. He did not need to seek opportunity, opportunity found him.

In Melbourne, radio station 3AW is the news-talk market leader and a sister station of sorts to Adelaide's 5AA, although there is no corporate link. They share resources and talent in the field of sports presenting. Their strength had always been their football broadcasts, but in summer, champion footballers Kevin Bartlett and Gerard Healy hosted a Saturday afternoon sports-talk programme. The station offered Hookes a minor role on the programme, as their Adelaide correspondent. Keen to establish himself further in what he regarded as the sports capital of Australia, Hookes accepted the position, even though it meant commuting to Melbourne every weekend. However, when Bartlett left unexpectedly in 1996, Hookes, was offered the full time role opposite Healy. He was also to do sports pieces in breakfast at 6.25am and 7.25am.

He had no alternative but to move, with Robyn and the children, to Melbourne.

David Hookes was in his element. The Victorians, be it in football or cricket, had long been the sporting enemy, but no city had a culture that fed the sporting appetite like Melbourne did. He even took up the position of team runner for the Fitzroy football club, which in 1996 was being coached by former South Australian Mike Nunan.

Sometime towards the end of 1996, 3AW's drive-time announcer was dismissed. The format had been current affairs and talkback. Steve Price, a hard-nosed, at times abrasive journalist, again from Adelaide, who at the time was 3AW's programme director, was installed as the drive-time host. When the three-hour shift between four and seven o'clock proved too much, the station looked for a fill-in for the hour between six and seven.

Strangely, for a city with such a unique sporting culture, there had never been a successful sport-based, talkback show in prime time. With the success of the Hookes-Healy Saturday afternoon programme, they decided to trial the pair in the hour between six and seven o'clock. It is a difficult time-slot, very probably the worst of the day, going head to head with the television news services.

They were a perfect combination: Gerard Healy, the Brownlow medallist, football champion who had played for both Melbourne and the Sydney Swans, and the flamboyant, outspoken Hookes, hero of Melbourne's Centenary Test. The station's gamble worked; soon, the programme was extended by an hour.

Gerard Healy is a qualified physiotherapist, but he has too much talent to be confined to a white coat and a manipulating table. As well as his radio commitments, he writes a column in Melbourne's *Herald-Sun*, commentates football on Foxtel, and hosts football's most informative, opinion-shaping hour on television, "On the Couch". He is also a national selector, and chairman of the match committee that tours Ireland with the International Rules All-Australian team.

He is intelligent, experienced and has strong opinions on sporting issues. Healy is a Victorian football icon, and Hookes could never quite shake off the South Australian stigma. They battled constantly over the merits of football compared to cricket. Healy's strong opposing views brought out the best in Hookes, and the conflict enhanced them both. Healy will say that it was Hookes's natural ability, rather than any research or preparation that made him a great broadcaster. He was an opinion-maker, not a statistician, and he had those occasional moments of madness that made him even more interesting.

His "hairy-backed sheila" comment about a South African lady who was accusing Shane Warne of some misdemeanor was a classical example, as was his off-the-cuff remark, "beware of Jews bearing gifts". The latter was made in reference to the respected businessman, prominent member of Melbourne's Jewish community, and benefactor of the Melbourne Football Club, Joseph Gutnick.

The Jewish community, who responded with expected hostility, received Hookes's "beware of" quote, a corruption of Virgil's Greek mythological prose, with outrage. The accusations of anti-Semitism briefly rocked Hookes, but he recovered quickly, and continued to speak out frankly on sporting issues that moved him. The targets of his criticism did not always appreciate his blunt honesty, but most, when they stepped away from the emotion of any personal attack, realised that even with the harshest criticism comes a modicum of truth.

It was not always complete harmony. The conditions of David Hookes's contract at 3AW were a source of constant frustration to Healy and the others who worked with him. The unique contract allowed him to be away whenever he was required to commentate on cricket tours, however obscure they might be. This presented problems with the continuity of his programme, although Hookes's absence allowed another rising media star, Gary Lyon, to gain his valuable radio experience.

Hookes was expected to file reports for his 3AW work mates while on these tours, but whether it was because of poor communication infrastructure or inconvenient time differences, he was often missing in action. However, they would see the funny side of his mischievous sense of humour, when a postcard would arrive from some exotic location in the Caribbean or the Maldives. Healy's comment was always, "How do I get a job like this?"

The point was, Hookes was doing exactly what he wanted do. The best times of his life were as a touring cricketer. Mateship is the quintessential characteristic of the Australian male. Sportsmen covet it, and cling to it, but only those who have been a Test cricketer would understand the bond that is forged between touring team mates. David Hookes's cricketing days were over, but life as a touring commentator extended those glory days.

David Hookes died at a tragically young age. He was at the height of his powers as a multi-media personality. Pay television had suffered through the pioneer days of Galaxy, whose method of delivering the signal through microwave transmission was always doomed. Galaxy had metamorphosed into Foxtel.

Hookes was still with them, both as a cricket commentator, and a panelist on the national Monday night sports wrap, "The Back Page". Having started from the lowest of bases, he and Gerard Healy started to dominate their time slot on 3AW. He also wrote more than an occasional column for the print media. A recent, cursory search of the News Limited archives showed more than 300 articles under his by-line, filed from all points of the sporting globe.

In the sporting media, he was omnipresent without being overbearing. When a prominent Australian lives his life in our full view, either on the sporting field or in the media, he symbiotically ages with us and the ageing process goes largely unnoticed. Occasionally the old photos of their youth will surface to remind us that even champions age.

There is one advantage of dying young. The media image is the one that is preserved in our mind's eye. There is no further withering of mental and physical capabilities, and the imperfections dissolve or are excused. David Hookes will age no more. He'd like that.

Welcome …
to Meltdown

GERARD HEALY

You rarely get good news from anyone at three in the morning. It's either a drunken mate or a serious problem, and unfortunately it was the latter on that Monday in January in 2004. The message was clear, Hookesy was in hospital and was not going to make it. How could it be so?

I was to begin our 11th year on air together later that day and yet here was someone telling me it was over, forever. Despite the passage of considerable time, the tears and pain that we all endure when someone close dies, it's still hard to fully accept. Hookesy had the best job in the world … although, if he told me once he told me a hundred times that it was actually Richie Benaud who had the best job.

But I reckon it was David. He was full time at 3AW as co-host of our sports talkback program, but the contract he signed with Steve Price and Shane Healy guaranteed him 100 days a year where he could be away doing cricket for Foxtel. He was always away for extended periods going to the exotic cricket destinations around the world; that's another thing that makes it difficult to accept the finality of his passing.

For some months afterwards, the programme continued as if Hookesy would breeze in as he always did, sit down at his desk and check his SMS messages, and then cheekily enquire why we'd dropped the cricket content in his absence. He didn't have any idea whether we had or not, but it was Hookesy's assumed charter to be the "keeper of the gate" for his sport.

Steve Price, 3AW's station programme manager through the 1990s, Shane Healy, the now general manager, and I had targeted Hookesy to be my partner on what we hoped would be a viable talkback sports programme on Melbourne radio. At our first meeting to discuss the format – a six-hour sporting talk fest between midday and 6.00pm on Saturdays – David was very concerned about two things, the contributors and, the time that would be given to cricket in the football-mad state of Victoria.

Hookesy got "his man", Ian Chappell, with no objection from any of us, but he had to fight harder for his "cricket time". Price had the "Scott Palmer approach" to sport in Melbourne.

[Scott is the long-time sports editor of Melbourne's *Sunday Herald-Sun* and is known to believe that in Melbourne only footy sells. He's often been heard to say: "You give them footy first, then you give them footy, and when they've had enough footy, you give them some more bloody footy."]

And David accepted that because he knew it to be true; he came from South Australia where the same rules applied. But he just wanted to make it clear that, in his mind, cricket was its equal. Unfortunately, from an emotional perspective it's not.

Often, as our relationship grew, I baited him that his sport lacked passion and I'd ask him, "When was the last time cricket threw up a topic that stirred the emotions of our callers?" That challenged David, and he responded as only he could. In the space of a couple of years he had instigated so many emotional cricketing debates that "his game" had gained substantial ground in the battle for air time.

Some of his issues debated on 3AW that stirred emotions and filled newspaper columns for months were:

Mark Taylor should resign as captain and be dropped.

Mark Waugh should be dropped.

Murali is a chucker, but the ICC is too divided by colour to do anything about it.

Steve Waugh demeans the Australian team by continuing to wear his dirty old cap.

The gambling allegations in India (Hookes broke the story).

New South Wales has too much say in national selection.

Michael Bevan gets too many "not outs".

And there were countless cracks at Cricket Australia on almost any decision it made. He'd pop them out at the most unlikely times; for instance, he'd wait until Steve Waugh had made an exhilarating century before having a go at his dress sense. You can imagine the effect that had on the talkback callers – and his radio partner. And, in the short term, it made for good radio when Hookesy set himself up to be slammed, yet more often than not his opinion was proved right over time.

That was his great strength; he was a world-class entertainer when he was talking sport or arguing about sport, either with the general public or his partner and a host of general contributors. His speciality was to antagonise soccer fans, who are large in number but remarkably sensitive to the state of the game in this country. Any time Hookesy launched an attack on various elements of the world game we'd receive countless threats to our safety.

He was at his best when he knew he had the measure of his opponent. The way he used to gong former Socceroos captain Paul Wade week after week, year after year, was at times magnificent listening. He'd lead "Wadey" into a verbal trap then pounce, leaving Wadey pleading "enough, enough!" If soccer lovers didn't always love it, nor did some of his targets in cricket. In some quarters his stance was seen as negative, but it was far from that, generating emotional responses from the converted and making the impartial more aware of the sport via discussion.

At 12.01pm on the Saturday of the 1999 Australian Open tennis ladies final between Amelie Mauresmo and Martina Hingis, Hookesy opened the program with this: "Welcome to Melbourne Park ... where 'Sports Saturday' will take you live to the battle between the half-man, half-woman of France versus the little lady from Switzerland ..."

The reaction to that introduction can only be described as meltdown. For two hours Hookesy sat there and was berated, belittled, insulted and derided. The women of Melbourne rose up as one with one message: "Hookesy, this time you've gone too far."

Of course, it was his way of buying into the debate about steroid or human growth hormone abuse, the allegations that were being directed at Mauresmo at the time. But his detractors had interpreted his comments as an insult to Mauresmo, whose physical appearance was, well, unladylike.

We got some relief during the match because it was a live call, but at 4.00pm they were there, still waiting for him. On that day we certainly established ourselves as an alternative to the ABC, who had a stranglehold on the Saturday afternoon ratings because of the cricket broadcasts. So, how ironic it was that after a couple of years we beat the ABC's "Grandstand" programme in the ratings – which meant fewer people were listening to cricket, Hookesy's game.

David had other "hot water moments", the most notable being the "hairy-back sheila" comment. When I heard it I had a little chuckle to myself, but I did wonder too if it was maybe "here we go again" time. When I got to work there were a few messages for Hookesy from the cricketing journalists but that wasn't unusual. Terry Wallace, former Western Bulldogs coach and a contributor to the programme, told me he thought the comment could be a problem.

Because David was in coaching mode he only arrived in the office 10 minutes before we were due to go to air. He bowled in and we asked him if he thought there was an issue, but he dismissed it with a wave of the hand. We still had our doubts when we walked into the studio and turned on the TV monitors to the BBC.

The first story up, you wouldn't believe, was about our very own "Hairy-back Hookes". Before the story hit our evening news television bulletins it was already headlines in the UK, South Africa and the rest of the cricketing world.

Our two-hour radio show was supposed to be all about the weekend of football, but we spoke about little other than the "hairy-back sheila" issue.

During the show we counted 16 mentions on International television channels, yet Hookesy remained decidedly calm, if perhaps just a touch uneasy as the enormity of the storm that was about to descend on the Victorian coach became clear.

When he came to Melbourne, Hookesy came to become a star. I suspect he had noted the incredible success of Sam Newman and Rex Hunt, former players who had achieved by being different and provocative. His original brief at 3AW was the "Sports Saturday" programme, calling football and doing the breakfast session with two hugely successful radio personalities, Ross Stephenson and Dean Banks, who had most of adult Melbourne listening to them every morning.

Dean loved cricket more than Hookesy so they hit it off well; Ross was a bigger stirrer than David, although he did it covertly, always loading the fun for Hookesy, who was silly enough to pull the trigger too many times. If ever anyone should be working as double agent for ASIO it's Ross, because he was one of those rare intellects who could do to David what David did to everyone else. Manipulate.

It was an enormously successful combination until it got too much for Hookesy working at both ends of the day. A colleague best summed up the experience, as giving David the chance to be insulting in the morning then apologise at night.

Sadly for "Pricey", who had never heard Hookesy call footy, he wasn't quite the total package because when it came to footy calling he was only a B grader, so the Hunt-Hookes double on Saturday never got off the ground. When Hookesy's dream faded he was more disappointed than he ever let on, but it forced him to look in other directions, inevitably leading to "Inside Cricket" and then the move into coaching.

The coaching was great for Hookesy, but it necessitated him doing a couple of major back flips on the hardline approach he'd previously taken on footy clubs and footy players. He got away with it, as usual; just argued his way through it until he got a position where people had had their say and everyone moved on. That was his great strength. He could argue his way into trouble, and then out of it again, upsetting people on the way but always being forgiven at the end.

No doubt he had his eyes on a higher honour in the coaching field; strangely, but typically, the man who often said that cricket coaches are for getting you to the ground, wanted to be the coach of the Australian team. I wonder if the Cricket Australia decision-makers could have coped with the full Hookesy package. And, wouldn't it have provided some emotional talkback topics?

Despite his ability to be influential his most enduring quality was his ability to make people laugh. For over a decade I would sit there and laugh at his ideas and the retelling of cricketing stories. He could extract the good line out of the majority of our callers and had me unable to talk I was laughing so much, numerous times during the year.

He was an entertainer with the cricket bat at the very highest level but behind the microphone he was in the cricketers' hall of fame.

Fame, then Friction

KEN CUNNINGHAM

My first meeting with David Hookes was lively. I think I was captain-coach of my club. Over the previous couple of seasons there had been a lot said and written about the outstanding ability of young Hookes. I was the bowler when David made his way to the crease for West Torrens. I thought to myself here is my chance to test this young whippersnapper … I've been around a lot longer than this kid … you know, that "old head is wiser than a young head" stuff.

I was lucky enough to put the first deliveries past the outside edge of his bat and proceeded in my follow through to give him the biggest sledge that I could, suggesting in my most colourful and expressive manner that he should go back and play with the Under 16s. His reply was silence accompanied by a long, cold stare. Then, after smashing my next two deliveries to the cover boundary, he walked down the wicket in an arrogant manner and said in a very authoritative way: "Listen, old man, if you continue to bowl those wobbly swingers the next eight (balls) will go over the fence." Not bad for a kid.

I was not surprised to see him play both first-class and Test cricket, but I was surprised – and disappointed – he didn't play more Tests. He was all class. He had the unique ability to destroy an attack, and at times in a very unorthodox fashion.

My link with Hookesy on radio and television began in 1977, when he was playing for the Redbacks (formerly South Australia or the Croweaters, take your pick) and I was hosting the talk-sports-drive programme on radio 5DN in Adelaide. Hookesy would do a daily spot on the show from wherever he was playing, and, like his batting he was never backward in coming forward. He called it as he saw it, which meant controversy, but that's how the sporting public wanted it and Hookesy gave it to them.

During the winter months he sat beside me in the call of the local South Australian

Football League matches and did extremely well. He was also a panel member on KG's Footy Show, which went to air at 5.30pm every Saturday night on Channel Nine.

Hookesy got into strife after his tour of Sri Lanka in 1981-82 where he made his highest Test score of 143 not out. It was an innings, in my view, that looked certain to make him a regular member of the Australian team. I was interviewing him on 5DN as a part of his contract with the station when I asked the simple question, "Who would make a better captain, Kim Hughes or Rodney Marsh?" Simply asked, yes, but when you think about it not a simple question! But it was the question any interviewer worth his salt would ask because there was a lot of debate out there among cricket fans about the issue of Hughes's captaincy. I thought David would be diplomatic for once because we both knew the Australian Cricket Board had strict rules in place about player commentary. In fact, if a player criticised another player, or officials, or some aspect of the cricket administration, then he could be liable to a fine.

But, Hookesy being Hookesy he didn't hold back; he said very openly and honestly that although Hughes was captain he thought "Marshy" would do a better job, and inferred the wicketkeeper could take over. Fair dinkum, you could have knocked me over with a feather. Immediately I knew Hookesy would be in serious trouble.

Sure enough, by the end of the week Hookesy had received a "please explain" from the ACB. Sadly, he had no defence and was fined a lot of money. Hookesy took it on the chin, but I still wonder if that slip caused him grief with the selectors.

The only time Hookesy and I "had words" was in 1987. David was still working with me at radio 5DN and told me that he had been approached to work at radio station 5AA, which was co-hosting a sports show in opposition to mine. At the time David still had a year of his contract to serve with 5DN. I explained to him that I had gone to a lot of trouble to get him the contract with the station and I would be bitterly disappointed if he decided not to honour it. I wasn't trying to act the big shot, but back then the station bosses were loathe to give long-term contacts to their announcers and they had gone out of their way to accommodate David. He told me that he would think about it for a couple of days before making a decision.

Next thing I heard on the grapevine, so to speak, that Hookesy had gone to 5AA, so naturally I phoned him to find out whether it was true. "Yes," he said, "and I'm about to sign." We exchanged words, mine as colourful and as expressive as that first time we met on the cricket field; I was most annoyed because he hadn't done the right thing and informed 5DN before the switch became public. Hookesy – with his co-host Ian Aitken – had become "the enemy". My anger didn't greatly affect our friendship, and we both got on with life.

Then, in one of life's little twists our paths in radio crossed again in 1989. My station 5DN had decided to drop its talk-sport format in favour of music and the ratings crashed. By mutual agreement, the station and I parted company and I suddenly found myself unemployed.

Soon after I was approached by 5AA management who wondered if I would be interested in co-hosting the 5AA Sports Show, which was hosted by ... Hookesy and Ian Aitken. I accepted the position. Who wouldn't have?

So once again I was about to work with Hookesy. Our first meeting was very strained; David, to his credit, was disappointed that Ian had been moved on. He told me in strong terms that the format of the show was not going to change for me. That was fine by me ... after all, the show's last few ratings had been quite good.

The ensuing five years working with David were terrific. The start was slow, feeling our way a bit, but then we got along famously and once again became good friends, not just personally but our families enjoyed good times, too. Still, I could always sense he needed a bigger challenge and I wasn't surprised that he received an offer to move to Melbourne and work with 3AW, and that he joined Fox, which offered him the opportunity to travel around the world to cover Test series. Even though we were no longer working together on the same radio station we often made crosses from 5AA to Hookesy on his sports show with Gerard Healy on 3AW.

The death of David was an enormous shock. I remember quite vividly getting the phone call from our general manager Paul Bartlett at 4.30am. It went this way: "KG – Bart here – sorry to wake you at this time but I have some very, very sad news. Hookesy's in hospital after an altercation at a hotel and will not get through. I thought it was better you heard it from me than on the radio."

I said, "Bart, you're joking. What happened?"

He said, "I'm not too sure how it happened but it wasn't good." The next two days were unbearable.

His memorial service in Adelaide is a day I will never forget. I have never seen so many people crying, from the young to the elderly. It is beyond any doubt that Hookesy touched so many people in so many ways, whether he was taking an attack apart at the Adelaide Oval or stirring people's emotions with his forthright and, at times, controversial comments on the radio.

Rough on Robin

TERRY JENNER

When I close my eyes and endeavor to gather pictures of Hookesy, the one that immediately springs to mind is of a round of golf in Melbourne. I had played a reasonable amount of golf with David in South Africa during the 1997 Australian tour over there. We were working for Foxtel, and Dean Jones, Greg Chappell and Barry Richards were also part of the commentary team, so spare moments revolved around golf.

Former England medium pacer Robin "Jackers" Jackman, also a golf nut, was part of the South African broadcasting team and joined us on a few occasions. We even played a "test" series between Australian and South African media representatives.

Playing for the South African side was Graeme Pollock, the man whose style of batting so many compared to David Hookes's style. One thing they definitely had in common was their lack of length off the tee! Amazing when you think how sweetly they used to hit the cricket ball.

Jackers on the other hand was sneaky long and had a very good all round game. He was the type of player one would like as a partner. So, when South Africa was touring Australia Jackers was out here, and a window of opportunity appeared for a game of golf in Melbourne at Yarra Yarra between Gerard Healy, Hookesy, Jackers and me.

It was game on, Healy and Jenner versus Hookes and Jackman. On paper it looked to be a pretty good contest.

Unfortunately for Jackers, his borrowed clubs were not to his liking and he failed to feature in the first three holes; Gerard and I were taking them apart. On the fourth hole, Jackers was again in the trees and was forced to chip out sideways. As he approached his ball a disgruntled Hookesy was angrily marching towards his own ball.

Jackers looked toward Hookesy and, in his exquisite English accent, asked: "David, how far is it from here to the green?" Without looking up, or changing stride or pace, David replied, "Robin, golf is a hand and eye coordination game!" Needless to say, Gerard and I went on to win the match.

No 'Gimme' for Greigy

JEFF THOMSON

Hookesy and I played a lot of cricket with or against each other, but it was on the circuit as commentators that we spent more time together as mates and got to know each other. How close were we? Well, not quite as close as our fellow guests at the beachside Sandals resort in Antigua must have thought on the tour of the West Indies in 2003.

It's a pretty exclusive joint but it's only for couples; for "couples", read holidaying husbands and wives, honeymooners, courting couples and, on this occasion ... Hookesy and Thommo! We'd bowl into breakfast together, we'd be at the bar every day together and we'd have a few beers in the nightclub together. We started to get some questioning looks, "Who's that nice couple?"

For us it became a huge laugh. "Okay, Hookesy, you be the bird today" ... "No, no, it's your turn." And so on. Well, what else could we do? Let it be known our wives had ditched us for the week? And inviting a few of the players back could only have made it worse.

As much as Hookesy was good to chill with away from the field, he did relish being immersed in the cricket, especially the big moments. We were lucky enough to be calling Brian Lara's centuries that swung that titanic series against the Australians in the Caribbean in 1999.

I say lucky because it was some of the best batting you'd wish to see. He made 213 at Kingston and hundreds in Barbados and Antigua and it was once-in-a-lifetime stuff. As Australians, you wanted the Aussies to win but it was sensational viewing to see Lara pretty much single-handedly make it two apiece.

We were there in 2003, too, when the Windies had lost the series but were set a world record chase of 418 to win in the fourth innings and got them with three wickets

With Robyn, Caprice and Kristofer. Robyn: "David was always amazing with the children; he never referred to them as his stepchildren, always as his children. He was just so proud of Caprice and Kristofer. He adored them, but at the same time he still managed to give them strong discipline and strong foundations in their upbringing."

DENIS BRIEN

David, and his mother Pat at the centenary dinner of the West
Torrens Cricket Club in 1997.

Robyn: "David walked me to the window. He had arranged for Les Burdett, the curator of Adelaide Oval, to have a birthday message placed on the scoreboard. It was all lit up."

Barbados, 9th April 1995. Wedding anniversary.

"Over the moon", somewhere between Dandenong and Melbourne in 2000.

Favourite photo. It's 1984 and Hookesy is with Robyn, Caprice and Kristofer on holiday at Kangaroo Island. Cricketing mate and good friend Ian Edgley remembers: "David once consented to come to the island for no fee, to play in a double-wicket cricket match to raise funds for the local cricket club. It resulted in the strangest scoreline ... "

Favourite holiday spot. Goolwa, South Australia, 2001.

Favourite dog. With Lucy, on the beach at Lorne. Robyn: "One day he came home laughing because Wayne Jackson, then the head of the AFL, saw him and called out: 'Why don't you get yourself a real dog?'"

"Throughout his playing career Hookes had flirted with the media, but it was always in the role of the subject rather than the commentator ..." He became a household name as a presenter in radio and television.

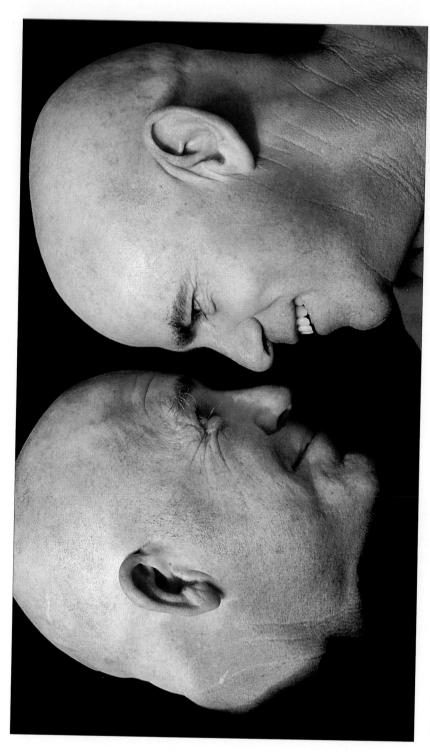

With 3AW co-host Gerard Healy, shaving down and raising funds for cancer.

Hookes got his first break on Adelaide radio in 1977, courtesy of Ken Cunningham, who remembers: "Later Hookesy would do a daily spot on the show from wherever he was playing, and called it as he saw it, which meant controversy, but that's how the sporting public wanted it and Hookesy gave it to them."

Stepping out as the coach of Victoria. Shane Warne: "He was keen but you could sense a very slight reservation. He wasn't sure about how it would all work out."

The coach was a crutch for Warne when the leg spinner was suspended and going through his toughest time over the drugs allegations.

Hookes comfortably handled the challenge of television. Subjected here to his wily questioning were champion golfers Ernie Els and Michael Campbell.

Not everybody gets a chance to do an ad for a favourite product!

Hookesy had an eye for a smart car. His penchant for thinking outside
the square, for planning, once got him into hot water in a car wash. A friend
remembers: "What he hadn't noted was that the machine, once it was activated,
moved over the car on a track. This oversight resulted in the open door of his
Alfa Romeo suddenly being jammed against the side of the car wash, and ... "

On the cricket field they were single-minded adversaries, very fast bowler versus very aggressive batsman, but in the television commentary box they were best friends – former West Indian cricketer Michael Holding and Hookesy in Antigua, 1995.

With Dermot Brereton inspecting the Sydney Olympics site in 2000.

David Hookes never forgot where he came from, just a barefoot boy from a working class Adelaide suburb. He was ever ready to help kids. With young cricket fans, Barbados 1995.

NEWS LTD

When the Melbourne Football Club went to Cambodia with Care Australia in 2001, Hookesy was there. As he was for The Grampians Disability Country League.

to spare. Ramnaresh Sarwan and Shivnarine Chanderpaul both got excellent hundreds.

Hookesy loved analysing the ins and outs of Muttiah Muralitheran's controversial bowling action. He loved running the gauntlet – don't forget that Hookesy's commentary to Australian audiences on Fox Sports would also be broadcast into Sri Lanka. I lost count long ago on how many freeze frames we've used of Murali's unorthodox action.

David had a keen eye for cricket talent. His big tip – Cameron White to captain Australia. I remember him saying it before I'd even seen the kid play for Victoria. He's a handy looking player and Hookesy had the chance to groom him through the Victorian captaincy.

Hookesy's commentary showed how deeply he thought on the game; he took great pride in his work. He was very good at it, too. In India, I remember doing my seven hours at the cricket and looking forward to some down time over dinner. But if Hookesy got together with Ian Chappell, there was more cricket talk over dinner. They were always at one another – who had the better historical knowledge on cricket, and so on. They loved it. He was a clone of Ian, the way he backed himself. Me, I had to switch off from cricket. I'd be the one saying, "If you talk cricket anymore I'm going to deck someone." But Hookesy could eat, sleep and drink it.

He was a commentator at the right time, with the Australians playing so much result cricket, but I wonder how he would have fared calling three tedious draws in a series back in the 1960s? He got a real kick out of witnessing another "leftie" Matt Hayden's prolific deeds with the bat overseas. He gets on with it and that was Hookesy's way, too.

And he was thrilled when "Boof" Lehmann's career eventually took off. I think for a while there he might have been worried that Boof might end up with a record like his own – brilliant first-class career for South Australia, but not as many Tests as he would have liked.

When Hookesy came into big cricket in the mid-1970s he was a brash kid. It didn't always work in his favour. Once he fell foul of my old fast bowling mate Lennie Pascoe in the nets. He could be a junior McEnroe with the smart chat and said something to Lennie and upset him; not such a smart move because that sort of thing was like a red rag to Lennie, who set about trying to knock Hookesy's block off. It was all good fun, but only if you were watching!

Everyone knows he christened his Test career with those five fours off one over from Tony Greig in the Centenary Test. Fewer people would know that Hookesy was still getting the better of the same bloke more than 25 years on. On tour, there's always time to enjoy one of my passions, golf. I was with "Greigy", Hookesy and Robin Jackman, playing at the Royal Colombo Club, Aussies up against the rest.

Greigy is not real good standing over a two or three-foot putt and it was only natural, given the "needle" in the contest, that Hookesy and I had stored away that little bit of knowledge. As sometimes happens in such matches, there were a few "gimme" putts around and, Greigy and Jackman had allowed us a couple of gimmes.

Then, crucial time in the match … Greigy has one of the same length, a two-and-a-half-footer. He's looking at us, expectantly. And, there was silence. Hookesy didn't say a word about a gimme, nor did I. Stony silence.

Greigy was ropable: "Right, that's f – – ing it … I know the rules of golf … " He went right off. Hookesy and I still said nothing, just watched him line up the putt and miss. Hookesy had got his man again. He was always at it.

In 1979, Hookesy was the young punk in that World Series Cricket Australian side that toured the West Indies. When we hit Georgetown, Guyana for the final Super Test, we'd already had play stopped in Barbados and Trinidad because the locals hurled bottles on to the grounds after controversial umpiring decisions.

The Georgetown experience was a little different. The capacity crowd was well and truly uptight about the start of the match being delayed because heavy rain had soaked the ground over previous days. Some had been queuing since 7.00am to make sure of getting even the most cramped vantage point. After the second or third delay the locals had had enough and bottles, metal seats, and broken fences, everything they could lay their hands on, were being flung on to the field. Then several thousand fans swarmed on to the field.

We had a bloody riot on our hands! The Australian team was holed up in the dressing rooms. There was broken glass on the floor by now because bottles, or whatever, had taken out a few of our windows. Lennie Pascoe and I had grabbed bats and were standing at the door. The first bloke through was going to cop it.

I remember Hookesy. He was just sitting there, wearing his batting helmet and wondering what to do. He wasn't alone mind you.

Any normal tour of the West Indies is about getting on a good boat and doing a spot of fishing. I've got my own charter boat business in Queensland and it's in the blood. Before all hell broke loose on that WSC tour we had a day out in Jamaica. A police vessel took a few of us, Trevor Chappell, Bruce Laird, Martin Kent, Mick Malone, Hookesy and me out off an atoll, where there was not much fishing but plenty of eating, drinking and some swimming.

On our swim to shore we all ended up with painful sea urchin spines in the feet and ankles. The locals thought this was very funny, the Aussies jumping about and calling for some urgent treatment for the stinging pain. The locals gave it to us straight – the best neutraliser for the pain was urine. That's right, peeing on your mate's leg. We went for it. The locals were laughing even louder – had we just been taken for the biggest ride or what?

When they made Hookesy captain of South Australia you knew how hard fought any Sheffield Shield game was going to be. He didn't mind using the rules to get an edge or overcome a setback. Did I say, use the rules? I remember one Shield match at the 'Gabba where the South Australians were well behind the over rate and facing a penalty.

Hookesy simply got in there, bowled overs off a single pace and was through them in two minutes apiece. He rushed the batsmen and generally did everything possible to churn through a dozen overs in 20 minutes or so.

I'd much rather forget the match at Adelaide Oval in the early 1990s when Craig McDermott and Carl Rackemann skittled South Australia for 130-odd in the first innings. There was no thought in the mind of the Queensland coach – me – that we were bowling for anything but a big outright victory. We set South Australia a massive 506 runs to win and they got them, even though Hookesy made only a handful of runs.

When we shared a microphone for Fox Sports in the far flung cricket corners of the West Indies, India or Sri Lanka, it wasn't the comments on air that kept us going through a stifling seven-hour stint in Cochin or Kandy.

It was the commentary off-air between balls; telling jokes, having a shot at certain types in the crowd, voicing blunt opinions, backchat, telling stories about players none of which would ever go to air – it was uncut if you get my drift. We always had our fingers on the blank button, but I warned Hookesy: "Mate, we're going to hit the wrong button one day and we'll be in the shit."

Early in 2004, I headed to Sri Lanka for the series against Australia. There was no Hookesy. I remember turning to our producer in the commentary box and saying, "It's not the same is it ..?"

No Picket-Sitter

PETER FITZSIMONS

As someone who worked with David Hookes for the past three years on a Pay-TV show for sporting loudmouths, I still cannot quite fathom that I will never again have the fun of crossing swords with him, or having a long chat in the make-up room, or sharing a meal afterwards. Never again share a laugh or enjoy his quick wit.

When the news of his end came through right as we were putting the opening show of the year to air, all of us were stunned into silence – an ironic first. What could we say, on the spot, that would make any sense of his death? What can we say even now? With the death of every famous sportsperson, there is a tendency in the media to eulogise in a fashion that is the exact reverse of Mark Antony's famous Shakespearean line over the body of Caesar: "The evil that men do lives after them; the good is oft interred with their bones."

Instead we are inclined to sweep away all hints of controversy, ignore their flaws and make submissions for their eternal sporting sainthood. Hookes was no saint as he would be the first to admit, and delight in pointing out, but he genuinely was a one-off in Australian sport. Does another come to mind who more perpetually had a twinkle in his eye, evinced a more pure love of his sport, and did more at so many levels to advance it, from playing to commentating to coaching?

Is there another who could sometimes say the most outrageous things but laugh off the ensuing hullabaloo in an instant, and clearly not care a continental who didn't like what he had to say? He was a bloke with an enormous appetite for life, who clearly enjoyed every moment hugely, and was perpetually keen for everyone else to enjoy it in the same fashion. Around him, they often did.

As a man, he was a bloke's bloke, and a bloody good one at that. As a cricketer, not for him the patient building of an innings, the painstaking pursuit of a score designed predominantly to lift his average. Rather, he was the embodiment of the greatest Australian sporting adage of them all, "Have a go, ya mug!" As a commentator, he was exactly the same. Just as he rattled the fences in cricket, he could never sit on them as a broadcaster.

According to Hookesy …

EXCERPTS FROM HIS COLUMNS

B ecause David Hookes arrived on the Australian cricket scene with the explosive impact of that other champion young left-hand batsman, Neil Harvey, the media soon wanted a piece of him. "Hookes brings a buzz of anticipation to the crowds whenever he takes his first steps out onto the arena," said the editors of the *Australian Cricket* magazine when they signed David Hookes up to write columns exclusively from 1978.

That opportunity was David's first tentative step on the way to what was to become his celebrated career in the media. Even then, there was no doubting his talent to get a message across. The columns, entitled simply "Hookes", concluded with a copy of his signature in a hand as flowing as his batsmanship.

On joining the breakaway World Series Cricket:
When you're 22 years old, and you've signed a six-year contract to play cricket for Kerry Packer, well, life has just got to be exciting – even if you are nursing a broken jaw! Boy, I don't know how I missed that Andy Roberts bouncer, but it sure hurt. I've always enjoyed playing against quick bowling and I just hope this incident doesn't affect my confidence.

Signing for the superstars has been a turning point in my life. And to think all this has happened in the last 10 months. I find I am still taking time to adjust to a whole new world. I don't think I will ever have any reason to regret my decision. I had a lot of talks with the Australian Cricket Board after my English tour and, for a time, I was worried and confused.

Then I spent a few hours in Channel Nine and that really solved my problems. You could see how much work they had done preparing to launch World Series Cricket. I realised they were totally professional. I was impressed with the long hours they were working to ensure the product would be the very best standard. None of us had really worked with full time professionals before and you can't blame the Cricket Board for that. But once I was caught up in this atmosphere all doubts dissolved. (January 1978)

On working for Kerry Packer:

I have found Kerry Packer a very fair sort of bloke. He's paying us and under the guidelines he's set down I'm sure he'll back us to the hilt. On the other hand, I wouldn't like to get offside with him. But who wants to get offside with their boss, anyway?

I believe working with WSC will open up new doors for me, hopefully in a business career. For instance, I don't want to play cricket seven days a week for the next 20 years. But I would like to keep working, preferably in the atmosphere of sport, perhaps in television commentating or as a sportswriter. It's just that sport is so much in my blood. I've played so many sports and I've gone through a physical training course.

My contract with Kerry Packer of course spells security for me. When you know you're going to get X thousands of dollars you know the money's there; you can plan your life that way. I've never had a lot of money before. It's not so long ago that I went four long years with the same cricket bat. My family couldn't afford a lot and if I wanted a new pair of shoes for school then it wasn't a case of just asking and they would be there next morning. We'd have to wait at least until the next pay packet came into the house. Security means that you know you've got a reasonable income, that you know where the next dollar is coming from. I have never had an ambition to be rich, to own fast cars and a luxury home. Now that I'm earning good money I won't be throwing it away. The money's there and I want to use it wisely. My wife Roxanne (she's just earned her master's degree in psychology) and I are living in a unit. It's nice and we like it but my ambition is to own an acre or two up in the hills, not too far away from Adelaide. Perhaps we can afford to buy a few luxury things – at least they're luxuries to us, but not to a lot of other kids. (January 1978)

On his first Ashes tour, 1977:

I feel lucky to already have an English tour under my belt. Was I disappointed with my performance? Well, I feel I could have done better. With my technique, which isn't all that perfect by any means, I needed a lot of cricket and the stop-start tour beginning (it hardly stopped raining for seven weeks) didn't help. After a while, I was hitting the ball in the middle but straight to fieldsmen. When you do that you get a bit flustered, then you get yourself out. A lot of times in England my dismissal was my own fault. I tend to play at the ball outside the off stump too much. Okay, I know I shouldn't, and when I'm in the practice nets it's easy to let a lot of those balls go past. But when you've batted for 15 or 20 minutes in a match, and you want to get on with it, you're tempted to have a go at them. I guess I've got to take my time and not try to score 50 in the first hour. But you only learn these things as you go along. (January 1978)

On that broken jaw:

Life through a straw isn't exactly my idea of a good time. I can tell you my first steak is going to taste just great, and they won't be feeding it to me through a vitaminiser, either! Will I join the crash-helmeted brigade? I'll certainly put on a helmet at practice because facing the odd bumper in a net is no fun at the best of times. I'll see how it goes from there.

Batting in Sydney (where I was hit), for instance, could influence you to wear a helmet. As far as helmets are concerned I feel their big advantage is with young kids learning the game, and players coming back from injury.

It will give the kids the confidence to hook properly and, if they ever face a "bumper war", then they will only hook the right ball and the bowlers will soon find it a waste of energy bowling ill-directed bouncers. (February 1978)

On professionalism and WSC:

The standard of players in the professional troupe guarantees that you can learn a whole lot. An example of this was when we returned on the bus from the first floodlit game at the VFL Park in Melbourne.

Greg Chappell spoke to me to help iron out a few problems of which I wasn't aware but which Greg could see from the other end. He told me how he had started in Test cricket with his century against the Englishmen in Perth, but had suffered a letdown the following summer against the World XI, when so much was expected of him.

The mistake he said he made was that he started to "look for the ball" instead of waiting for the ball to come to him. This is what happened to me in a match in Sydney. I was just getting tense in the first quarter of an hour and trying too hard to get my first 20 runs on the board. I am a good cricket watcher and ready to learn from these great players. (February 1978)

On being banned from "official" cricket:

So, the Australian team has been named to tour the West Indies (Bob Simpson's team, 1978) and our World Series fellows are not included. Well, I wouldn't be telling the truth if I didn't admit I am disappointed. When I first signed for Kerry Packer I was naïve enough to hope that I would continue to hold my place in the Test side. I guess that is wanting to have your cake and eat it, too. Once the big split came, I knew then that it was one or the other. A pity, because it would have been an education for me to have played in front of West Indian crowds. Having played so much cricket this summer against the West Indians, it would have been a chance to consolidate to take them on again in the Caribbean. (March 1978)

On the standard of World Series Cricket:

I am feeling a lot happier after my comeback after that broken jaw. I am particularly grateful that I was able to get back into the game. If I had stayed out for the rest of the season I would have spent an anxious winter wondering about my ability to pick up where I left off. At VFL Park I hit a couple of half-centuries, played pretty well. I'm my own hardest critic, so I can say that I'm not all that happy with my footwork. It's not as good as it should be. I'll do a skipping routine in the winter months. Maybe I should try the old Bob Simpson technique – ballroom dancing!

Next season? Well, we don't know yet what formula World Series will take, but whatever it is it will be tough. This has been a hard-grind summer, a real strain. Every ball is a fight; there is nothing easy. You simply don't go in to bat against a weak bowler, nor does a bowler operate against a less than efficient batsman. The younger players are making immense improvement in such a demanding school.

Where World Series is really tough is for the batsman who has a run of failures and loses his place in the Super Tests. In "official" cricket you can rely on recovering confidence at Shield or club level. But there is no let-up in World Series, not even in the up-country games (the WSC second competition).

I returned after my broken jaw to play in a match at Hamilton (Victoria) against Michael Holding and John Snow! (March 1978)

On World Series Cricket, and its detractors:

At the end of the first season the drawing of small crowds to all our games upset the players as we felt we were playing attractive, entertaining fiercely fought cricket. The stigma created by sections of the media widened the gap between players and media representatives. We felt we were being harshly and unfairly treated with regard to the cricket we played and the general concept of World Series.

It wasn't so much the lack of constructive support from the media that irked us but the hypocrisy shown by representatives during our extremely successful second year. From a complete lack of communication for 15 months to a situation where we were expected to speak freely to those who had written and said we were "mercenaries, pirates and traitors to our country" certainly didn't come easily.

During the break between the first and second year the players put a lot of work into both the fitness and basic skills of cricket in a determined bid to prove to the sceptics we could successfully stand on our own two feet.

The public responded by continually turning up to the matches. It was this continued support that led the players further away from the media and the "establishment".

What did I learn in the last two years? As a batsman the pressure of facing continual fast bowling can only improve one's stature. There is a very high level of concentration required and it did not matter whether the matches were played in front of 2,000 people at Morwell on a soft, green pitch or at the SCG in front of 50,000, the bowling, fielding and batting were of world standard.

Waking each day realising there would be no respite on the field caused each player to strive that little bit harder to succeed and be a better cricketer than his opponent. It can be seen that success would come only if attention was placed on even the finest detail with regard to the skills of cricket. I learned that because a degree of success has been obtained it is not possible to take things easy. (October 1979)

On the trials of touring the Caribbean with WSC:
I went to the West Indies full of confidence and after a couple of scores early the runs deserted me (127 runs in the Super Tests at 14.11 – ugh!). The West Indies fast men, notably Andy Roberts and Michael Holding, got it into their heads that I wasn't a particularly suave player of the short ball climbing into my ribs, and they gave me a steady diet of this type of bowling. They put two men deep on the leg side and two others close in on the off with the result that if I hooked I was likely to be caught in the deep, and if I fended the ball away I was likely to get caught by the close-in men.

That meant that I was doing a lot of ducking and weaving – and getting hit. For the last Super Test I had a couple of cracked ribs. It was like Bodyline.

I needed some long sessions in the practice nets to try to overcome my deficiencies in handling this type of bowling, but there are no practice facilities of any use in the West Indies. I kept making the same mistakes day after day, and by the end of the tour I even tried to change my batting style. This was something I always said I would not do but under the continual self-pressure of making mistakes it is amazing how one's ideals change.

It is up to me to work on the faults the West Indies bowlers exploited and hopefully come up with an idea that eliminates the errors that kept causing my dismissal. Ron Barassi, Australia's best known Australian rules identity states: "The professional sportsmen are not the ones who are paid the most but that group of people who are dedicated to the eradication of errors." (November 1979)

On losing a domestic double-header:
Why and how did South Australia lose both McDonald's Cup games in November? We played 14 hours of cricket that weekend and outplayed both Victoria and Western Australia for a total of about 11 hours, but weren't good enough to win either match.

It is the sort of situation that arises in One-day cricket and the inexperience of some of our players showed towards the end of each of our bowling stints. In the last few overs, when it becomes helter-skelter cricket, it is imperative all fieldsmen "walk" the ball into their hands – they grab the ball before they attempt to throw it back.

That may sound all very basic, but basics tend to be overlooked in tense situations if they haven't been experienced before. (December 1979)

On his first "official" Test after World Series was disbanded:
I was quite happy with my form in the first innings of the First Test against the West Indies in Brisbane. At stumps on the first day I was 33 not out and I was pleased that in compiling those runs I had played each ball on its merits. The next day I progressed to 43 before skying an attempted hook off Colin Croft. Some critics had a go at me for getting out in such a fashion, but that doesn't worry me in the slightest.

Okay, it wasn't my best shot but the hook has been a good friend to me over the years and there's no way I'm going to cut it from my repertoire. I figure that in the next few months I'm going to play the hook 100 times. For that I'll score about 230 runs and get out twice. That's not a bad percentage if you ask me. The particular shot that brought about my dismissal was the result of changing my mind in a split second.

It was high outside off stump and my first reaction was to cut rather than hook. After I'd decided that, I realised there was a fieldsman at third man, which presented a danger because I mostly cut in the air. At the same time I remembered there was no one at fine leg so the hook seemed the safer shot.

That it wasn't doesn't mean a thing. I would have played it at nought or 150 and I would have been out – or, I would have had four.

The hook is a shot that a number six batsman should be expected to play with confidence. There are a lot of runs to be taken from it. The bowlers should be that bit more tired, the ball's a bit softer, and their bumper isn't as lethal. That's the time to hook. I'm not going to stop hooking. I tried that in the West Indies with WSC and I ended in a complete mess. (January 1980)

On the importance of crease occupation:
I suppose one of my shortcomings is that I tend to go stupid when I get on top and try to hit every ball for four instead of treating each according to its merit. I was greatly impressed at how Viv Richards (in the First Test in Brisbane) could suddenly open out and hit three consecutive fours, then play the rest of the over out calmly, and perhaps the next three or four overs. Simply, he picked the ball to hit.

After I've hit three successive fours I tend to want to repeat the dose on the fourth, even if it's a beautiful delivery.

One thing I'm going to start doing to try and improve my self-control is to simulate a match situation during practice in the nets. This may sound fairly basic but practice for me has always been a "bat hit ball" session – crunch! Occasionally it should be "ball hit bat". Really, I'm not the crude, full-throttle-out batsman some people seem to think I am. Last season when I was captain of West Torrens in Adelaide grade I played some very disciplined innings. One day we were chasing 230 to win and I batted for five hours in scoring 90. When I was out we were just a few runs from victory and we coasted home. That innings gave me a great deal of satisfaction. The responsibility of captaincy is good for me. (January 1980)

On the benefits of One-day cricket:

We've read plenty about limited-overs cricket and the bad effect it is having on the cricketing education of the young players. Very little has been written about the other side of the coin. From a player's point of view I contend any cricket is good cricket and can contribute to the learning process. This applies especially to batsmen.

In One-day games the start the opening batsmen get determines the fate of the lower order to a greater extent than in Test matches. Batsmen in the three to five slots play a game that is generally based on caution, with the right to play shots at their discretion.

The number six batsman is assigned the hardest job of all. Generally he comes in at a time when shots are required virtually from the first delivery he faces. His ability must be such that he can immediately punish the ball in the middle of the bat and find the gaps. One of the aims of the batting side should be to make sure they bat out the 50 overs. It is a cardinal sin to be dismissed with three or four overs still in hand.

From the bowling point of view, One-day matches are an object lesson in the finesse of line and length. The bowler learns to bowl to his set field and to probe at a particular weakness of opposing batsmen. Possibly the most positive aspect to come out of One-day cricket is the improvement, worldwide, of the standard of fielding.

If the fielding side is capable of saving a run every over, or so, that's a shaving of 40 to 50 runs off the target score. Possibly the one type of player who is disadvantaged is the attacking spin bowler, whose preference for a slip and bat pad fielder in the longer game, isn't always possible in a One-day game. Consequently he has to become a defensive type bowler.

Overall, the ultimate value of One-day games for players can be seen from the spectators' point of view. The fans flock to these matches and that puts money in the coffers, which, in turn, puts money in the players' pockets and so on down the line to the district clubs. (March 1980)

In more recent times David Hookes wrote columns for Melbourne newspapers *The Age* and *The Sunday Age*.

On Bradman's Best:

Don Bradman knew his "best team", released by author and Bradman biographer Roland Perry, would create enormous discussion and genuine interest. But there are some unanswered questions. Having known Sir Don, one of his greatest strengths, and one that was perhaps a little underestimated, was his ability as a selector. Entertainment was his philosophy and approach, and he always backed players who were prepared to play to win. Team balance was critical to him, as indicated by his right-hand, left-hand opening batting combination.

If, as Perry suggests it is a fair dinkum team, then five batsmen and five bowlers, of which only one Ray Lindwall could bat at all, must represent the most unbalanced team in history. Bradman went for Lindwall because he made two Test centuries, So what! Bradman is on record as saying Pakistan's Wasim Akram is the world's best left-arm fast bowler. Perry suggests Alec Bedser was selected because Bradman already had Sobers to bowl left-arm pace and therefore needed a right-arm, medium pace bowler capable of bowling long spells into the wind. What nonsense! Bradman already had two right-arm fast bowlers in Lindwall and Dennis Lillee, so where is the logic of selecting a right-arm medium pacer over Akram?

Akram has taken more than 400 wickets in both Test and One-day Internationals and ranks as an "all-time great" – Bradman's words not mine.

And then, supposedly, Bradman selected Clarrie Grimmett before Shane Warne. The other leg spinner Bill O'Reilly picks himself, as Bradman always said he was the best bowler he ever faced and saw. Bradman did not select Grimmett for the Ashes series of 1936-37 so why would he pick him in front of Warne, one of Wisden's five cricketers of the 20th century? It is also interesting to note that Bradman apparently selected three players who disliked him. So much for team spirit and harmony. Head to head:

BRADMAN'S TEAM	HOOKES'S TEAM
A Morris (A)	J Hobbs (E)
B Richards (SAf)	G Greenidge (WI)
D Bradman (A)	V Richards (WI)
S Tendulkar (I)	G Pollock (SAf)
G Sobers (WI)	V Trumper (A)
D Tallon (A)	G Chappell (A)
R Lindwall (A)	A Gilchrist (A)
D Lillee (A)	K Miller (A)
A Bedser (E)	W Akram (P)
W O'Reilly (A)	M Marshall (WI)
C Grimmett (A)	S Warne (A)
W Hammond (E)	D Compton (E)

(August 2001)

On Steve Waugh's captaincy:

Steve Waugh did not captain particularly well in the West Indies, his first tour as captain. Australia won the First Test in Trinidad by bowling the home side out for 51 in the second innings. It was the Windies' sixth consecutive Test loss, yet under Waugh Australia managed only to draw the series even with winning every toss.

Australia then went to England to snatch an unlikely World Cup victory, heralded as much for Waugh's positive captaincy as for Herschelle Gibbs's dropped catch. Waugh is captaining Australia during the country's most impressive period; his strength lies in allowing his players to do their own thing.

When a young left-hander played his first match for South Australia in 1975 he had trouble against the off spin of Lance Gibbs. At the other end his captain, Ian Chappell, was ducking and weaving against some quality fast bowling from Andy Roberts and Michael Holding. After three overs of embarrassment of playing and missing at Gibbs, the debutant started to walk down to his captain for some help and guidance. He was greeted with a gruff: "Don't bother coming down this end, son, I've got enough troubles of my own."

It was in the days before coaches, assistants, fitness trainers and medical staff and Chappell's simple philosophy was a couple of disciplined nets during the week, and a quick "good luck bowlers, good luck fielders" as the team went on to the field. Unless one is privy to the private world of a change room, judgement on the captain may only be assessed from afar. A good test on a captain is to monitor his behaviour, demeanour and body language throughout a long, hot, unsuccessful day.

Waugh moves from his position at gully to cover and back with no apparent change to his steely approach. Waugh may be conservative with a bat in his hand but his development over two years as captain has been profound. From a staggering, wobbly start in the Caribbean Waugh has etched his name alongside the greats.

He is open and honest at pre-match news conferences, quite happy to publicly target opposition players and captains.

It is a ploy that can be accused of "giving ammunition" to the enemy, but it is one the Australian team back with considerable success. Others will judge Waugh, but a good leader does not captain by committee nor does he worry what others think.

Waugh can stand tall. His batting is still world class (three Test centuries in the past four matches) and his ambition to captain Australia in the 2003 World Cup in South Africa should be realised. (March 2001)

On the methods of John Buchanan, Australia's coach:

"There's a fraction too much friction," sang Tim Finn. And following recent comments by Australian coach John Buchanan, the phrase could apply to the national cricket team. Buchanan's thoughts regarding the state of Shane Warne's fitness, and his general fatigue and weariness, smacked of a coach attacking a senior player. With Warne not succeeding, Buchanan's post-match comments could have taken the "I told you so" path. Had Warne bowled Australia to victory in the Third Test (against India), the coach may have said, "It worked, I was just trying to gee him up."

Unbelievably, Buchanan had not seen the pitch in Madras before suggesting Warne may not play. Conversely, Steve Waugh said he was sure that after looking at the pitch Warne was a certainty to play. Coaches should always address player's problems in-house and not in the public domain via the media. Buchanan's actions should have resulted in swift action, first from Waugh and then from the Australian Cricket Board. At the very least, Buchanan should have been censured and denied access to any media outlet for the rest of the tour pending a Cricket Board investigation.

On the strength of Buchanan coaching Queensland to its first Sheffield Shield victory, he was appointed Australian coach following Geoff Marsh. His attention to detail and understanding of the use of computers in helping a cricket team were factors in his favour. Soon after his appointment Buchanan engaged the services of a manager, a move not understood by those close to the team. Buchanan thinks laterally and out of the square, two traits that are very important, but it must be remembered that cricket is an individual game developed in a team structure.

The coach should coordinate training, ensure that the stumps and balls are there and if he has had extensive top level playing experience, he can contribute in tactical and technical discussions. Buchanan's left-field approach sometimes requires players to stand up and address the team on non-cricket related issues. It might be the life and times of Abraham Lincoln, a subject that most players would need to research. But Buchanan must remember he is dealing with International sportsmen and it can be more than a little annoying for them to spend precious free time in a library.

The current tour of India is a long one in hot, humid, dusty and trying conditions. The crowded itinerary allows for just two days off for the players. On that basis it was strange that, on the last day of the Third Test after the Australian players had spent days in the field, the players warmed up for half an hour in 35 degree heat and 90 per cent humidity. There are some rumblings from within the ranks, particularly among the senior players, and a coach must be aware of the signs.

Having been sacked as captain, this columnist understands the need to be aware of player power. It can be a dangerous virus within a team, but nobody signs a contract that stipulates everyone must get along with everybody else.

If Buchanan is to retain his job he must learn to be flexible in his dealings with senior players. That is not to suggest he should lie down and be treated like a doormat, rather ascertain and implement some of their thoughts.

Part of the romance of cricket is the captain being in charge. He must remember how opposition players cope, what shots they have and what shots they don't play. Computers may help in theory but Steve Waugh needs to react on the ground. Australia does not want to get to the stage of playing boring predictable cricket (like that) trotted out by the computer-induced robots from South Africa. Buchanan must learn that Australian cricket will always depend on its captain. He will ignore that at his own peril. (March 2001)

On the role of Adam Gilchrist:

Regardless of what people think, Adam Gilchrist cannot continue to fill the roles the selectors ask of him if they want him to be Australia's next captain. Following Australia's three-day victory in Bombay captain Steve Waugh supported Gilchrist's role at number seven, but in the near future there needs to be a change in thinking.

Let's be honest. Being such a fine wicketkeeper and skilful batsman the demands of coming in at number seven are simple. There is little or no pressure on the batsman. Flashback to day two of the Test last week and think what would have happened had Gilchrist failed when he came to the crease at five for 99.

The post-match witch hunt would have been directed at the top order, not the wicketkeeper who came in at number seven and went out cheaply. With Australia struggling, Gilchrist went to the crease and did his own thing and no one would deny what a wonderful part he played in helping to win the match.

But with so much cricket being played it is important the players maintain their enthusiasm as much as their fitness. On this tour the players have only one scheduled free day in two months. It's hot, humid and very demanding, not the sort of tour a captain needs to squeeze between a full summer in Australia and an Ashes tour, particularly if he has to stand up at the stumps.

Should the selectors, with the approval of the Cricket Board, decide on Gilchrist to lead the country after Waugh's retirement, then they must look for another Test wicketkeeper. Gilchrist could captain Australia and bat at number four, with the next best wicketkeeper coming in at number seven.

During the limited-overs matches Gilchrist could captain, open the batting and keep wickets. It should not prove too much of a task, provided he is not expected to do the same in Test cricket. (March 2001)

On the death of Bradman:
In 1987 I sat next to Sir Donald Bradman at a pre-season dinner to launch the South Australian cricket season. After a number of speeches about the team's sponsors, the new players in the squad and the side's ability, the fitness coordinator spoke on the merits of pre-season training and how fit the squad was after months of weight work, sandhill running and sprints.

I quietly asked Sir Donald how he got fit for cricket in the 1930s and, in his voice that would shatter a glass, he told me: "I got fit running between the wickets." Cricket's greatest player has gone and how ironic it is to be penning this piece in India, a country of more than one billion people, most of whom know the name Bradman.

Yet, Bradman never set foot in this country. The nearest he came to this part of the world was waving from the deck of a boat carrying the Australian team nearly 70 years ago. Contemporary cricketers loved talking to him. Unlike many of his peers he appreciated the modern game and, indeed, admitted he would have worn a helmet during the Bodyline series.

One of cricket's best-kept secrets was the signing of 55 players to join Kerry Packer's World Series Cricket in 1977. I had signed and a couple of weeks later I had a telephone call from Sir Donald inviting me to lunch at the exclusive Adelaide Club on the eve of the Ashes series. As a kid from the western suburbs, I had never contemplated going to the Adelaide Club. My mother pressed my only suit and it was a nervous young man who met Sir Donald at the front of the heritage-listed building.

After trying to work out which knife and fork to use, lunch turned out to be just a ham and tomato sandwich. The conversation was intimate and cricket-related and Sir Donald thought I hit my cut shots in the air too often for his liking. It was, however, his parting comments that linger.

As he waited for his car, he told me that the only thing worth playing for was the baggy green cap. At the time I thought nobody knew about World Series Cricket, but I still believe Bradman knew.

Bill Jacobs was approached by Bradman to be a manager during Australia's series against the Rest Of The World in 1971-72. It was Bradman's stance against apartheid that led to the cancellation of the South African tour (to Australia) and the formation of the Rest Of The World side. On the eve of the last Test match, Bradman told Jacobs: "Tomorrow will be the saddest day of my life; my son is going to change his name." John Bradman had struggled to cope with the pressures surrounding his surname, so he changed it to Bradsen.

Sadly Sir Donald's reclusive lifestyle meant his contribution to latter-day cricketers was minimal. In the early 1980s I asked him to attend South Australia's practice one evening. I said I would lock the gate, thereby keeping the media away, and not tell the players until that day.

The precautions didn't matter; he said "no". As captain I felt let down and disappointed for the young players. Bradman saw nearly every day's play at the Adelaide Oval and I felt he could have assisted our training session.

His legend will carry on. At Australian training in Bombay the day before Sir Donald passed away a young Indian boy told me his favourite cricketer was Bradman. (February 2001)

Face-to-face with Darren Lehmann:

Hookes: There seems to be a preoccupation with your weight and fitness and that every cricketer needs to be like Anthony Koutoufides (Carlton Australian rules footballer). Do you feel that is fair?

Lehmann: Oh, mate, I feel like "Kouta" at the moment! No seriously, I feel cricket fits a totally different fitness scenario to what most people think. I know I can bat for long periods of time. Mentally, I'm ready to do that. Obviously, I'm not the skinniest bloke around. I've worked hard on my fitness with the ACB's fitness guy; he's a bit of a "Hitler" on the training track.

H: The mental aspect; what is that?

L: That's what I call "cricket fitness". More than anything else, that to me is the most important form of fitness for cricket. Granted, there is a physical component required but as long as I'm ready to play, then I feel I'm fit to play.

H: Do you feel your "look" has kept you out of the Australian team at times?

L: I don't know, I hope not. Look at (David) Boon and (Greg) Ritchie. I know that times have changed. I'm not massively overweight. I'm a pretty solid bloke so I wouldn't think that has been a factor, perhaps just poor shot selection at times.

H: Has an Australian selector or a member of the Cricket Board ever told you that if you lost weight it would increase your chances of being selected for your country?

L: No, never.

H: You have scored 49 centuries at an average of over 54 runs per innings, an unbelievable record. You will shortly break the Australian first-class record for the most number of runs. Is there a time, perhaps when you are changing a nappy, when you think, "Why haven't I played more Test cricket for Australia?"

L: Sometimes I do, but a lot has to do with the fact they are a very good team.

H: You came to Victoria for three years. On reflection was it the right thing to do and would you do it again in the same circumstances?

L: Yes. I may decide to stay a bit longer next time. I think the MCG pitch could have rounded off my batting if I had stayed longer.

H: What is your future?

L: I have another couple of years at Yorkshire and, because I am still enjoying first-class cricket here, I will play for at least another three seasons for South Australia and then I'll have to sit down and think about what to do next.

H: What, get a real job?

L: Yeah, I suppose so. (April 2001)

On player rotation selection policy:

Rotating players in the Australian cricket team needs to be revisited. The system was introduced when Australia was playing well and winning and gave senior players a chance to rest. The philosophy and intent may have had some merit but it seems to have lost some credibility in India.

Australia began its quest for two consecutive victories to break the West Indies record for most wins in One-day Internationals by leaving out three players recently arrived from Australia, Darren Lehmann, Bracken and Andrew Symonds.

That selection followed Steve Waugh's comment after the Test series loss that, although the first limited-overs match was in two days, he could not get his head around the Test match loss and would need some time to regroup.

His feelings were understandable, which made the selection for the first One-day match even more puzzling.

After losing consecutive Test matches in oppressive conditions, the team needed an influx of fresh minds, fresh legs and a dose of enthusiasm. Quite rightly Hayden was retained and continued his good form, but Ricky Ponting's selection at number three was baffling. In sporting teams there must be a reward and penalty for performances.

Hayden was rewarded but Ponting suffered no penalty after a poor Test series in which he averaged 3.4 in five innings. Ponting deserved to be dropped. That he played in the first One-day match and failed again was no surprise. The surprise came when he was left out of the second match in Pune. Having played the first game in Bangalore he should have been in the second team.

There appeared no reason to drop him after carrying him through three Test matches and one limited-overs match. And, the sight of the world's most high-profile cricketers, Shane Warne and Ponting, running drinks to their team mates every time a wicket fell in Pune smacked of a rigid system not encouraging any flexibility. Australia has 15 players in India plus a support staff of six.

At any One-day fixture just two players are required to handle any off-field duties, leaving space for the remaining two rested players to lie by the pool, play golf or go to the races. If Warne and Ponting were rested under the rotation system then they should have been rested, not acting as glorified, millionaire water boys. (August 2001)

On Ricky Ponting:

The Australian cricket selectors have got it wrong again. What were they thinking when they decided to appoint Ricky Ponting as Australia's vice-captain? At this moment Ponting is the wrong man for the job. In fact, there is no right man for the job. The vice-captain's job is the most overrated in Australian sport. Any captain worth his position will consult several players throughout the course of a day's play in his decision-making process.

Ponting should not have been selected for three reasons. First, the position is overrated. Second, his form warrants him being dropped from the Test side, not promoted to a position of power and importance. Even allowing for the loss of Waugh because of injury, a sequence of six Test matches without a score in the 20s means Ponting must be dropped.

When a player retains his place after an extended run of not making runs or taking wickets it creates an imbalance and disquiet within the team. The continued selection of Mark Taylor when he was batting like Glenn McGrath is still spoken of in mutinous terms by his former team mates. A player out of the side and in form wants to get selected and can't.

In Ponting's case, Mark Waugh, batting number four, might not actually sit by the player's gate when Ponting walks to the crease, but he will put his thigh pad on earlier than normal. Third, and perhaps most significantly, Ponting is not mature enough to do the job properly.

It has nothing to do with any off-field misdemeanour. He has worked extremely hard to rectify his public persona but a number of on-field actions have indicated an angry man not calm in his approach to the game. While fielding in Adelaide last year he threw the ball in a fit of pique at West Indian batsman Daren Ganga, an act not befitting the vice-captaincy position. In the stifling cauldron of a Test match, an angry young man out of form and in a position of power is a dangerous and volatile mix. (August 2002)

On the Zimbabwe crisis:

Henry Olonga and Andy Flower wearing black armbands at the World Cup to mourn the death of democracy in their country is an amazingly courageous stance. If I was an Australian player who was wavering about playing in Zimbabwe on February 24 and I saw that happen, I'd be pretty keen to go and see the team management and say: "Look, I'm not going."

A moral stance, to my mind, should be extremely strong with the players and yet it doesn't seem to be. Apart from a reasonably strong stance from Matthew Hayden, saying he wouldn't shake Robert Mugabe's hand, every other player has toed the party line and talked about safety and security. These blokes are on a global stage for two months; they've got a real opportunity to make a worldwide statement by refusing to go. They've just won the Laureus world sports team of the year award in Monaco, they're not just "Mickey Mouse" Commonwealth country sports people – they have world stature. Maybe they should support Olonga and Flower and wear black armbands, but withdrawing altogether would be an enormous statement globally.

In 1979 we played World Series Cricket in Guyana with the autocrat Forbes Burnham ruling the country. On reflection, I shouldn't have played there. I would like to be able to say I was worldly enough to work that out at the time, but I wasn't.

Even though the "Jonestown massacre" had occurred six months before we went there with WSC, Guyana didn't have the worldwide focus that Zimbabwe has now. This is a world story and if the players aren't talking about it in the change rooms what are they talking about?

There is a great affinity between the Australian and Zimbabwe players, who have similar attitudes to life and a love of the outdoors. A lot of the Australian players had stayed at Heath Streak's farm before Mugabe kicked his family off the land; I've stayed there with Carl Rackemann. Maybe Zimbabwe players are saying, "Please come and play", which would make it an even tougher decision to make.

The story of Edison Mukwazi, who was arrested, beaten and later died because he was protesting against World Cup matches being played in Zimbabwe … what more do people need? When does this become a moral issue?

Everybody has hidden behind the safety and security angle. I understand the Australian Cricket Board's policy statement, that safety and security are its only concern, but I would have thought the moral issue was the primary consideration.

My argument about safety and security is that the Australian team will not go there unless it is safe, so once they fly into Bulawayo it has been deemed safe. Declaring that it's safe to go there doesn't make it morally right. If Fox Sports sent me to Zimbabwe to commentate I wouldn't go. They might say, "Go and show the plight of Zimbabwe to the world", and, if you knew you could do that you'd be happy to go. But I can't believe pictures coming out of Zimbabwe are going to show a million people a week starving. They'll just show a cricket ground with blokes hitting fours and sixes.

If the players are still ho-hum about going there after all that's happened then that would be disappointing. But I would deem a cricketer weak if he feels strongly about a moral issue and doesn't make a stand. (February 2003)

CHAPTER
VIII

Hookesy was nothing like any coach before him. He had no interest in how to conduct a training session; his fielding drills were straight out of the 1970s. But he was always looking for something different to bring to the members of the Victorian squad, such as his stories from the "what-it's-worth basket".

'The Sky-Hookes'

DARREN BERRY

As a coach, David Hookes was simple but complex; left field but conservative; he was aggressively hard, but also fair. In fact, he was as he always was, the mixed bag of tricks we all knew as Hookesy. When David was appointed coach of Victoria at the start of the 2002-03 season, it certainly raised a few eyebrows among the players. After all, as a proud South Australian where the rivalry across the border has always been strong, he grew up hating the Vics.

He had not, of his own volition, been back in the dressing rooms since his retirement, and you could say was out of touch with the modern methods of coaching. However, David Hookes wasn't silly; he was as street smart as they come.

Not long after that appointment, Greg Shipperd, the coach of Tasmania for the past decade, was appointed as Hookesy's assistant. Once again, eyebrows were raised. How could two completely opposite personalities possibly work together? As a player Hookes was aggressive, entertaining and at times simply outrageous. Shipperd, on the other hand, was conservative, meticulous and at times just bloody boring.

I remember playing against Greg at the end of his career; mine was just beginning. He waddled to the wicket at Bellerive looking like the "Michelin man". He had more padding on than anyone I had ever seen. Merv Hughes took the new ball and did everything he could to upset this man, little in stature but, as it turned out, a man big in temperament. Merv called Shipperd every name under the sun but the one that we found most humour in was his reference to Shipperd as the "human mattress". Shipperd was determined and gritty and played every ball like his life depended on it.

The combination of Hookes and Shipperd at the helm of Victorian cricket proved to be a wonderful one. Together they worked beautifully, and we players had the best of both worlds. Coach Hookes was nothing like any coach before him; he had no idea, nor interest for that matter, in how to conduct a training session. His fielding drills were straight out of the 1970s and caused the boys many a sore hand. His theory on catching practice was if you dropped one, the next one would come at you twice as hard.

It was hilarious watching the boys try to avoid being in Hookesy's fielding group pre-match. Young Cameron White played the majority of last season with padding on the palms of both hands as Hookesy turned him into our first slip specialist.

Hookesy also added a bowling coach, Rodney Hogg, to his coaching staff; and on to the selection panel came Ray Bright, who played more than 100 games for the Vics, John McWhirter, a former State Second XI batsman, and Mick O'Sullivan, an accomplished district wicketkeeper, who was chairman of selectors. This group was from the same era so it seemed only appropriate to label them the "Sky Hookes" – we reckoned they were all "living in the 1970s".

Hookesy acted more like a director of coaching than the coach. As far as training was concerned he was the ringmaster and left the specifics to Shipperd; on match days he left it to his leaders within the team. He never spoke all that often, but when he did the boys listened. He was respected for the way he played the game and brought that same attacking style to the Vics.

The MCG dressing room is our sanctuary and within it is the meeting room, or coach's room. You would be called into this room if you did something wrong like playing a poor shot at a crucial time in a game. David Hookes didn't mind letting you know exactly what he thought of your efforts if they fell short of the mark.

This room achieved notoriety after Brad Hodge was on the receiving end of a Hookes barrage one day. "Hodgey" is one of the funniest blokes I have played with, good at the straight-face line so he's usually at his best when he's trying to be serious. This day, face a mask of contrition, he labelled the room "the wrath room". Eventually, because we all feared a visit to the room, we put a sign above the door, *The Wrath Room* – much to Hookesy's amusement.

Hookesy was always looking for something different to bring to the boys. He would often tell us stories he referred to as, coming from the "for-what-it's-worth-basket". These were usually experiences from his career, and entertaining. Or, they might have related to something he'd heard when among his circle of friends.

A favourite was his tennis analogy – you can lose more games than your opponent, but still win Wimbledon. This theory, which of course is true, sums up the never-say-die attitude of David Hookes.

At the beginning of his tenure as coach, he was extremely keen to introduce what he called "set plays" in the One-day game and, eventually in four-day cricket. We ran with this theory but it did take a while to grasp. Early-season in Perth we tried it every ball in a block of four overs; every player had a piece of paper in his pocket so we knew what ball was coming up next and the field would change according to the type of ball that was to be bowled. It took us forever to get it right.

With some perseverance we got it down pat and, as wicketkeeper and captain, I would signal for a certain delivery and the boys would automatically change positions. It sounds complicated, but after we had mastered it, we found it quite easy and, at times, very successful.

What I liked most about Hookesy as a coach was you could have some wonderful debates with him over cricket issues; at times, our strong opinions clashed but the next day it was business as usual. He frustrated me at times with his stubborn resolve on certain things and his black-and-white approach, but he always told you exactly what he thought. It's the style most players prefer – upfront and honest. At least, that way there are no hidden agendas.

In Hookesy's first year as coach, we played a One-day game against Queensland up at Ballarat. We were all out for 65. Hookesy was fuming at game's end and gave us an almighty spray. In the heat of the situation he ordered all of us to 6.30am training sessions every day the following week in Port Phillip Bay. There was more; he said anyone late would be dropped for two games. I must admit, at the time I felt he had gone too far, that his anger had overwhelmed sensible decision-making. It was an old fashioned punishment for poor performance. And, the boys were flat. But the coach had spoken so we copped our medicine.

You won't believe this; on the fourth morning, the one after the Allan Border Medal night, my wife and I arrived home late – naturally – and I was very conscious to set the alarm so I'd be at the Bay for the early morning swim. Next thing I wake up – to my wife's alarm at 7.00am, to get her to work. What happened, why didn't my alarm go off? I'd made the mistake of setting the alarm for "pm". I knew I was gone. I met Hookesy at lunchtime and explained my innocent mistake. But he had set the rules and I had broken them, end of story. I was dropped for two matches. To Hookesy, a man of his word, it was a matter of principle. Harsh, but fair – that was Hookesy.

He believed victory was possible from any position and this mentality rubbed off on the team in the famous run chase on the last day in Newcastle against New South Wales. He drew on his experience from his playing days when South Australia chased down 506 in the last innings to win a game.

On the white board that he rarely used he scribbled: "Score 225 runs in 55 overs followed by 225 in 55 overs and we win the game". Somehow it seemed a lot easier to think about than wondering how on earth could we chase 450 in one day.

The boys left the ground that night with a real belief that we could win and a focus on how to do it. The next day, after the first 55 overs, overs we were right on target, but still we couldn't quite come to grips with believing we really did have a genuine chance of victory. But David Hussey played one of the best innings I have ever seen to guide us home with eight overs to spare.

It was one of the greatest victories of all time, and masterminded by our coach. The celebrations started with a walk from the ground to our hotel. This was after the sponsor's entire product had been consumed at the ground. I'll never forget the stroll home. Most of the boys, led by Hookesy, stopped off at a quiet pub for a quick drink to break the journey. The publican asked David if he had something all the boys could sign as a souvenir of our visit and the amazing events of the afternoon. Hookesy took the shirt he was wearing off his back and inscribed on it, *The Great Chase*. Then, all the boys signed the shirt and publican was rapt. Tragically, this would be the last Pura Cup game Hookesy would coach. The publican must now cherish that moment commemorating that day as much as we in the Victorian team do.

The events of the next week still seem too unreal to comprehend. The death of our coach mid-season was a shocking tragedy that cut the playing group to the core. A few of us were with Hookesy the night it happened. How can you, as long as you live, ever forget something like that. Captaining the team during that difficult time was one of the hardest tasks I have ever faced; trying to explain to the media how we would move forward as a group was bloody difficult, but something within drove me.

Perhaps it was the memory of my friend that gave me the strength. I was unsure how we would recover from losing David so soon after the death in the previous off-season of our former coach John Scholes.

We travelled to Adelaide for David's funeral then had to get together just a few days later to start our next match. I remained on edge; how would I cope, and how would the boys regroup? But, from that moment on we got stronger and stronger. We won both the ING and Pura games played at the Adelaide Oval where David's memorial service was held. Then we went within a whisker of making the ING Cup final, which was a big improvement on our previous few seasons; then we lifted the ultimate prize, the Pura Cup. Some will say after what we had endured we were destined to be Pura Cup champions, that it was fate. Truth is, it took a lot of bloody hard work.

After the final, when we sang our team song in the dressing room, we purposely left a space in our tight knit circle of players for our coach Hookesy. We knew he was right beside us in spirit. I know how proud Hookesy would have been that we won the title. It had been 14 seasons since the Vics had won the trophy and, without doubt, the influence of David Hookes, our friend, mentor and coach had played a significant role in the victory.

Reaching for the Stars

GREG SHIPPERD

I'm told that Cricket Victoria spent some time cajoling David Hookes to "have a go", to get involved in putting the polish on the Victorian Bushrangers team. I suspect life seemed busy enough with more than the average number of commitments on his plate – family, radio, television and community events.

But once in, he was determined to make a difference and he attacked his challenge much the same as he did "that day in 1977" at the MCG.

He wanted the players to re-establish respect which had been lost, not for them as people but in terms of the team. There was a feeling abroad that the State had little interest in its cricket team. Its players had forgotten to reach for the stars.

The environment he nurtured was one of enjoyment, to play positive, entertaining and, what he called "win-from-any-situation cricket". He wanted the players to support the spirit of cricket. To learn about its history. And, he wanted them to respect and value the infrastructure around the team.

He was an orator of rare talent with a rich history of tales to tell an awakening group of men. He had a story about them all, from Bradman to the Chappells from Packer to World Series Cricket, and about his times with South Australia. He was in tune with the deeds of the past as well as the trends of the modern game. He was ready to say what he thought, and defend it stoutly.

Some 18 months prior, we former foes in the Sheffield Shield had been united, "by appointment to Victoria" you might say. We were wary of how the seasons, and relationship, would unfold. As I listened I learned, as he watched he learned and, as people flourished, a team improved.

He built a good cop, bad cop routine with his players that allowed for directness, honesty, toughness, but succour when necessary. He reminded us, after having completed an appointment with the ill, needy or dying, how privileged we were to enjoy what we had, a lesson that now shapes the thoughts of many people affected by his untimely death.

As he watched his team grow, and the players responding to his style and personality, it gave him great satisfaction and encouragement to continue the journey. David had begun negotiations with Cricket Victoria about continuing as coach, despite frustration when his comments caused consternation at Cricket Australia and other places. He championed freedom of thought and speech. Ironically, we hear Cricket Australia is relaxing the code of conduct regarding player comment on the issues of the day.

I think it surprised him how attached he had become to his "new family". As a coach of some experience I can reveal it's like that; you share some very strong bonds, have some great moments, ups and downs. It's as though you've adopted 30 or so people.

He was both alarmed yet tickled that he could still physically match it with his players in the bench press and other physical pursuits. He looked forward to those sessions and had spent hours walking and swimming rehabilitating his knee post-surgery. An early morning call on tour – "see you at the ground" – would signal that a walk to the ground was an opportunity to mentally organise that demanding schedule.

Through his industry contacts and colleagues the team was exposed to a range of guest speakers, all likely to provide a broad perspective on elite sport and life: Gary Lyon, Mick Malthouse, John Fitzgerald, Tim Lane, Mark Bickley, Rod Hogg, Merv Hughes, Charlie Walsh, Neil Craig and more. And, the media, former players, mums and dads and kids, country talent, sponsors, employers all shared an environment generally not easily entered – the dressing room. The interaction was something to behold.

Without a doubt his most brilliant individual coaching moment was the Victoria versus New South Wales fixture in Newcastle in January 2004, when Victoria chased a last innings total of 455 on a fourth day wicket against a quality NSW attack including Stuart MacGill, Matt Nicholson and Simon Katich, all of whom had bowled for Australia.

His whiteboard plan was rather an original one: imagine the chase as two One-day matches. Importantly, he had made them think; he had promoted the possibility of an outrageous victory, which I am confident no one initially thought possible.

The ensuing victory was founded on that wonderful individual innings by David Hussey (212 not out in 218 balls – 26 fours, five sixes, truly Hookes-like!). The win was celebrated with gusto and a determined reminder – never forget how to win. It consolidated the "Hookesy way".

Backhander at the Nets

SHANE WARNE

I was at the AIS Cricket Academy in Adelaide when David Hookes came up, introduced himself and told me I'd be welcome to come down to the South Australian squad training sessions at the Adelaide Oval. It was 1990. Of course, I'd seen him play, and I have a good memory of watching him in World Series and, whilst he wasn't my hero or anything like that, I did have a David Hookes bat called "The Hurricane".

Naturally, I took him up on the practice offer. I knew I'd only be a net bowler, but I also knew that the odds were I'd learn a bit more about the game bowling to all these squad guys. It's the sort of thing that used to happen everywhere, senior players inviting promising, keen young cricketers to spend some time with the senior players.

The trick is not to get above yourself; in other words, be seen and not heard, and just listen and do as you're told. When Hook, as the other squad members called him, came in I'd already bowled to a few batsmen and was pretty happy with the way they were coming out.

But now I was about to bowl to the one and only David Hookes; I remember suddenly being very nervous; in fact, thinking back as I am writing this makes me nervous. Nerves never do much for the suppleness a leg spinner needs in his fingers.

The other bowlers in my net were seamers. Hook faced them first. The first ball he got he spanked right off the middle of the bat and the second seam bowler got the same treatment.

My turn. I tried to relax but couldn't. Even so, I bowled a pretty good leg break but it was too straight, too much at the great man's pads and turning further to leg. He sort of pirouetted, then one-handed hit the ball back to me from behind his back. I was stunned and thought, "What ..!" The look on my face must have been sheer amazement. He glanced back up the pitch at me and said: "Don't bowl there, son."

When the talk started about him coaching Victoria, he was keen but you could sense a very slight reservation. He wasn't sure about how it would all work out. That's certainly not to say Hook lacked any confidence in his ability to do the job, it was more a case of clearly understanding what he had to work with.

Before he was appointed, we had a game of golf, just the two of us, which turned out to be a sort of fact-finding mission.

He asked me: "Okay, tell me where the Vics can improve ... tell me your thoughts on each player ... what are your plans?" That last bit came from left field. I asked him: "What do you mean?" He said, "Well, you should be the captain and I want you to be the captain. But you have to be committed to the Vics."

"I always have been," I told him. And I added that I was considering retiring from One-day cricket so I could play Test cricket for longer and therefore spend more time with the Vics. "Good," he said. "Let's go for it."

Hook touched everyone in the squad in a very special way. He was never one to let a problem fester and would confront it in the best way he knew – front on. His style was pretty much "in your face". A player would be invited to "have a quick chat" in The Wrath Room. I think deep down Hook enjoyed that little bit of player dark humour. It meant that his methods had been "accepted". And, more than that, it showed the squad was able to retain a certain spirit when there was a bit of heavy stuff around.

Our Pura Cup final win was a fitting tribute to Hook. The legacy he has left for Victorian cricket is one of passion and a never-give-up attitude and I'm sure that this is a start of a great era for us. A lot of our younger guys have grown so much as cricketers and are starting to realise how good they really are. We are in a great position to push it all the way now. Let's hope the Hook way will live forever.

Over the years Hook and I had some real humdinger arguments. We were friends, but never really close until we had a good chat in Sri Lanka in 1999. We cleared the air. We talked for hours about plenty, some personal issues, but about cricket more than anything else because he loved cricket so much. He always had challenging ideas about the game and rule changes. Some of his theories where pretty radical but more often than not he'd raise a point that you hadn't really thought of. He made you think outside the square.

It's no secret that Hook supported me through everything, and especially the last 12 months, on and off the field. That really meant a lot to me, and my family, because it was a tough time. Behind all that bravado he was a very loyal and caring person.

Hook was a guy it was good to be around because he instilled a lot of confidence into a lot of people, and made them think that anything was possible because nothing was a problem; you walked away feeling good about yourself.

A Sentimental Bloke

ALAN SHIELL

For all his daring, for all his bravado, for all his forthright ways, David Hookes was a sentimentalist with an encyclopedic knowledge and understanding of people generally, not only sporting people. And he respected history and tradition, even if his sense of humour dictated that he had to be cheeky about them sometimes.

He would have been humbled by the emotional tributes and the sincere outpouring of grief – locally, nationally and internationally – accorded him in death. He would have been humbled, too, by his funeral service and we can only begin to imagine some of the one-liners he would have come up with about being in a coffin for his last day at his beloved Adelaide Oval where he swatted sixes and fours as if it were his own little backyard; and, where he scored 20 of his 29 first-class centuries for South Australia.

He would have delighted in the irony of being made to resemble a rose rather than the prickly thorn he often was perceived to be – and sometimes was – during his time as South Australian captain, and then as a forthright media commentator and, most recently, as the Victorian team's coach. The only satisfying thing about the numbing days that followed his death was that so many good, decent people were so generous in their praise of Hookesy.

It ought to have convinced the doubters, who want to resent those who move in the limelight, that he really was a man of substance, one who crammed so much into his 48 years and who always gave of himself so generously. That, I think, was probably his greatest claim to fame. He responded warmly to men and women, boys and girls, and they returned the compliment – and they never forgot the experience. He was very good with names and he did his homework to ensure he was. People appreciated that.

The great Ted "EJ" Whitten became an even bigger, more much-loved character and so-called "identity" after his illustrious football career, because of the power of his personality and his ability to communicate and identify with people. EJ could charm the birds off the trees, as they say. Hookesy might have lacked some of the incomparable Whitten's all-consuming charisma but he left a similar feel-good impression with those he met. Suddenly, he was their friend, their mate, and they all had a nice story to tell about him. It was as if Hookesy knew everyone and everyone knew him. Of course he was no angel. Who is? He could be stubborn, opinionated, argumentative, and even reckless. Who isn't? He thrived on company and conversation, and it didn't always have to be stimulating, particularly if he was cradling a beer.

He wanted to be with people and, fortunately, they wanted to be around him because he was always entertaining and challenging, just as he was as a cricketer. That's one of the reasons he was such a natural, supremely competent media performer on radio and television. He was just being himself. He didn't have to put on a different hat when he went into a radio or television studio. He was still Hookesy being Hookesy and if you didn't like it, well, too bad.

He loved the media, the challenges and rewards it offered, the outlet it provided for him and the people he met through it. He deserved all of his success because, as a cricketer – as Whitten was as a footballer – he was very good to media people, and they liked and respected him for it. The finest tributes to Hookesy came from Australia's leading cricket writers and sports columnists.

Robert Craddock, News Limited's Brisbane-based national cricket writer, got it right when he wrote: "The game has lost not only a fine man but perhaps its last great loose cannon. In a sport choked blue in the face by political correctness, it takes a man brave enough to work inside the system but take it on at the same time. Hookes did, and we loved him for it. It says everything about his genuine nature that often the people he occasionally challenged were those who liked him most because they accepted him for simply being the colourful maverick that he was."

Phil Wilkins wrote in *The Sydney Morning Herald* that "in a nation without aristocracy, Hookes was one of those rarities, a prince among men", and described him as "handsome, athletic, humorous, invariably sporting a cheeky smile", and said he "positively shone out in a crowd, his personality radiant". They were able to write so insightfully, and with such emotion, because they were his mates. They had all shared good times with him and they knew him well enough to know and understand what made him tick.

Never did Hookesy's honesty and modesty shine through more than when he talked about his cricket career and the frustrations of not becoming a dominant, consistent run-scorer at Test level as he was for South Australia.

He opened his 1993 autobiography with these words: "I want to get one thing straight from the start. I don't have any delusions of grandeur about my cricket career. How could I when I played only 23 Tests in a first-class career that started in 1975-76 and finished in 1991-92? My overall aggregate of 12,671 runs (av. 43.39), with

32 centuries and 65 half-centuries, in 178 first-class matches is satisfying and productive enough. Yet, with only 1,306 (av. 34.36) of those runs coming in my Tests, I have much to be modest about at the game's highest level."

And he closed the book this way: "I suspect history will judge me harshly as a batsman because of my modest results in Tests, and I can't complain about that. It was always going to be a struggle, trying to live up to that freakish period early in 1977 when I scored the five hundreds in six Shield innings and had that explosive five-fours-in-a-row stint in the Centenary Test. Injuries might have hampered me at times, but they cannot be the definitive reason or excuse for not achieving more because most successful sports people must, and do, overcome injuries.

"They are also expected to learn from their mistakes, and some people will maintain I didn't learn enough from mine. But, as a batsman and as a captain, I tried to be aggressive and entertaining, and succeeded occasionally. As a team mate and as an opponent, I'm confident I made many more friends than enemies. And if, in South Australia particularly, I have left some small legacy for those fortunate enough to be involved with cricket's future, then at least I have made a worthwhile contribution to the game to which I still owe so much."

Quite a few observers thought that World Series Cricket came too early for Hookes and that he never recovered fully from the effects of having his jaw broken by that bouncer. Hookesy never disagreed with this and, indeed, admitted that he had difficulty concentrating when he resumed playing, sought hypnotherapy treatment to try to overcome the memory of the injury and subsequently "didn't hook much".

And he criticised himself for not using his feet enough to advance down the pitch to slow bowlers. He was most critical of himself, though, for that performance against England in the 1982-83 home series, in which he made 344 runs (av. 49.14) with scores of 56, 28, 66 not out, 37, 53, 68, 17 and 19. No century, no Test future was his reasoned self-criticism.

For all that, an in-form Hookes would have walked into Australia's One-day team now, and how thrilling would it have been to have seen him in full flight with fellow left-handed thrashing machines Matthew Hayden and Adam Gilchrist? Rarely, if ever, has a cricketer had a more appropriate play-on name – Hookesy – for it embodied everything bold about batsmanship. And Hookesy was as bold as they come.

CHAPTER
IX

Why is it that the thought of never seeing someone again is such a powerful emotion? Why do we suddenly think of all the things we should have said? Why do we link it to something we failed to do, or should not have done? Why does it have the power to please, but grieve?

A Boy's Anguish

BEN SHIPPERD

I was woken by the sub-conscious desire to empty my bladder. The comforting lime green glow of my digital radio alarm clock revealed the time, 4.57am. I pulled back my blue striped doona, stumbled to the moonlit bathroom, then headed back to bed. As I turned into the hallway leading to my bedroom, I heard that familiar rattle of a key entering a lock.

A pang of fear ran through me; were we being burgled? Suddenly I was wide awake. To my relief, the shiny beacon-like head of my father came through the door.

I thought to myself, "I know the Bushrangers have just won the cricket ... but out until five in the morning?"

I warned Dad, "You're going to cop it in the morning – Mum won't be happy." "Don't you worry, you wouldn't understand," said my father, who looked quite drained. Without remonstrating with him, I trudged back to bed. But before I fell asleep again I wondered, "What wouldn't I understand?"

That morning the sky was blue. I threw on a tracksuit and headed to the lounge room where beams of golden light filtered through the leafy canopy of my backyard. I flicked on the television. There was my dad standing with Shaun Graf, and there was Darren Lehmann, too. Then my ears heard what I never wanted to hear; my eyes saw what I never should have seen.

My dad's good friend, the man who only 15 hours ago was showing me aeroplanes, our good friend David Hookes, was now in a critical condition in hospital.

I sat down, dumbstruck. In shock. "I'll go tell Dad," I thought to myself. Then the pieces fell into place. That's why Dad had come in so late, that's what I wouldn't understand. I burst into my parents' bedroom. Dad was sitting on the bed with my sister; Mum was amusing my three-year-old brother. No one had to say anything; they knew that I had just learned the truth. It was obvious to me that I was the last one to find out the news.

I crawled up to my Dad. "He's going to be okay, isn't he?" I pleaded. "The news said he was 'critical, but in hospital'."

"No," Dad said, "he's not getting up from this one." I was close to hysteria: "But they said he was going to be all right." Over and over again I repeated it, and beat my fists against Dad's chest.

In the days that followed, I felt a huge range of emotions. Anger, sorrow, denial, self-guilt and emptiness. I ran laps around Caulfield racecourse until I collapsed in a wave of exhaustion and lay on the fragrant grass.

I passed time with my family, without really doing anything or going anywhere. I spent time with a friend, Lachlan, whose father also worked with David. As we carelessly watched the Dowling Shield, or any other cricket that was on, Lachlan and I reminisced about the good times we shared at the cricket, or at our home with David. When I was in the Bushrangers change rooms, I'd expect David to walk around the corner and say suspiciously, "What are you up to, Benjamin?"

I formed my timeline of events from many sources. I took part of the story from the media reports, most of it from what my guarded father told me, and some from Lachlan, as his dad had been there, too. My interpretation of the incident was like the Bible, a patchwork quilt of stories and rumours, rolled into one until they made remote sense. I was interested to observe that at a time of great sorrow, humans think the worst of other humans.

So life continued to roll on, and I had to keep up with it. I played cricket on the next weekend, and only two things were different. The black tape on my left arm, contrasting with my white sleeve, was one difference. The other was a gutsy determination deep inside me.

I gripped my bat tightly, tapped it against the pitch behind my feet, those feet that were just itching to move. The "beast" charged in, breathing fire and seeing red. I rocked back, hook shot, four runs. The beast was tamed. I could've faced Brett Lee that day, with some assistance from Hook.

Why is it that the thought of never seeing someone again is such a powerful emotion? Why do we suddenly think of all the things we should have said? Why do we link it to something we failed to do, or should not have done?

Why does it have the power to please, but grieve? It happens to everyone but until it happens to you, you don't understand or realise that it will befall you.

And yet, after the traumatic event, after the sorrow, the anger, the salty tears and stifled cries, it makes us stronger, and closer to the people left around us.

Being the great man he was, the generous, humorous and quick-witted human that he was, David will never be forgotten. Sure the tributes have stopped pouring in and the media have removed his picture from the front page, nonetheless, he lives on.

I tried to write a letter to David's widow. For hours I sat at my desk, frustrated that I could not spill the words in my head on to the paper. A few days later they just came to me, and I wrote and wrote.

And how is my family coping now? No one acknowledges it, but they feel it – we are a stronger unit, and better equipped to deal with anything like this in the future. We may never fully get over it. I found Dad lying on his bed the other day, staring at the ceiling. I had to call out to him three times before his concentration broke and he acknowledged me. I know what he was thinking about.

Why does death have the power to please and grieve? I am pleased that I had the chance to meet David; two years ago I barely knew who he was. I am aggrieved by the fact that I will never be able to get to know him better.

A Mate's Emptiness

Darren Lehmann

Rarely do we have the opportunity of meeting someone so special that they make a profound and lasting impression on our life. For me David was one of those special people; he moulded me not only as a cricketer but also as a person. To lose someone so close in such sudden, tragic and difficult circumstances leaves a deep and painful void. Cricket has helped to fill that void but the journey has been a long and emotional one littered with sadness and uncertainty.

What David meant to me, and how life has been without him, was probably best summed up by my century during the First Test in Sri Lanka in March 2004. I had missed four months of International cricket because of an Achilles injury and only had two or three games back for South Australia when he died. When you're just two metres away from such a violent incident, and standing next to someone ringing the police and the ambulance to get someone there, you go through a whole range of emotions.

I wasn't 100 per cent mentally right when I came back to play. I had been confronted with his death, and the funeral, and then going through that whole grieving process. But it's like "getting back on the horse" and doing something you love, and trying to make it work. The relief of getting that century was like a big weight had been lifted from me, mainly because I felt he was with me a lot of the time when I was out there playing.

When someone you're close to dies you have thoughts of them being with you all the time, and a real calmness and sense of relief came over me as a person. I can remember looking up and just saying, "Thanks, mate. I know you're here with me whatever I'm doing but now I feel I can move on, a little bit."

Getting back playing was one stepping stone; a realisation that David's not here, there's nothing you can do about it, you can't change it, all you can do is appreciate your family and friends more and try to make every post a winner.

I remember sitting in Galle (Sri Lanka) after each day's play having a beer and thinking I didn't really have a mate to ring and chat about the day's play; that's because I used to ring him a lot.

He'd say, "You're being too defensive, or attacking, or how's your family?" Simple things like that. I was going through the wringer so I can only imagine what his family must have been feeling. His wife Robyn sent me text messages right throughout the Test series, and they were really supportive. I wasn't just batting for Australia, but also to show Hookesy that I could still do it at that level.

It felt like I was there playing for a lot of different people. It's amazing how much support I had from throughout Australia and England. The phone didn't stop and there were lots of messages – "keep going", "one day at a time" and so on.

Kandy is the only venue where David made a Test century and thoughts of him overwhelmed me after the Second Test there when we had won the match and the series. I sat out on a ledge at the front of the change rooms for an hour or more and cried. I kept thinking, "Is it all worth it?" I was going through all these emotions. You're away from your family all the time, you've lost a close mate, you're playing somewhere where he made his only Test hundred, and we'd won the series.

I spoke to my captain Ricky Ponting and vice-captain Adam Gilchrist after that night saying, "I don't know whether I'll stay; I think I might go home before the Third Test." They pressed me to reconsider, were pretty adamant that I had to move on from the tragic circumstances of David's death. They also made me feel comfortable about going out to pubs again, and being around bouncers and crowds. That had been very difficult because of the way David had died.

The other very difficult time had been in the week immediately following his death. South Australia trained a few days after it all happened, preparing to play against Victoria in a four-day game. I remember batting in the nets and the first five minutes were fine, then I just started crying. That's when I knew this was going to take a lot longer than three or four days to get over.

We had a meeting with Cricket Australia that afternoon to decide whether we would play the game or not. They postponed the game, thank goodness. With David as their coach, the Vics were in same boat. They just couldn't play either. That's the sort of effect he had on a lot of people who knew him. He wasn't just David Hookes the outspoken media commentator, the bloke who loved a beer and enjoyed his time. It was more about the things he did away from the spotlight.

For the effect he had on me as a person, you only have to see by the way I act. I'm quite confident with people. That comes from him. I played a lot of cricket with him and he turned me into a more confident person. He was my first captain for South Australia. He put me under his wing and took me to places that you'd only dream of going. He moved with the rich and famous and he really got me out into the social scene, which broadened the country boy mentality in me.

I believe that like so many things David did this was part of a plan, because I'm sure he felt I was a chance to captain South Australia later in life. I have a lot of his traits in me. I'm glad I played most of my cricket before I lost him. I've still got his number in my phone. I just can't delete those things. I still can't do it. I've heard stories of hundreds of people ringing his phone to hear his voice one last time.

I wasn't able to do that. I said my goodbyes to him in the hospital … that strange feeling when I went into the hospital and they were just about to turn off the life support system and it was just him and me … he was lying there so peacefully that I thought he would wake up. I was mumbling because I was crying the whole time. From that moment it has felt like he comes everywhere with me.

I still think about him and his family every day. I just can't stop thinking about all those who were affected by his death, particularly those who were with him on the night, and wonder how they're all going. It's changed me. I really take time to talk to everyone and help out anyone I can. I always try and do a bit more than I used to, and I'm always ringing friends to make sure they're all right. I'd never been through this before. I'd never seen death so close up.

There are times when I can still hear him talking to me. When I'd play a stupid shot and he was annoyed with me he'd call me "Darren". I can still picture it, him yelling "Darrennnnn" in a grumpy voice.

There were things he did on the field that were dynamic and different. True, he might try to stretch the boundaries, but he did respect the traditions of the game. Not long after I started playing for South Australia Andrew Hilditch wanted me to throw him some balls. We'd been in the field all day so I took a beer down.

Hookesy came down and tore strips off me. Now if I see anyone who I think is not showing the game respect I'll say, "That's not the right way," or "Do you think you should be doing that a different way?" I'm trying to be a mentor to all the young guys coming through. That's the legacy he's passed on.

Apart from missing the phone calls and the jokes, it's not being able to sit face to face and have a good argument with him. We'd argue about certain players or teams, who should be in and who should be out. David taught me other things like cricket etiquette, confidence and backing yourself. And, most of all make sure your family comes first.

A Good'un
Farewelled

PETER FITZSIMONS

In the realms of Australian sport, did anyone ever have a better send-off to the place where "the one great scorer comes to mark against your name"? Maybe, but surely few have had a grander funeral than David Hookes's farewell at Adelaide Oval. Conducted beneath brilliant sunshine in front of 10,000 of those people who love him best, it was like the man himself – that odd combination of the magnificent and yet casual.

Yes, it was nominally a formal religious service with all the trappings despite his own avowed atheism, but it wasn't the religious trappings of "bells 'n' smells" and hymns and prayers that made the occasion.

Nor even the symbolic touches, such as the stumps on the wicket behind his coffin, bedecked in flowers, with his bat and South Australian cap resting on them, and the bails at the base placed in the shape of a cross. It was the feeling in the air of, "Jeez, this bloke was a one-off good'un and, as well as grieving for him, we must celebrate his life".

There were seven eulogies, including ones by his singularly eloquent brother, his two children, Ian Chappell and the South Australian coach who was with him on the night he died, Wayne Phillips. All tried to capture the essence of David Hookes, using such phrases as "family man and friend", "loyal", "intense passion" and, most pertinently from Ian Chappell, "David was always a reminder to us that cricket is a game."

Among the crowd were such luminaries of the sports, political and media worlds as Richie Benaud, Mark Taylor, Kerry Packer (reportedly), Allan Border, Tony Greig, Greg Chappell, Dennis Lillee, Ray Bright, Martin Crowe, Russell Crowe, Billy Birmingham,

Steve Bracks, Mike Rann, Anthony Mundine, Eddie McGuire, Ray Martin, Steve Price and the entire Australian cricket team, as well as the South Australian and Victorian sides, including Shane Warne.

Hookes's wife, Robyn, felt unable to participate in the funeral but was watching the proceedings from one of the corporate boxes at Adelaide Oval with one of her closest friends. Then to the climactic moment of the whole funeral.

The hearse bearing his body did a slow half-circuit of the same ground that Hookes had graced as a Shield player from 1975 to 1992, and an Australian player from 1977 to 1985, past an honour guard of former great cricketers and current representatives of South Australia and Victoria.

At the moment David's body left the turf of the Adelaide Oval for the last time in all eternity, slowly exiting beneath the Victor Richardson Gates on the far side of the ground, someone began to clap. Then another joined in. And it spread from there.

There had been other applause in the course of the funeral, but not like this. The clapping got progressively stronger as the throng caught the enthusiasm of the moment and began to cheer and whistle. At another funeral it would have been highly inappropriate but here it was perfect. Nothing was said but everyone there knew why we were applauding and what we intended by so doing. We meant to say, and we did with gusto: "Well played, David."

CHAPTER IX

CHAPTER
X

The memorial service for David Hookes at Adelaide Oval left an indelible impression ... three stumps, a bat leaning against them, a cap atop, roses, memories in the form of eulogies, ten thousand mourners, maybe more, and a guard of honour formed by his cricketing mates.

Two Mates, Three Stumps

BARRY GIBBS AND LES BURDETT

During the emotional, unforgettable and absolutely appropriate memorial service for David Hookes at his beloved Adelaide Oval on 27th January 2004, there were countless images that will have left an indelible impression in the minds of many thousands of people.

One in particular that stood out was the poignant sight of three cricket stumps in place at the northern end, Hookesy's trusty Gray-Nicolls bat leaning against one stump, his red SACA cap hanging from another, the bails on the ground in the form of a cross, and a bouquet of roses – yellow ones from his family and friends and a red one for David from Robyn.

That scene filled the whole front page of numerous newspapers the next day, transcending the need for anything more than just a few simple words. It has become something of a legacy of the life of David Hookes.

The story behind the three stumps that were the centre of that powerful picture is something we would like to share. The day after Hookesy died, we gathered with a group of his mates at a pub, as he would have demanded of us all, to share a beer, perhaps shed a tear and reminisce about a mate while trying to come to grips with the shocking reality of his senseless death.

Many David Hookes stories were being recounted, one of them by Les who fondly talked about this vivid picture he had in his mind of David's penchant, if he was batting when the lunch or tea breaks were taken, for leaving his bat leaning against one of the stumps, his cap on another and his gloves on the ground to dry out.

Hookesy would head off to the dressing room bare-headed and, as he walked through the open players' gate, the only visible clue to the fact that he had been out in the middle batting was that he still had his pads on. A short while later the discussion got around to the stumps from David's final first-class match at Adelaide Oval in 1992, when he became the highest run scorer in Sheffield Shield cricket history, breaking the record of 9,341 runs previously held by his good friend and former captain, John Inverarity.

Winding the clock back about 12 years, it should be explained that because we both really rated Hookesy as a good bloke and a great player, we felt that when he retired from the game it was only appropriate to find something special to give him to commemorate his remarkable cricketing achievements.

So we came up with the idea of "retiring" those stumps from his final match at Adelaide Oval at the same time as David retired, having an engraved brass plaque fixed on each of the six stumps and numbering them so that, at an appropriate time, a tangible memento could be given to the leading run scorer in Sheffield Shield history. To the best of our knowledge this had never been done before, not by the SACA anyway.

Hookesy was chuffed at the gesture and gladly signed all six stumps. He ended up with three of them to do with as he saw fit; one went into the SACA archives while Les and I became custodians of the remaining two. David received the first of his stumps at a function held in the Bradman Room at Adelaide Oval at the end of the 1991-92 season. On that occasion, SACA president Jim Grose presented the solitary stump to Hookesy who, in typically roguish fashion, remarked, "Is this all I get for slaving my guts out there (pointing in the direction of 'the ova'") for the last 16 years?"

What Hookesy didn't say at the time was he knew full well that he was going to receive more than a cricket stump from the SACA at the end of his outstanding career. At a farewell cocktail party tendered in his honour a short time later, held appropriately in the Captain's Bar of the Sir Donald Bradman Stand, David was presented with a magnificent portrait of himself, commissioned by the SACA and painted by the renowned South Australian artist Robert Hannaford. He had several sittings with Hannaford, so the oil painting was hardly a surprise. Hookesy was very proud of that painting and the tragic events of January 2004 will have undoubtedly made it an even more cherished possession for his wife Robyn, and children Kristofer and Caprice.

It was during the discussion about that first little presentation to Hookesy, more than a decade earlier, that the seed was sown that led to those three stumps at the northern end becoming such a powerful symbol at David's memorial service. Barry recalled that he had one of the stumps "somewhere", so he decided to go off in search of it. He soon located it and brought it back to the pub. While we were having this farewell drink for Hookesy, the stump had its place at the table. There was a strange, but very real feeling within the group, that he was somehow there with us as we toasted his memory.

The stump, complete with a plaque containing this inscription, became the central point of discussion.

NUMBER 5 OF 6 STUMPS USED IN

DAVID HOOKES LAST FIRST CLASS MATCH ON ADELAIDE OVAL,

SOUTH AUSTRALIA V VICTORIA 21ST-24TH FEBRUARY 1992

WHEN HE BROKE THE RECORD FOR THE HIGHEST RUNS SCORED IN

SHEFFIELD SHIELD CRICKET.

DW HOOKES SHIELD RECORD:

MATCHES 120, INNINGS 205, NOT OUT 9, AGGREGATE 9364,

HIGHEST SCORE 306 NOT OUT, AVERAGE 47.77

Les knew that he had the stump he was looking after in a safe place and that somewhere at Adelaide Oval the SACA had a third one to make up a set.

Even at that time, less than 24 hours after David died, we quite naturally got around to wondering where his funeral would be held. Although nothing was said at the time, Les had this thought in his mind that if the family chose to have the service in Adelaide, then Adelaide Oval would be the place to hold it and the stumps in some way could be a part of it.

After talking through the various options, one of which was St Peter's Cathedral in Adelaide, Hookesy's family felt that the most appropriate place to hold a memorial service for David was his spiritual home, the beautiful Adelaide Oval. They approached the SACA, who readily agreed and the date was set for 27th January 2004 – the day after a crowd of 30,000 were expected to attend a day-night One-day International match between Australia and Zimbabwe in Adelaide.

Les, who had the massive job of having Adelaide Oval ready for the memorial service less than 12 hours after the One-day International finished, was heavily involved in the detailed discussions about arrangements with funeral director, Simon Berry and representatives of the South Australian government's protocol department.

Through them Les, knowing Hookesy as he did, had the opportunity to convey his suggestions to David's family on what he thought his mate would have wanted to take place. High on the list was his idea of using the three stumps, the bat and the cap and re-creating the scene from David's playing days when he left the ground during a break in play if he was batting. The family thought it was a great idea and fully supported the concept, so Les's vision was about to become a reality.

To make the scene as realistic as possible, the SACA ground staff swept, cut, rolled and marked the pitch that had been used the night before. The three stumps from David's last match were set in place at the northern end of a pitch that was by now fully prepared for International cricket. The memorial service commenced at 11.00am, time for the umpires to call play in a Test match. For us, there was even more significance in the choice of that time to begin Hookesy's memorial service.

For many years we got together up in the Bradman Stand to watch the first ball of each cricket season delivered – at 11.00am. The fact that we watched from the Captain's

Bar was incidental, but as we were in there we always seemed to have a beer to toast the new season. Okay, the sun wasn't over the yardarm quite yet, but sometimes you have to make these sacrifices in the name of tradition!

When he retired from playing, David told us that one of the things he was really looking forward to was joining us at our usual meeting place at the start of each match. No point just marking the start of the season according to Hook, let's do it for each home match of the season! True to his word, Hookesy was on hand for the first ball of the 1992-93 season in his capacity as a radio personality on Adelaide's 5AA.

There was one small problem: the match was a Mercantile Mutual One-day fixture against New South Wales on a Sunday in October, but it commenced at 9.30am! Traditions must be observed, we thought, so the three of us saw that first ball from the Captain's Bar. Enough said.

So at 11.00am on Tuesday 27th January 2004, David Hookes arrived at Adelaide Oval for the last time. After a memorial service that will never be forgotten by the 10,000 people who were there, as well as by a vast television audience, Hookesy left the scene of many of his greatest cricketing triumphs.

By now it was after noon. The crowd began to disperse, but the three stumps, two crossed bails, the bat, the cap and the bunch of roses were still there, standing like a beacon in the centre of this magic place that David Hookes loved so dearly.

It was time to drink a toast to a departed friend. And we did. Hookesy would have been proud of us.

My Little Brother

TERRY CRANAGE

What can I say, looking around, about this unbelievable support for my brother David. From the bottom of my heart, thank you. For you who don't know me, I am David's only brother, older by 13 years, but I always had three things over him – taller, better tennis player and more hair.

David William Hookes … my little brother from Clifford Street, Torrensville, the boy who attended Thebarton Primary and Underdale High. The West Torrens Thebby Oval kid taken away at the tender age of 48.

Over the past week, it has been so difficult to absorb from the Cranage family side, and keep separate from the fabulous Hookesy profile, the tragedy of this insane incident. I have heard so many times over the past few years that one of the saddest things in life is for a parent to have to say farewell to one of their siblings. Well, in my case, as David's brother, I am the only person left on this planet who saw David come into this world on day one and, to be with him when he left us behind.

It is fortunate in a crazy way that our Mum Pat, who passed away less than 12 months ago, has not had to go through this painful experience. But, David, there is one reserved seat in the stand today – it's where Mum sat to watch you play. She is here.

So therefore, my eulogy today is about David, my young brother with whom I was fortunate enough to share those treasured early years of his life before I left Adelaide when I was 17. The very justified tributes to David the cricketer, David the hero, David the loving person so many people from all walks of life loved, will be more than adequately covered by following speakers.

This is a transcript of the eulogy made by David Hookes's brother at the memorial service at Adelaide Oval on 27th January 2004.

I remember by specialist's orders David was not allowed to wear shoes until he was five years of age. He was born with one leg shorter than the other; imagine what he would have achieved in cricket and other sports with two equal legs. I remember, as if it was yesterday, kicking an Aussie rules football, playing paddle tennis in the driveway at home and, of course, introducing David to backyard cricket, all in bare feet. Even in his book, he acknowledged I was responsible for his ball coordination.

I remember him crying his eyes out when, in December 1964, I left the Adelaide airport for my first overseas posting with the Australian Government. And likewise, in 1966 he was so distraught at our wedding he wouldn't leave my side during the entire ceremony because once again June and I were going overseas the next morning.

As time went on David loved and cherished being an uncle to our two children, Adrian and Melinda; he was such a tease to them, as we all know only David could be, pinching and pulling their toes and so on. Only two months ago he gave our grandson Mitchell the same treatment.

There has been so much written and said this past week about David the hero, the human, loving, compassionate, down-to-earth larrikin guy. We all have many examples of this but one that has really driven it home to me is that two months ago, June and I were in Melbourne for the Davis Cup with some friends from Brisbane. We met David at the MCG and after the day's play he took my friend and me into the centre of the hallowed turf. My friend was so honoured and blown away by this gesture that he and his wife are here today to honour David. What else can I say?

In conclusion, I would like to reflect with some poetic words adapted from Ralph Waldo Emerson given to me by an extraordinary man I met in Melbourne last week, Father Bob McQuire, as a tribute to David's life of love and achievement. David was a success, who lived well, laughed often and loved much, who gained the respect of intelligent men and women and the love of children, who filled his niche and accomplished his task, who leaves the world better than he found it, who never lacked appreciation of earth's beauty or failed to express it, who looked for the best in others and gave the best he had.

David my brother, my mate, my hero, rest in peace as we that are left behind can only ask "why?"

My Rock

CAPRICE GELLMAN

Where should I begin? How do I possibly put such a wonderful life into words? It is impossible. To speak about the contribution David made to our lives could never be summarised in a few minutes, but any more and David would be saying, ""'Capricey' – just get on with it!"

He loved telling stories and being with people – but also hearing other people talk about their experiences. As a midwife, I recall performing a reenactment in our family lounge room of how a baby is born using a teddy bear, and David was pretending to be the woman giving birth. There was David, flat on his back with a teddy bear under his jumper, beer in one hand, moaning and groaning … anything for a good story, David.

Everything David did he did head first at 100 miles an hour. He never read an instruction manual and, if there were three jobs to do, he would find four. It was because of this that we affectionately referred to David as "Forrest" from the movie *Forrest Gump*.

But as amazing as his capacity for hearing stories, and for endurance, it was his ability to do quirky things that drove us crazy and made us love him. I recall the recent Robbie Williams concert in Melbourne. My partner Matthew and I were having a quiet night at home and he called us from his mobile phone at the beginning of *every* song. David, you *were* driving us crazy but we know you just wanted to share your wonderful experience with us.

David was my rock.

I cannot say any more about him than that.

This is a transcript of the eulogy made by Robyn Hookes's daughter at the memorial service at Adelaide Oval on 27th January 2004.

Although he would love being the centre of attention today – he would want every single person here to go away at the end of the day and not dwell on things, but "Just get on with it!"

It is so incredibly difficult to make sense of the event that has taken place, and so much has taken place in such a short period of time. The positive side of this tragedy is that David did not suffer for a prolonged period of time and was not in any pain.

We are so grateful to those people who were present with David at his hour of need. It may sound unusual but it is difficult to express the amount of comfort we as a family have received to know he was surrounded by his friends at this time. We all know who you are – it is such an honour to have such loyal, caring and devoted people as friends of David and our family,

This last week has reinforced an old saying: "Life is too short". So in a time such as this, when it is almost impossible to make sense of what has happened – remember we must live life to the full and make the most of each day. Otherwise, David would be on your back saying, "C'mon, mate, you're here for a good time not a long time!"

And he absolutely wouldn't tolerate it any other way.

True Blue

KRISTOFER GELLMAN

Despite his high profile, David always maintained his true blue persona and never forgot where he came from. I remember as a child, wherever we might be, people would come up and say "Hi, David," and his usual response would be "G'day, mate, how are you going?" We would keep walking and I would say, "Who was that?" and he would say, "I don't know." Being so young I was confused as to why he was talking this way to complete strangers. I understood that with David, every man stood on the same playing field.

David had a great love for animals, especially dogs, of which he had many throughout his life. I would like to make mention of our previous family dogs Indiana and Jessie. Currently there is Lucy in Melbourne and my dog Sascha in Adelaide.

In particular, I would like to talk about Jessie, who was our family dog until 1995 when Mum and Dad moved to Melbourne and she had to be given to our Nanna. Jessie died at the age of 16 in November last year and David wrote to me after her death.

Receiving letters from David was not uncommon, especially given his hectic travel schedule that always kept us apart. So much so that this formed the basis for a lot our communication, whether it was two lines on a postcard or a two-page letter. In this instance it was a short note while he was in New South Wales with the Bushrangers, and I would like to share it. It was dated 28th November 2003, and reads as follows:

"Hi, sport, hope you are okay. Sad news about Jessie, but at least she was walking and eating up until the last day, and she was such great company for Nanna. Give Sascha a hug from me, you never know what might happen. Love you, David."

This is a transcript of the eulogy made by Robyn Hookes's son at the memorial service at Adelaide Oval on 27th January 2004.

Only now can I fully understand the significance of this letter, scratched out on a hotel compliments slip.

As everyone knows, David's commitment to friends, family and professional life was second to none; he was a completely selfless person whose generosity often bordered on the ridiculous. It was almost as if he had to make up for being away so much by being totally non-stop during the times we were together.

Having said this, it would be easy to assume that we often did things together like play backyard cricket, but sadly that was rarely the case. What I would give now to have those times again.

David, I'll miss your stories, your love, your nicknames, your jokes, the laughs and the advice. I will miss having a beer with you whether it be at a five-star hotel or in a front bar wearing shorts and thongs.

Although you and I are still very much kids at heart you have taught me so much about life and how to be a man.

I love you and will never forget you.

Not Really
'Enemies'

Wayne Phillips

I can see, and hear him singing that song[1] – poorly. It is quite an honour to be asked by the family to speak today, especially to tell you about those final hours with Hookesy. Many will ask why the captain and coach of the opposition team would be enjoying themselves with the enemy. Not only was it permissible, it was mighty important that we did. Two of David's many strengths were his passion for the game and his passion for the people involved in the game.

He loved the game and its history and he felt strongly that part of that history ... a part that had sadly been diluted ... was to encourage those involved in the game to get together, win, lose or draw ... he hated draws ... to talk about the game, learn about the game and, as a result, ensure the game prospered.

We had enjoyed a terrific game against his Bushrangers, played in wonderful spirit on the ground. We wanted to ensure that the spirit was maintained off the ground and, as a result, we accepted his invitation. We were always going to, it was as important as playing the game – he taught me that.

The night of Sunday, January 18th, saw two groups of good blokes enjoying themselves as one. Three hours earlier they had been opponents. When we were out we talked about the game, he reminded us of the result ... which I thought was unnecessary! ... we watched that magnificent group of men, the Australian team play their game in

---

This is a transcript of the eulogy made by David Hookes's friend and former team mate at the memorial service at Adelaide Oval on 27th January 2004.

[1] "I Do It For You" by Bryan Adams, which was David and Robyn Hookes's "song".

Brisbane … he is thrilled to know you guys are here.

He got such enjoyment from the Australian team, as a player, a commentator and as a supporter. He talked with genuine enthusiasm about some of my younger players, he was excited with what he saw, and he spoke with an almost warm devotion about his Bushrangers and his support staff. What happened next was tragic and will be addressed in the right and proper way.

The ensuing hours in hospital were challenging but full of hope and support; we expected him to come around the corner with a typical "whose buy is it?" When hospital staff confirmed David's condition was dire, the hours then became full of love and pain, although there were some smiles; it always happens when you get cricketers together.

David was his own man, and this is why we respected and appreciated him and his ideals. He would want us to move on with our lives, but he would be thrilled to know that when stumps were next drawn you grabbed a beer and headed next door to talk, and learn about the game, and ensure the spirit of the game is strengthened.

I left Robyn at eight o'clock Monday morning and went outside to face a world that was, and is, a lesser place for us all.

A New Beginning

Dr Leonie Zadow

When my husband Rob was called to Melbourne last Monday morning, I remained here in Adelaide. As that day, and the subsequent days, unfolded you can imagine that the family, and others close to them like Rob, were surrounded by a sort of cocoon. They really had no idea what the outside world was feeling. In Adelaide, however, I was privileged to share in a community that reeled under the enormity of the tragedy which had occurred.

I think it was only when I arrived into the Melbourne cocoon that Robyn, Kristofer, Caprice, Matt, Terry and others began to realise the impact their tragedy was having upon so many.

Robyn had a specific request for me with regards to the service. She asked me to convey to everyone, in as personal and simple a way as possible, the heartfelt thanks of David's family and friends for the care and understanding offered.

Thank you.

The outpouring of grief has left its mark upon us all. It was only as the depth of feeling was realised that Robyn came to the conclusion that David's funeral needed to embrace everyone. The family so humbly and sincerely hope it does.

Their only request in return is that, through the words offered by "Flipper", "Chappelli", "Zads", the children and Terry ... through The Dean's insights ... and, in the many images, visual, musical and just the sheer physical presence of being on the awesome cricket ground ... that you will find the beginning of whatever you need today to move on. Be it the beginning of forgiveness, be it the beginning of healing or of hope.

This is a transcript of the eulogy made by a close friend of the Hookes family at the memorial service at Adelaide Oval on 27th January 2004.

I'm going to finish with the last verse of a poem entitled "The Summer Day", by Mary Oliver. David, I know, would be rolling his eyes; we always had words about words. But David would allow me this, because I won't be able to phone him any more and correct him when he says "magneeta", instead of "magenta".

> *Tell me, what else should I have done?*
> *Doesn't everything die at last, and too soon?*
> *Tell me, what is it you plan to do with your one wild and precious life?*

When Victoria swept to an extraordinary Pura Cup victory over New South Wales in Newcastle early in January 2004, by scoring more than 450 runs in the last innings, captain Darren Berry said it was all made possible by Hookes producing a whiteboard – "something he hardly ever did" – and writing down a magic, winning formula.

"Ever lovin' Adelaide". The famous oval was the centre of Hookesy's universe and he was the centre of its stage. When he retired – "Funny, eh? I made the decision to go on then suddenly, two nights later, I just knew I'd had enough" – the photographers had only one thought, pose him there.

And, when the "prodigal son" came back to Adelaide, but as the coach of the natural "enemy", Victoria, the photographers ... posed him there.

Hookes the coach at work, planning. Darren Berry recalled some thinking from outside the square: "He was extremely keen to introduce what he called 'set plays' in the One-day game. We ran with his theory. Every player had a piece of paper in his pocket so they knew what ball was coming up next and the field would change according to the type of ball that was to be bowled. It took us forever to get it right."

In September 2003 the Melbourne Cricket Ground accorded Hookes legend status. Naturally, he was in fine company. Back row: Ted Whitten jr, Ted Hopkins, Wayne Harmes, Kevin Bartlett, Phil Manassa, Shane Warne; middle row: Trevor Chappell, Graham Yallop, Robert Dipierdomenico, Hookes, Graeme Jenkin, Stephen Silvani, Merv Hughes; front row: Ross Dunne, Barry Breen, Max Walker, Neil Crompton, Alex Jesaulenko, Ron Clarke, Betty Cuthbert, John Landy, Ron Barassi, Shirley Strickland-de-la-Hunty.

Feeling feisty. Hookes argues for an extension to play during a Pura Cup match against Queensland.

Feeling frazzled. Watching the Bushrangers from the strange surrounds of the visitors' dressing room at the Adelaide Oval.

The victorious Victorian Pura Cup team, 2004. Said captain Darren Berry: "When we sang our team song in the dressing room, we purposely left a space in our tight knit circle of players for our coach Hookesy … we knew he was right beside us in spirit."

"And the news came through, the news that we had been dreading all day, David Hookes had passed away ... " The Australian cricket team observed a minute's silence before their match against India at the SCG, just after Hookes's tragic death.

Kristofer, Caprice and her partner Matthew at the memorial service.
Robyn Hookes said: "The strength and compassion they showed in writing and
reading their own eulogies, in such a public forum, was a tribute to
the wonderful parenting skills David had and the love that was shared between
them. He was so proud of them, adoring them totally but being a strong
advocate of discipline and character-building to give them a solid foundation
for whatever life ahead was to bring."

Among the mourners were actors Russell Crowe and Gary Sweet and former Australian fast bowler, and fellow commentator, Jeff Thomson.

Guard of honour. Former players.

It was Adelaide Oval manager Les Burdett's idea to use the stumps, the bat and the cap to re-create David's habit when he left the ground during a break in play if he was batting. Three stumps from David's last match were set in place at the northern end of the pitch.

At drinks on day two of the Third Test against Sri Lanka in Colombo in March 2004, Darren Lehmann "did a Hookesy" as a gesture to his late mate.

"That one's for you, Hookesy ..." Lehmann passes his century in the First Test against Sri Lanka in Galle in 2004.

Gesture. The crowd at the World Series match between Australia and Zimbabwe at the MCG two days after the memorial service in Adelaide.

BOWLERS 0

1
2
3
4
5
6
7
8
9

DAVID

HOOKES

1955 - 2004

REST

IN

PEACE

"The most appropriate place to hold a memorial service for David Hookes was his spiritual home, the beautiful Adelaide Oval, this magic place that the kid from Torrensville grew to love so dearly ..."

Media chief Sam Chisholm, a transplant recipient, has been prominent in raising awareness of the organ donation program and The David Hookes Foundation. He is with his daughter Caroline. Robyn Hookes says: "The Foundation has been important to the family. It is the only positive thing to come out of it. Without question I know that David would see that as an absolute positive; that he would say, 'Go out there and do it.'"

CHAPTER
XI

David was not a person who showed his emotions easily. He grew up without sisters in a male dominated sport; he was a bloke's bloke and perhaps he felt intimidated about showing affection. But in maturity he did open up; he cried when AFL legend Ted Whitten did his lap of honour at the MCG.

My Man of Surprises

Robyn Hookes

David and I met through work about 25 years ago in Adelaide when he bought into the Lifestyle chain of fitness clubs. I was working as a membership consultant, teaching aerobics and running the aerobics program.

My first impression was that sometimes he rubbed people up the wrong way; they thought he was arrogant, because on the surface he appeared very confident. But underneath it all he wasn't that confident. I think it was a front to overcome almost awkwardness. It's strange, because David became a very good communicator.

Our friendship grew from the time David was in charge of the centre; that was when I saw a different side of him. When we first met I knew of him because my nephews wore David Hookes T-shirts. I knew they thought he was a big deal, but I didn't think he was a big deal at all.

I had two brothers and grew up playing backyard cricket in a household where the radio was always on the ABC, listening to the cricket during summer. I knew all the old players through the radio.

I remember the first Christmas we all had together and I think my brothers were pretty chuffed that they were spending the day with David Hookes, but everyone treated him as "just David". That was the thing about the family; he was always just David to us. They always watched him play, of course, and followed his career.

David had grown up without sisters in a very male dominated sport; he was always a bloke's bloke, a man's man. Because he never had to deal with sisters meant, I think, that David wasn't too sure about some things. Perhaps he felt intimidated about showing affection. Something I saw grow in him as a person as he matured was being able to show more open affection to me, and to the children.

Bringing up Caprice brought out a softer side in him. He loved and appreciated her dedication to ballet and drama. And he loved his dogs; we always had dogs, but I insisted we had female dogs. One of the few times I ever saw David cry was when we had to put our beloved Indi down. She was a German shepherd, named after the movie character Indiana Jones, and we had her from a pup.

He also adored Lucy, our cocker spaniel. David used to run around "the tan" with her every morning. One day he came home laughing because Wayne Jackson, then the head of the AFL, saw him and called out: "Why don't you get yourself a real dog?"

David was not someone who showed his emotions easily, but he cried when AFL legend Ted Whitten did his lap of honour at the MCG just before he died. Another time, Kristofer went overseas to work for two years. I was sobbing as we left the airport and, to my surprise, I saw tears running down David's cheeks as well.

David was always amazing with the children; he never referred to them as his stepchildren, always as his children. He was just so proud of Caprice and Kristofer. He adored them, but at the same time still managed to give them strong discipline and strong foundations in their upbringing.

In the very early days cricket didn't play a big part in our life. David had been dropped from the Australian team and wasn't even playing for the State. But, when David was playing cricket again, the Adelaide Oval was like our backyard. We would go to a State game and that was virtually our weekend, all day Saturday and all day Sunday at Adelaide Oval. Kristofer loved to go to the change rooms. That was his favourite thing. We were a family together.

After living together for seven years we did get married and had the most amazing wedding, an incredible party. It was in Adelaide with family and friends and, of course, all the cricket team and their wives were there. We didn't have to do it, we were already a family, and so getting married was more a celebration of us.

Home was David's sanctuary. When he came home he could really be himself and it kept him on a level field. At home, David was a very loving and caring person. If we were watching television he would hold my hand, but if you went out on the street with him he wouldn't want to be seen holding hands.

I think that came from being well known from a very young age when he had the world looking at him, especially in Adelaide. Wherever he went people would call out, "G'day, Hookesy". I never took his fame seriously. I knew how fickle it could be.

Our favourite thing as a couple was to go to the movies. We did that a lot. You didn't feel like you were on display. When we went into the theatre people would say "Hi" to him, but the minute the lights went down he would reach across and grab my hand and we were just David and Robyn at the movies. If ever we were out to dinner or whatever, though, invariably a fan would ask for an autograph and although David didn't mind that, in a sense you felt you were on show all the time.

When we moved to Melbourne nine years ago, his playing days were over; it felt like we were out of the goldfish bowl. It started to develop again with his profile on radio, and Foxtel and the Bushrangers, but Melbourne is a big city. It was not so intrusive.

One of the biggest things for us as a family was that every Christmas, for as long as I can remember, we went to Goolwa in South Australia for the holidays. David planned for that holiday all year and we had to work it around cricket. For all the things he did in his life, the holiday in Goolwa was what he adored the most.

We would rent a place for two weeks maximum in the beginning, but over the last 10 years or so we would take three and four weeks. In all the time we were in Melbourne, we'd pack up and drive, take Lucy, and organise to have the kids and their friends come there at some stage. We would also take our mothers to stay for some of the time. There were lots of laughs, especially when we played cards and charades.

We laugh about it now, but David was such a stickler for preparation. He would virtually start planning the next trip as soon as the last one was over. He would tape movies all year and he kept pages of detailed notes about what to take. There would be reminders, and lists of things that he must not forget; the corkscrew was most important and he would add cards, and lots of games, as well as books, a torch, sandals, and goggles, anything that he could think of. We always took our dogs; they were like children.

We met up with a group of friends from Adelaide – football people, cricketers, and media people, just friends who, over the years we had got to know. We also had a lot of time on our own. It was a very relaxed, happy time.

The Goolwa holiday was always at Christmas time. All year, the big thing for David was to get presents ready because he knew the kids would have their pillowcases ready to be filled. He would go to great lengths to have as many presents as possible. If he had been to England or the West Indies, doing something for cricket, he would bring back the travel pack from the flight, or a T-shirt or cap and wrap them up. Any little thing he had been given he would stash away. The pillowcases would always be overflowing.

David loved big surprises. The year I turned 50 David was going to the West Indies for two months in the February. The day before he left he kept nagging me for the Christmas card list and was getting really agitated about it. He said he had lost his and wanted mine so he could send everyone postcards. David was a great postcard sender. Anyone who knew him as a friend would have received a postcard from him at some stage. That was his way of keeping in touch.

I was really irritated with him about the Christmas card list. I couldn't believe that he was going away for two months and seemed more worried about the Christmas card list than not seeing the family.

My birthday is in July and I found out later that he needed the list to organise a simply wonderful 50th birthday party for me at Melbourne's Crown Casino. David was in the West Indies for two months, and then came back home for only three weeks and then, because it was the World Cup that year, he had to go to England. And while he was on tour he was planning and organising what was going to happen at my surprise party! How I never cottoned on I don't know, but everyone was just blown away.

On my actual birthday, David had taken us over to Adelaide for the weekend. We stayed at the Hilton and had a suite there with a silver service dinner with the kids and friends. He'd also arranged for us to catch up with all the family for a celebration. It must have been difficult for them not to let slip what David had planned.

The following Friday, friends had arranged for us to have dinner at the Casino – at least that is what I thought. David had it all planned, even down to the tiny detail of getting our friends to pretend we were only having dinner at some new restaurant at the Casino.

There were to be 120 guests, 60 of them from Adelaide. He had sorted out cars to pick up people from the airport, and had organised accommodation for them in east Melbourne. And I knew absolutely nothing about it!

On the day, he took me to lunch at a restaurant in north Melbourne with a friend of ours who was over from Adelaide, "for some work thing". At 4.30pm we were still sitting in the restaurant. I wanted to go home and get myself organised because we were going out that night, but David was worried some of the girls from Adelaide might be shopping, or walking down the streets of Melbourne, and I might see them. Then, when we finally left he took a really bizarre way to where our friend was staying, as another precaution against me running into all these people

The party that night was in the River Room. David opened up a door and there were all these people and balloons, and I recognised some 3AW people so I thought we had walked into a 3AW function – until they all started singing, "Happy Birthday". The next thing my mother walked towards me. It was such a shock, such an unbelievable shock. It was just an amazing night; and lots of heavy heads afterwards.

It wasn't unusual for David to surprise me on my birthday, if not every year, then every second year. He just had these amazing organisational skills. When we were living in Adelaide, he blindfolded me at home on my birthday then got me into the car and drove me through the streets. It was pitch black and freezing cold and I couldn't see a thing. I felt like a real dill with absolutely no idea of what was happening.

We arrived somewhere, but I didn't know where; I could hear voices, but I didn't recognise any. David guided me into a lift and walked me into a room … and took off the blindfold. I was standing in one of the private boxes in the new Bradman Stand at Adelaide Oval; he had arranged a dinner party with friends in the box. Then, as I was taking all that in, David walked me to the window.

He had arranged for Les Burdett, the curator of Adelaide Oval, to put a birthday message on the scoreboard, which was all lit up. Les had written, "Brave Lady living with David, Happy Birthday". It was lovely.

I hadn't thought about that until I started thinking about my memories of David. He loved surprises, big or small. He often organised these catered dinner parties at home and wouldn't tell me who he had invited.

The silly part is that I never really learnt. I would think, "Oh, he has outdone himself this time," only to be amazed at his next big surprise. David did spoil me and he did spoil Caprice and Kristofer, but that was the way he was. There were lots of things he probably felt he missed out on because of being away with cricket so much.

On Sunday morning 18th January 2004 I was supposed to have gone to Rye, on the Mornington Peninsula, but changed my plans and decided instead to drive to our holiday house with David the next morning. That night, I had been very restless for some reason, tossing and turning in bed. I looked at the clock and it was just before 1.00am.

I knew David would be celebrating the Bushrangers win against South Australia in a One-day game in Melbourne. He always left a message on the phone to let me know where he was. He did that for more than 20 years, whether he was here or overseas.

When the mobile rang I didn't recognise the number and did not answer it. Then, the house phone rang. It was a friend telling me to go to The Alfred Hospital. I was frightened, because I was told David was critical. I drove myself to the hospital and remember walking into the casualty ward and seeing David's friends and players from the Bushrangers and Redbacks. I knew it was bad. They were all crying. I just sat there, thinking, "This can't be happening."

We were hoping and praying they had made a mistake. Caprice and Kristofer arrived. Caprice had driven from Rye with her partner, Matthew, and Kristofer was on the first flight out of Adelaide. We went in to see David and he was warm, a good colour; he just looked like he was sleeping, but he was on life support.

What did that mean and how could we change it? We couldn't. The shock, the numbness and disbelief would not leave us, and we just had to wait and have our worst fears confirmed. The clearest thing in my mind was being told that the best-case scenario for him was that he would be severely brain-damaged.

Being on the life support allowed us to be with him. He seemed like he was breathing and he just looked beautiful.

When it got to the stage where they were going to declare him dead, a social worker raised with us the issue of organ donation. We were aware of how David felt about it for he had passionate views on the donor program and, as a family, we had discussed it many times. He used to tell us that he thought it was such an incredible waste not to donate your organs.

When the children were going for their driver's licences David told them it was their decision on donation, but would always add, "What do you need your organs for after you're dead?" He didn't pressure the family to sign up, but made it clear what his views were and how strongly he felt.

When I moved from Adelaide to Melbourne in 1995, I had to exchange my driver's licence and felt that if I didn't tick the box agreeing to become a donor,

I would be letting him down. It was just a big thing with us. I was doing it for David.

That all helped to make it easier for us to agree for him to be a donor. For us, there was really no decision to be made – of course we would donate his organs. We were so comforted by the fact that we wouldn't let him down and we could do that for him. In a strange sense it gave us longer with him.

We didn't realise just how much detail was involved; when they got to the liver we all smiled a little and thought, no one would want his liver. He loved a beer. As it turned out he had a perfect liver. He would have appreciated that. It was one of eight life-saving organs David gave.

It was all done in a very caring and respectful manner. We stayed with David through Monday night and the early hours of Tuesday saying our goodbyes. David was larger than life and we are still in shock about his death.

The David Hookes Foundation is a positive out of all of this, and we hope it will encourage families to at least talk about organ donation. It was founded to promote organ donor awareness. One organ donor can save the life, or dramatically improve the life, of up to 11 people.

There is a comfort in knowing there are so many other people who can't believe he has gone. Caprice has a photograph on her fridge of David and Kristofer when the Crows won the premiership in 1997. He looked so happy. We look at those photos and just can't believe David is not here.

I was talking to a friend in Adelaide and she said she was thinking she hadn't heard from David in a while, and I know exactly what she meant. He was incredible with the contact he had with the kids and me. It was nothing for him to ring me six times a day or, there would be a message on the machine. The minute he found out something he would have to tell me.

My mum remembers the morning after "September 11", the terrorist attack on New York. Gerard Healy and David had been at a sports night. When David came home it was about 11.30pm and I was half-asleep. He was on the phone and when I asked him what he was doing he said Gerard had just called and said to put the news on.

We stayed up all night watching and, early the next morning, about 6.30am, David told me to ring my mum. She lives on her own and David didn't want her to hear the grim news and be alone. Mum was talking about that just recently; she never forgot that he thought of her at that time.

Sometimes I'll come home and think his voice will be on the answering machine. He was just in your face. There is a numbness that just doesn't leave you and I don't know how long that will be there for.

David had a knack of making people feel special, making a bit of a fuss about them. He was very special.

At first I thought being involved with The David Hookes Foundation would be too painful, but I have worked through that now.

The Foundation has been important to the family. It is the only positive thing to come out of it. Without question I know that David would see that as an absolute positive; that he would say, "Go out there and do it."

CHAPTER
XII

David Hookes's true memorial will be The David Hookes
Foundation. If the awareness of organ transplantation can be
raised and more people make that donation commitment then
an enormous amount of suffering and illness can be avoided.

In Death, Inspiration

JOHN SINGLETON

W e were sitting at The Flower Drum Restaurant in Melbourne after a particularly wasteful meeting with the racing industry. The only good thing was that in our company was Sam Chisholm, as feisty and as stroppy as ever, which was pretty amazing. Why?

Well, only 6 months before Sam had been a dead man walking, his lungs shrunk to 3 percent of capacity. He was living on oxygen and hoping that every phone call might be his last chance – a chance for a lung transplant.

His only chance, and not a good one ... because it registers with so few Australians that should they lose their own lives someone else could live through their organs. Worse, those who do register have their wishes overruled by family who are too much in shock with the loss to focus properly on anything except their own very natural grief.

Anyway, against all odds and against all logic, Sam got his new lease of life and who gave a stuff about the idiots running television racing in the scheme of things? As if God had pre-ordered, as we sat there in the world's best Chinese restaurant we were served up the world's best headline in the Melbourne *Herald-Sun*.

It related to the premature death of cricket great David Hookes and his magnificent gesture of giving all his organs to others. The *Herald-Sun* headline read: "Champion's Gift of Life".

It summed it all up. As one we agreed we ought to form The David Hookes Foundation and use his senseless death to give life to others through increased awareness of organ donations.

The phone calls flowed. It was impossible for Kerry Packer to say "no", his life renewed by a donated kidney. John Hartigan, CEO of News Limited is always first to back a good cause. Alan Jones doesn't have "no" in his vocabulary at all. Sam was so excited his wife Sue thought a heart attack was a new risk. Robyn Hookes agreed immediately, and what a week it was.

The launch of The David Hookes Foundation saw the biggest increase in organ donors ever. In the next 20 years a lot of people will live because David Hookes gave us inspiration, even in death. Thanks, David, and thank you to the sub-editor at the *Herald-Sun* whose front page inspired us all.

The Foundation

OFFICIAL LAUNCH

The David Hookes Foundation was launched at Sydney's St Vincent's Hospital in February 2004. Radio personality Alan Jones was the compere. Among those present were organ recipients Kerry Packer and Sam Chisholm, Robyn Hookes, her daughter Caprice, and her partner Matthew, Rob Zadow, a friend of David Hookes, businessman John Singleton, John Hartigan, chief executive officer of News Limited, Professor Allan Glanville, the head of lung transplantation at St Vincent's Hospital, Dr Josette Eris, director of renal transplantation at Sydney's Royal Prince Alfred Hospital, and Dr Michael Wilson, who was the surgeon for Sam Chisholm. This is an edited version of the launch.

Jones: We are here because Australia has the second worst organ donor record in the world. We donate 10.4 organs per one million of our population; we beat only New Zealand. A country like Spain is about 33 donations per million.

Singleton: I didn't realise the rarity of donations. I just assumed that everyone gave, assumed that if you weren't going to be around – not that we can focus on that – that we want others to be around. I called Kerry … he said, "How's a bloke gonna say no?" I called Alan … ditto. Sam called Hartigan. It was just the usual gang, but then we needed to talk to Ian Chappell, who put me on to Rob Zadow, who put me on to Andrew Hilditch … and there was such an outpouring. We're all going to die, but when it's someone like David Hookes … he's never going to die, he's an immortal.

If you're a friend, or a fan or family, at that moment you think, "We have got to make something of this – is it going to be for disadvantaged cricketers that come from the wrong side of the tracks, is it going to be this or that? And then somehow we pulled together and we got this thing, and it happened, and it happened because of the front page of the paper that said David Hookes made it happen. David Hookes made sense of this senseless situation because he gave, through his family, life to others.

Jones: There are two people here, Sam is one and Kerry the other that have, as you know, been beneficiaries of this whole process of people generously donating their organs.

Packer: David was a great sportsman, but his true memorial will be in this Foundation, in changing so many people's lives. If, through his generosity, we can get the awareness of organ transplantation to be recognised in this country, and for people to make that donation, then there is going to be an enormous amount of suffering and illness that can be avoided. I've been lucky enough to be the recipient of a transplant and the change in life is astronomical.

What stops most people from getting an organ is the fact that there just aren't enough of them. That is what we are all about today, to try and make sure people understand what a truly fantastic gift it is. And, for families of people that give organs to understand that they have to agree (to do it) quickly, otherwise the timing is against everything. And it is a matter of getting people to understand that if their family member has made that decision then they should honour it. I wouldn't be here without what has been given to me, and I can't tell you how lucky I feel. I hope we can offer other people that luck.

Jones: Kerry's point is The Foundation is not here to raise money; we are here to raise awareness. Even with family approvals, 46 per cent of families in Australia veto the procedure. We are way out of kilter with the rest of the world. Many of us here lived through many years with Sam Chisholm, locked up and caged, unable to go anywhere, and we saw him grow weaker and weaker. And suddenly, the appropriate organ came along and here he is today.

Chisholm: I don't think there is any better way to commemorate the life of David Hookes than to become an organ donor; I really do think that it defines Australian mateship. I thank my donor every day of my life; I just can't put into words my gratitude. But it recalibrates your thinking, and you are just so aware of this amazing gift that a selfless donor has provided for you.

Having gone through years and years of unspeakable torture to suddenly get relief is absolutely amazing. And, it would be remiss of me not to add that Michael Wilson and Allan Glanville helped put me here today. The great thing about this Foundation is that it will go on in perpetuity and, if we can do all this, then the lives that we save will be countless and David Hookes will never be forgotten.

Jones: There are two very dedicated transplant physicians here today, Professor Allan Glanville who is the head of lung transplantations at St Vincent's Hospital, and Dr Josette Eris who is the director of the renal transplantation at Royal Prince Alfred Hospital.

Glanville: The issue here is one of supply and demand. Clearly in Australia we have a high demand for organ transplantation and, at any one time, there may be up to

2,000 people on the waiting list for one form or another of organ transplant. As Alan has mentioned, we have about 10 per million head of donors per year, which means about 200 per year and, due to the fact that you can't use all organs from all of those donors all of the time, it means that we do about 700 transplants per annum.

That means that there are 1,200 people each year that miss out. All the people that are waiting for transplants are all very, very sick and many of them don't survive to receive their transplants. We simply have an issue of demand over supply; we don't have enough organs available to help all the people that we would like to help.

Anyone who is a lover of the noble game knows that David Hookes played the game in the spirit that cricket was meant to be played. In life he was a champion sportsman, and in death he retains the ability to be a champion because of the actions of the family who cared for him. In fact, every Australian family who makes that important decision at the death of a loved one, to let them become an organ donor, is a champion. And everybody who signs up to become an organ donor is a champion.

Who knows who will benefit? It may be you, it may be the person that you love, and it may be your family. We don't know, but it is through this Foundation that we will conceivably help very many Australians to have a better quality of life and a better duration of life.

Jones: Statistics can confuse as well as inform, but if I just give you one "stat" that Professor Glanville alluded to: in 2002 there were 133,700 deaths in Australia but only 206 were organ donors.

Dr Eris: We are organ transplanters and, day in day out we see the people who need transplants, and the missed opportunities if they don't get the transplant, and the outcome of that. Kidney transplants are not a matter of life and death, but it is a matter of staying on dialysis, which is certainly an inferior type of treatment that does not provide either the quality or the quantity of life that a transplant does.

I guess, as a physician, my plea to the public is to at least consider this Foundation and talk to your families about it. That is a message that we have been trying to get out for a long time. It is difficult for the families of people who have just died to make that decision in the short time that is available but if the issue has been spoken about and the patient's wishes have been made clear to the family, then it makes a big difference.

Jones: One of those families that didn't veto is represented here by David's widow, Robyn Hookes.

Robyn: When they came to us in the hospital we just said, "Well, of course." It's been hard to come today and focus but we got here; we are doing it tough, but we have had so much support from so many people. Now we have something that will be his legacy and through that we will get back to all those people.

Jones: When "Singo" made that call to everyone here, the response was immediate. Our biggest media proprietors decided they would do whatever needed to be done. Channel Nine has assisted very significantly in trying to get the message across. John Singleton

Advertising is responsible for all the advertising presentation and the logos that have been developed. And, John Hartigan insisted that News Limited newspapers right across Australia would promote this with all the authority possible.

Hartigan: I think David's generosity in death certainly inspired me to become a donor, and Ricky Ponting, the Australian cricket captain, was equally inspired. He has given his time to do a series of community service television advertisements.

Jones: Any questions?

Q: *John Singleton, with this campaign, would you consider taking it further and lobbying governments to change the rules to perhaps an opt-out system for organ donation instead of an opt-in, which we have at the moment?*

Singleton: In a number of countries, Europe, it is assumed that once you are brain dead you do want your organs to help others, unless due to religious, moral or any other reasons you specifically want to opt out. If that leads to legislative change here I, for one, would be happy. But as a board, we are not making any formal attempt; we are just hoping that public pressure may lead to such a consideration.

Q: *Mr Packer, can you understand how people may feel uncomfortable or frightened to sign up?*

Packer: Not really, no. It's an option. Everyone has to do it or not, but when you are dead you are dead, and if you can help someone in death that is the greatest gift you can give.

Singleton: The thing I think that is very questionable when you think this issue through is the fact that half the people that have overtly chosen to be a donor, through the register or through a licence, have that choice taken away from them by their family. Why a family should want to do that, or would have the right to do it, is a very personal issue. Life and death – is there anything more emotional? Some people who have a loved one dying or dead can find it hard to accept an autopsy. On the other hand, once we are dead and we can give life, there should certainly be no question.

Jones: Professor Glanville, I think you have had to address these issues in the past, certain fears that you yourself have talked about.

Glanville: One of the issues that is not fully understood or appreciated in the community is that we are protected by legislation. The dead person, and their family, is protected by legislation because the transplant team cannot be involved with a process of declaration of brain death. So the two teams work absolutely independently, and usually they work in different States or different hospitals at the least. But even if by chance there might be a potential organ donor in one's own hospital, the transplant team cannot by law be involved in the decision making process to declare that person brain dead. That's in legislation; we can't do it.

When it comes to individuals or families, who may have fears organ donation may be done before the patient is dead, it's not. We have very clear and 100 per cent proven records of independent physicians declaring people brain dead.

People may fear that disrespect may be paid to the dead body, but this is a very respectful procedure done properly in operating theatres, by caring medical nursing and aesthetical teams and intensive care unit teams, who are very respectful to the potential or actual donor.

When we carefully address all these fears they can be broken down, one by one by explanation and education, to show that this is a very respectful process. It comes down to education, and one of the things we hope that this Foundation will do is broaden people's awareness, and take away some of the mythology and some of the fear that Australians have, so that they can become better Australians and better mates to their fellow Australians.

Jones: Professor, one other point that might just assist everybody … after that procedure has occurred and the organs have been taken, how is the body then presented in death … you might just explain how that happens.

Glanville: Well, the body is prepared so that the individual person would look just like the person; they just wouldn't have those organs inside them. If we think about the organs that may be taken out, for example the heart, the lungs, the kidneys and the liver, those body cavities are then closed up properly, surgically. Then the patient is presented as a deceased person so that if the family wishes to view the body, as some do, then they are able to do that and see the person that they loved and continue to love.

Q: *Dr Eris, can you tell us what the proportion is for kidney donations from living persons, how that has changed over time and what is the potential for other living donation in areas beyond the kidney.*

Eris: Living organ donation in kidneys (one kidney is perfectly sufficient to carry on life providing that your kidney function is normal) now makes up about 50 per cent in the larger centres, but that may vary between 35 and 50 per cent if you look at particular centres. That compares to a rate of about 20 per cent about five years ago, so there has been a dramatic increase in the amount of living donors. That is a worldwide trend, certainly in the western world. The potential for living organ donation in other solid organs is medically more difficult.

With kidney patients there are about 1,800 on the waiting list at any one time; the average waiting time is about four years in Australia and many patients wait in excess of 10 years. You can see that there is a great need there.

Q: *Mr Packer, could you tell us whether you would hope there would be an encouragement of more live donors and, perhaps you could tell us how you feel about your own donor.*

Packer: Of course, I would love to see more, but it takes a brave man to be a live donor. My eternal gratitude goes to Mick Ross, who was the person that helped me. I'm just in favour of transplantation in whatever form it comes. I think that people who donate are wonderful people, dead or alive. All I can tell you is that it is the greatest gift you could ever get, and everything else pales into insignificance, and for people to do it and mark it on their licence. I have marked it on my licence … God help anyone who gets any of mine, but I am willing. There may be a liver that is in reasonable shape, but outside of that … I just beg you all to do it.

Jones: Robyn, what would you say to families in the future that have to make that same decision as you did, what words of encouragement could you give them?

Robyn: I would urge all Australians to discuss it around the dinner table as a family; if they are donors, make it known to the family how strongly they feel about it. We are not advocating that you have to do it, we are just saying think about it and talk about it as a family.

CHAPTER
XIII

A life touched by any aspect of transplantation is a life open to review. People begin to wonder about the meaning and purpose of life in general, and their life in particular. Strong questions surrounded by strong emotions begin to challenge some of the underlying beliefs of life.

It's All About Hope

JENNIFER MCGUIRK, OAM

We seldom see it coming, the moment that changes forever who we are; the life event that causes us to wonder "about life". David Hookes, in his death, has gifted us all with new awareness of the fragility of life, the gift that life is and what becomes possible when all that is good about humanity works to ensure that a life has meaning. Out of this seemingly senseless death, countless other people stand now on the threshold of new life through successful surgery, and many more wait with deepening hope.

For donor family and recipient there are meeting points, far beyond the giving and receiving of precious donated organs, which offer hope; hope that the death of someone precious has not been in vain; hope that new life may be possible; hope that someone you loved will be remembered beyond life; and, for everyone who is part of this story, hope that life can move on and once again have meaning.

For 15 years I was privileged to work as a pastoral care chaplain to a transplant unit. It is an amazing place, where hope is born in the uncomfortable, unbreakable connection between life and death. I was honoured to be allowed to walk with others in their sacred spaces.

Transplant teams are made up of many skilled professional people, who all help the families touched by transplantation bring their lives back together. These families may meet a chaplain, not because this is a religious place, but rather because this is a sacred place. This is holy ground.

It is difficult to be in this place where life and death meet. For the donor family, death comes with such unexpected force. For the recipient and their family, death has been a shadow over life, hovering, waiting, always waiting.

A life touched by any aspect of transplantation is a life open to review. In this place of endings and beginnings, of goodbye and hello, people begin to wonder about the meaning and purpose of life in general, and their life in particular. Strong questions surrounded by strong emotions begin to challenge some of the underlying beliefs of life. Even though they have consciously or unconsciously governed life's choices, until this moment such beliefs are rarely taken out and examined:

> *I will be secure as long as I have a job.*
> *I am the head of the house, everything depends on me.*
> *I must always be in control.*
> *As long as I have money I'll be okay.*
> *I am only worthwhile when I am doing something other people value.*
> *I must plan my life for the future.*
> *I believe in God so God will protect me.*

For donor families, and recipients and their families, these are commonly held maxims. Suddenly, everything that has been taken for granted is gone. The world has become an uncertain place where life's goalposts have been dramatically shifted. In this transplantation experience the journey to a changed world begins. Recipients of organ donation often feel overwhelmed by the generosity of the donor families who have made a most difficult decision in the midst of trauma, and grief and said "yes" to donation. They wrestle with the inadequacy of the words "thank you", for they seem unequal to the challenge of acknowledging such a life-changing event. Most people I have worked with struggled to write their letters of thanks to donor families. Forming words of gratitude to grieving families holds a delicate tension.

One of the difficulties with death is that most of us live as if death is something that happens to other people, never to me, or those I love. So it is for donor families, and for those in need of transplantation. By the time the transplant comes, most recipients have wrestled with some essential questions of preparation. They are not your ordinary, everyday questions of life:

> *Why do I want a transplant?*
> *What will longer life mean for me?*
> *How will I live with a donor organ in my body?*
> *What does it mean for me to have my hope of life linked to another*
> *person's death?*

In the best of all possible worlds most donor families would also have wrestled with questions of preparation. Ideally, in family discussions the options and choices would have been explored, so that each member of a family knows clearly the wishes of the other in the event that circumstances bring organ donation into the final questions of life.

The intensive care waiting room is not the place to think about this issue for the first time, just as going into theatre for a transplant is not the time to be addressing the larger questions of life for the first time.

The teams who work to bring the miracle of transplantation to reality also work out of the "place of hope". For the staff who undertake the difficult task of donor operations, there is hope that the outcome will bring something good to the life of another. I was very moved to be present at a donor operation and to witness the love, care and respect given to the donor by all the staff.

For the staff of the recipient transplant team, there is the ongoing commitment to work with the patient, and their family, to hold life and maximise health, physically, emotionally and spiritually, in readiness for that long-awaited phone call which tells them that a matching organ is available. The phone call triggers deep feelings, not least of which is an awareness that in this place of hope for themselves, another family is grieving.

In 15 years of ministry, almost without exception, members of the recipient's family talked to me about their awareness of the impact of transplantation on another family, without whom they would not be in a place of cautious hope. Most feel overwhelmed by the extraordinary generosity of the donor, and their family, towards complete strangers. The celebration of successful transplantation touches everyone. It is easy to celebrate.

I first met Sarah[1] when she was 17. Her illness had come suddenly and her need for a transplant was urgent. There was a generous donor and health returned to Sarah, and all the normal aspects of life returned for Sarah. Several years later I was privileged to celebrate Sarah's marriage and in time to name and bless her newborn son. Today Sarah is eagerly awaiting the birth of her second child. Yes, it is easy to celebrate.

But where is hope when death intervenes? At first glance, Tracy's story and Sarah's story walk hand in hand. Tracy[2] was a young man with a newborn son, a newly transplanted organ and a new life beckoning. Three more children came into Tracy's family and he and his wife planned for the future. The future that came was not the one they hoped for.

After a second transplant Tracy died. At the 2003 Victorian annual Service of Thanksgiving and Remembrance[3] Tracy's wife and children spoke about their gratitude to both donor families. Their gratitude was not linked to the outcome. It was enough that the generous spirit of donation gave them hope. It was also an acknowledgement that the gift of donation lives on beyond the life of the recipient. Wonderful things become

---

[1] I am indebted to Sarah for allowing me to tell something of her story.

[2] I am indebted to Tracy's family for allowing me to tell something of his story.

[3] Each Australian State holds an annual Service of Thanksgiving for all people whose lives have been touched by organ transplantation.

possible where once there was no hope. Marriages happen, children are born, careers are developed, and the world expands in ways once only dreamed about.

It is difficult in the midst of loss, and the grief that accompanies it, to believe that the darkest experiences of life may in time be life giving. The people I know who emerge from close encounters with organ donation and transplantation, who have seen death face to face, speak with gratitude of the new awareness they have for significant relationships, for their life choices and for their life. Moving on from such experiences requires determination, strength and courage.

This meeting place of life and death is an uncertain place. In those instances where organ donation is the only way to hope of ongoing life, transplantation forms a bridge between death and life. Two distinct events have occurred. Someone has died, and contrary to how we would sometimes express it, the person who died does not live on in the recipients. Their death needs to be honoured, for a life is complete. After death, up to eleven people may have cause to remember the donor with deep gratitude. They may see the world with a new cornea, they may engage life without dialysis with a new kidney, they may run a marathon with a new heart or liver, they may walk with a new bone or stretch with a new muscle, their heart may beat with a new valve.

After these tumultuous events, donor families and recipients face a place of choice. They choose life in the face of death, but a changed life. Recipients can once again trust the new experience of health. Donor families trust that life will again one day hold meaning. For those whose lives are touched by transplantation, the commitment to giving, or receiving a donor organ is always an act of faith. On the one hand, faith that life will be extended, and on the other, faith that the opportunity for a second chance at life will be honoured.

It is faith that allows the embracing of hope as the foundation of the present, within the reality of the past and the uncertainty of the future. With hope, the unbearable becomes bearable and the un-nameable can be named.

The Surgeon's Story

PROFESSOR DON ESMORE

In December 1967 the news of the first human heart transplant performed by Christian Barnard in Cape Town, South Africa, stopped the world; the unachievable had been conquered. Barnard was instantly elevated to celebrity (temporary) status, one he would have happily traded for fame (permanent) and peer group acceptance. The patient, a 55-year-old male, survived 18 days before succumbing to rejection.

In the two years after Barnard's historic first operation some 200 heart transplants were performed worldwide by eminent surgeons in respected cardiac surgery units. But survival was abysmal, with 50 per cent mortality at one month and a confronting 11 per cent survival at one year. Cardiac transplantation was deemed a clinical experiment that had gone wrong, not able to live up to the great expectations of an initially adoring public and, subsequently, some said, "an indictment of the medical profession."

The complexities of post-transplant management had been overlooked, and the ravages of infection and rejection had wrought havoc with the recipient population. There was much work to be done. That work was to take a decade and a half, physicians and surgeons chipping away at the imponderables of the diagnosis, prevention and treatment of rejection and management of ever-threatening infections.

Shumway (Stanford, Ca.) and Lower (Richmond, Va.) were largely credited in the late 1960s as the doyens for perfecting the heart transplant procedure, Reitz (Stanford, Ca.) for the combined heart-lung transplantation technique in the late 1970s and Cooper (Toronto, Canada) for single lung transplantation in the mid-1980s and subsequently double-bilateral lung transplantation in the early-1990s.

It was not until these surgical procedures were technically possible, that transplantation became a viable therapeutic option as a care-pathway for gravely ill patients with congestive cardiac failure and, latterly, end-stage lung disease.

Nonetheless, those poor results were the platform for future research and clinical successes. The serendipitous discovery of a new, more selective immunosuppressive agent, Cyclosporin A, paved the way for clinical deployment with an immediate improvement in survival with less complications in the few heart transplants being performed.

The development by Caves (Stanford, Ca.) in 1973 of a technique for sampling the transplanted heart, was pivotal to further successes with immunosuppressive drug doses being specifically tailored to individual patient needs.

So, it is not surprising that transplantation had its humble beginnings with the surgical fraternity. A heterogeneous group of transplant pioneers, who recognised the need and with "The Courage to Fail" (Personal communication: Sir Terence English, transplant pioneer, Cambridge, 2004) evolved the surgical techniques in the research laboratory.

The Oxford definition of "transplant" is "to take from one and place in another" – that is, two operations, the donor and recipient, to achieve the clinical outcome for the patient. In the modern era, the surgeon's role in transplantation has changed significantly but his or her contribution and skill remain pivotal to the completion of the transplantation process. The surgeon's is the final decision as to who will be transplanted and the assessment of the donor organ or organs: will they tolerate the out-of-body period stored at four to 10 degrees Celsius, often for many hours; will they function adequately?

To decline the offer of a donor organ is to rob the donor family of the expected and desired outcome of their most altruistic of gestures. It is always the transplant surgeon's responsibility to finally accept or decline organs on offer, the difficulty of the "marginal" donor organ, with the knowledge, perhaps surprisingly to many, that the commonest cause of early death following heart or lung transplantation is primary graft/donor organ failure. The transplant surgeon remains the definitive advocate for the donor family.

All of the above rests on the shoulders of the transplant surgeon, not the physicians, anaesthetists or nursing staff. Clinical experience goes a long way, but the bravery to push the frontiers, to challenge contemporary norms, question protocols means the transplant surgeon remains the definitive recipient and advocate. When all the decisions have been made it finally comes down to the operation, the removal of a terminally diseased organ and the transplantation of the previously healthy donor organ from the compromised brain death environment into the gravely ill recipient.

For patients with end-stage heart or lung disease life is uncertain; physical capacity is of the order of 10 to 20 per cent of their peers, quality of life and "happiness" almost non-existent, the waiting list period daunting and the risk of sudden death confronting. The impact on family members, loved ones, friends and colleagues is likened to caring for the terminally ill: what to say, what to do, how to make the patient's life better?

Meanwhile, "the wait", with the attendant progressive deterioration in wellbeing and loss of self-determinism, is an inexorable journey into the unknown. "To be or not to be?" is very much the question the waiting-list patient and transplant surgeon face.

The only prospect for survival, better quality of life and happiness is the transplant operation, a life-saving surgical procedure that relies on the untimely death of another human being.

At this time of extreme family trauma and grief, the possibility of organ donation is broached usually by members of the medical team in consultation with a donor coordinator, on occasions at the behest of the family. In the most altruistic demonstration of thought for others – something good out of bad, family members give consent to organ donation.

I dislike the reference to "organ harvest". Human organs are not farmed with the intent of harvesting. The organ procurement process, as I prefer to call it, is subsequently put in train, yielding the increasingly rare and precious donor organs without which transplantation remains only a virtual option.

The donor offer only comes once, often in the early hours of the morning with a response/acceptance time of 20 minutes. In this time frame, relevant members of the transplant team are contacted, the waiting list status of potential recipients reviewed and the most suitable recipients highlighted.

The definitive decision is then made as to accepting the donor offer, putting in train the organ retrieval process and contingencies for the subsequent transplant procedure or, as is often the case, multiple transplant procedures.

Over the last decade there has been a trend towards multiple transplant procedures; that is, a heart transplant and two single lung transplants from the same donor, being performed sequentially in adjacent operating theatres. The scene charged, the recipients gravely ill, the odds great. The transplant team(s) has frequently been working all day, involved in elective open-heart surgery procedures, only to front again in the early hours of the next morning for the transplant operations.

There has been some conjecture about the organ allocation process in Australia. Government bodies, independent reviewers and the public through various avenues have broached the issue of "equity" in organ donation: that is, the fair and reasonable allocation of donor organs to the most appropriate recipient. An undertone of favouritism, cronyism, and "insider-trading" has sometimes been implied in the questioning.

Organ allocation is complex, but fair and equitable – "beyond reasonable doubt". Once the specifics of blood group, size comparisons and antibody matches are taken into account, the potential recipients' waiting list status is of overwhelming importance in the definitive organ allocation, with the sickest patient who has been waiting the longest in general being chosen. "Blind Freddy" would have little trouble in recognising the robust and transparent equity of access to organs for the Australian waiting list patient.

But herein lies the transplant conundrum: the near perfect functional substitute for a terminally diseased organ is plagued by a supply-demand imbalance that can never be redressed by human-to-human organ transplantation. For heart transplantation alone this imbalance is brought home by the International Heart Transplant Registry data: 3,500 heart transplants performed annually worldwide and falling, with an expanding potential world market of 100,000 to 200,000 congestive heart failure patients who could benefit from heart replacement annually.

It has been this increasing supply-demand imbalance that has stimulated ongoing research in artificial heart technology; that is, the Australian Ventrassist artificial heart clinical trial, and the farming and potential utility of genetically modified pig organs.

There is no other initiative in contemporary medicine to parallel the transplantation process. Gene therapy and stem cells offer exciting prospects for the prevention and treatment of disease in the future, but in 2004 organ transplantation delivers the goods to an otherwise doomed population with irreversible and terminal end-stage organ failure.

Although the advances in 21st century health lie in the realm of the "evidence-based" clinical trial, much of what has been achieved in thoracic organ transplantation over the last 20 years, the so-called "modern era", has been built on one fundamental – the need to succeed.

Nearly 40 years on from Barnard, solid organ transplantation is regarded as a miracle of 20th century medicine; the product of surgical ingenuity, clinical trial and basic research, with principally the surgeon's belief in self and the clinical need pushing the frontiers of conventional wisdom in life-saving surgical treatment strategies for end-stage organ dysfunction.

Today, Melbourne's Alfred Hospital and other contemporary peer programmes' transplant outcomes have improved dramatically with a five per cent mortality at one month, a one-year survival rate of 87 per cent with a 15-year survival rate of 50 per cent; a remarkable achievement by the transplant team.

In the future, transplant immunologists may engineer more specific immunosuppressive agents with consequently less infection and patient-specific immunosuppression which, hopefully, will lead to the Holy Grail of transplant immunology: the achievement of lifelong transplanted/donor organ tolerance.

For the transplant surgeon, in the end it always comes down to the message inherent in the Nike slogan – "Just do it!" Or, as David Hookes said so many times to so many: "Just get on with it."

CHAPTER

XIV

The doctors persisted, a transplant was Jason's only chance.
The operation took 15 hours and involved seven surgeons and
their support staff. Jason will never forget day three after the
operation: "That was when they took away the breathing tube
and I had to use my new lungs for the first time."

Weird, but Wonderful

JASON GREY

When I think of what life was like just before my transplant I remember two things: constantly struggling to breathe and, barely having enough energy to get out of bed. Mum says it was like looking after someone in their 90s, even though I was only 25.

Back then I couldn't plan even one day ahead because I'd never know how I'd be feeling from one day to the next. At my worst I was living my life pretty much between the couch and the bed.

I was born on 28th February 1978, in Manly, New South Wales weighing a fairly chunky nine pound three ounces. Mum said I was about one month old when she realised something was wrong.

I wasn't putting on weight, I wasn't keeping any food down, I was hardly sleeping and I was crying all the time. It was as if I had a non-stop cold, and I kept losing weight even though Mum knew she was doing everything right. Mum was taking me backwards and forwards to the doctor every week. At the age of 10 months I only weighed 10 pounds, or just 13 ounces more than my birth weight.

The doctor, and the nurses at the baby health clinic reassured Mum that everything would be okay, but she ignored them and decided to take me for tests at the Children's Hospital and, as it turned out, everything wasn't okay. After a whole range of tests the doctors told Mum and Dad that I had cystic fibrosis, and that I'd be lucky to live to the age of five. Things were not looking too good.

Cystic fibrosis is a condition where the mucous glands cause normal mucous to change into a thick, sticky substance that clogs the lungs and traps bacteria, causing repeated infections and blockages. It also causes problems with the digestion of food because the pancreas has trouble releasing enzymes.

Mum and Dad were cautioned against having more children, but fortunately they ignored the advice and my brother Christian was born in 1980, Mitchell in 1982 and Lee in 1986.

When I was little the cystic fibrosis didn't really worry me that much apart from a bit of breathlessness, not that much different from asthma. And, during the 1980s our family life was pretty much like anyone else's. I'd occasionally have to go into hospital for what they'd call a "tune up", which involved having antibiotics through a canula in my arm, and intense physiotherapy.

I didn't enjoy the hospital visits much so Mum started doing my treatments at home, and that helped to minimise the impact on me. Until I was about 12 I could do pretty much what everyone else could do, and I was starting to think about going on to do a career, maybe architecture. I suppose it helped that I wasn't really into sports; I was more interested in doing creative things like drawing. The thought that I might die just didn't occur to me.

Then everything started to change. I was getting really tired all the time, and shorter and shorter of breath. That was when I began to feel really left out. There were lots of things I couldn't do any more, like playing cricket or just walking around with my mates. A few more years went by and I was spending more and more time in hospital. I'd go into hospital for treatment, go home and be back in hospital two weeks later. It was hard on our family.

Because I was constantly having physiotherapy and heaps of medication, not a lot of time was left for anything else. My brother Mitchell also has mild cystic fibrosis. He's managing it himself now, but Mum was pretty busy in those days keeping on top of our medication and treatment.

Just after my health started deteriorating I was having really severe stomach pains. Tests showed that my bile duct was compressed and the bile wasn't draining properly, a common condition in cystic fibrosis sufferers. So it was back into hospital again, this time for a bile duct bypass operation. That settled everything down, but generally my health was going downhill fast.

I wasn't living my life, I was struggling to live. It occurred to me that things weren't going to get any better.

When I was 22 I reached a point where I could walk just a few paces; I needed a portable oxygen machine to go anywhere. In 2000, my doctor at Westmead Hospital's cystic fibrosis clinic told me it was time to think about an organ transplant. Without a transplant, he told me that I'd probably live only another 18 months to two years.

I thought, "My God, I'm going to die!" As far as I was concerned a transplant wasn't an option. I just thought: "I'm never going to do that." That may sound odd, to think about a transplant as a death sentence. Of course, what was happening was I suddenly realised just how little time I had, and how few options. The doctors persisted: a transplant was my only chance; I kept putting off a decision. Eventually, they asked to have a meeting with my parents and after talking it through we decided to go ahead. But making the decision was the easy part.

After a range of tests at St Vincent's Hospital in Sydney the news wasn't too good: the doctors didn't think I was a candidate for a lung transplant because my liver was diseased. There was a big chance I'd die on the operating table.

Things looked a bit grim, but then my own doctor told me there was another option: to see Professor Keith McNeil, the Director of Transplant Services at the Prince Charles Hospital in Brisbane. My doctor said Dr McNeil might consider me for a triple transplant.

Dr McNeil told my doctor he wanted to "eyeball" me first – his exact words. So Dad and I flew to Brisbane and Dr McNeil explained the procedure; I would come up again for an assessment to see if I would be a suitable recipient. After the assessment we didn't hear anything for a few weeks, then Dr McNeil phoned to say, "Move up to Brisbane and we'll put you on the list." Then the mad rush started.

In September 2002, Mum, Mitchell, Lee and I moved to Brisbane before we'd actually found a house. We were booked to stay at Rainbow House, which provides temporary accommodation for cystic fibrosis patients and their families.

On the day we arrived in Brisbane I had a bleed in my oesophagus and ended up in hospital for two weeks. In the meantime Mum found a house and moved in. When I came out of hospital everything was done, so at least I didn't have to unpack any boxes. After that it was just a matter of waiting.

I knew that finding a donor wouldn't be easy because of my blood type, and because the donor would have to fit my general build of 162 centimetres and 50 kilograms. I spent Christmas 2002 in a wheelchair and on oxygen, and wondering where I'd be for Christmas 2003. Eight months passed and I was at my lowest point.

There was nothing dramatic about the way Dr McNeil told me they'd probably found me a heart, lung and liver donor. I was in hospital at the time with a collapsed lung. I had a chest tube in to re-inflate the lung and I was preparing to go home the next day. That didn't happen.

It was about 8.30pm when Dr McNeil came into my room, put his hands on my feet and said, "Guess what – we may have found a donor for you." He said he'd be back in about half an hour, after he'd checked a few things out. My mind was churning with all sorts of questions: Is this the end? Will I survive? Who will I ring?

I phoned Mum. She told me later that I was crying, but all I remember is saying, "Mum, get up here!" She said, "Why, what's wrong?" and I said, "Keith just came in …" That was it; she said, "I'll be right there!" and hung up the phone. Mum had been in her pyjamas getting settled for an early night. She remembers she changed and got up to the hospital in five minutes with Mitchell and Lee.

The nurses were waiting for Mum to arrive, everybody was hugging everyone else and the tears were really flowing. Even Mitchell and Lee were crying. Everyone was crying except Mum. She said she was holding back and staying strong because she knew she'd be able to do her crying later.

Then Dr McNeil came back and said, "Okay, it's all under way. We've got the surgical teams about to come in." He said the donor organs were being flown to Brisbane, and in the meantime I'd be "prepped" and have blood tests. By the time I'd had the tests, taken some pills and had a shower it was about midnight when they wheeled me away for surgery.

That four or five hours felt like about half an hour for me, but Mum said it was an eternity for her. When they took me into "pre-op" for that last half hour the nerves really set in, but one of the cystic fibrosis nurses held my hand and we had a joke around until they were ready for me in surgery.

Then they wheeled me into theatre, moved me off the gurney and on to the operating table, the anaesthetist made a joke … and that's about all I remember.

The operation took 15 hours and involved surgeons from the Prince Charles and Princess Alexandra hospitals. There were four cardiac thoracic surgeons, three liver transplant surgeons and three anaesthetists, along with all their support staff, working in shifts to get everything up and running.

Even though I was given the donor's heart, lungs and liver, my own heart was okay, so I'd already agreed to donate that to whomever needed it, or for research. I don't know what happened to it, but I'm sure they found a good use for it.

"Post-op" is all a bit of a blur. I remember being wheeled into a lift, but I could have dreamed that. I woke up in the intensive care unit with tubes and pipes everywhere. One of the doctors asked me how I was, and all I could do was give him the thumbs up. I slept for most of the first week, but I'll never forget day three after the operation.

That was when they took away the breathing tube and I had to use my new lungs for the first time. It was a really weird feeling. I'd been used to taking such small breaths and suddenly I had this huge lung capacity. I was scared, and not sure if I was doing the right thing. Even learning how to cough again was a whole new sensation. I think people were a bit amazed at how quickly I regained my get-up-and-go, but I just wanted to live a normal life and felt I had so much catching up to do.

I know that I was part of medical history and that my operation represented a huge breakthrough for transplant technology, but what it means to me on a really basic level is being able to breathe and to have energy.

Sometimes I find myself reverting to taking those short, shallow breaths like I used to do, and I have to remind myself to breathe properly.

Now I live my life according to how much I can fit in, rather than according to how much energy I have left after making the effort just to breathe, get out of bed, eat and walk around the house. The transplant hasn't just given me a gift of life – it's a quality of life that I never thought I'd have. It's something I'll never take for granted.

My family and I will always be grateful to the donor family, who made all of this possible. I have a duty to live life to the fullest, to show how much this means to me and my family.

Life is really full at the moment. I'm doing a 12-month Diploma in E-business Support on scholarship with Spherion Information Technology Institute, and I've done a few website design courses. People ask me if I have any plans for the future and I just tell them I don't want anything outrageous – a job, a house, just the normal sort of stuff.

One of my priorities after the operation was to keep working on my Mitsubishi Lancer, affectionately known as "The Gremlin'". It's a full show car and I've been slowly doing it up for seven years. It was that project that sometimes kept me going in the tough times, but in the months before the operation I had no energy to do anything with it so it just sat in the garage. But in the first 10 months after the transplant it did 13,000 kilometres, including three trips to Sydney!

I still have some health problems to deal with, and because of the anti-rejection drugs I have to be really careful when I go out in the sun; but I'm only taking a fraction of the medication I was on before, and my quality of life is 110 per cent. To be honest there are still some days when I just lie around and do nothing – but it's because I can, and not because there's no other choice.

"I Saw a Miracle …"

FIONA COOTE

It's now been 20 years since my lifesaving heart transplant at St Vincent's Hospital in Sydney. At the age of 14 I was living on a farm in Manilla, near Tamworth, New South Wales, with my parents and sisters. Tonsillitis turned into viral cardiomyopathy. Within weeks I was air lifted to Sydney and put on total life support.

Only five weeks earlier the team at St Vincent's had completed their first heart transplant. My parents have since reminded me of the irony. Watching the news on television of the miracle of Peter Apthorpe's transplant, I had turned to my parents in our lounge room and said, "If anything ever happens to me I'd like to donate my organs."

Thanks to the brilliance of the team at Royal North Shore, who kept me alive, the team at St Vincent's who performed my transplant, and the generosity of the families who made the decision to donate their loved one's organs for my first and second transplant (20 months later), 20 wonderful years have passed and I'm looking forward to enjoying a long and healthy life.

Today I am blessed with an astounding level of health and I enjoy a wonderful lifestyle in the lucky country.

People often ask me my thoughts on transplantation, organ donation and life after transplantation. Over the last 20 years, I've been happy to share those thoughts in thousands of conversations, media interviews and speeches in the hope that my story might encourage others to understand the wonders of this miracle, and give support wherever they can.

I believe that my thoughts and feelings were best expressed in a speech I made at the "Time of Remembrance and Reflection Service" at St Andrews Chapel, in Sydney in 1999. I'm happy to share it with you in full:

"Today I witnessed the most incredible things. Things that astounded me. Today I saw a miracle! I saw the sun rise over Coogee Beach. I saw a child laugh. I saw a family kissing each other. I saw a flower in my garden.

"Every one of these was a miracle – because they are the miracle of my life.

"And every day for the last 15 years I've enjoyed and appreciated the second chance at life that organ transplantation has provided to me.

"But it's not just the miracle that the human body can have a part replaced, although that is pretty incredible. The real miracle is that there is enough love in the world that hundreds of unrelated people join together every day to deliver the miracle of life to people they've never met, to people they may never know.

"They have each been a vital link in a chain of events that delivered life to me and 30,000 other Australians like me, so that every day we can witness a sunrise, or a child laugh.

"It never ceases to amaze me that the images that fill our television screens most nights are mainly about acts of thoughtlessness or cruelty, yet, every day go unheralded millions of acts of people who are lovers of life. So today, I'd like to recognise and thank those lovers of life who are each critical links to the chain of life that is organ and tissue donation:

- Police officers and other people upon whom the process depends.
- The NSW Roads & Traffic Authority and their staff who enable the decisions of millions of people to be accurately recorded.
- The health care staff that make organ and tissue donation and transplantation possible.

"These are the people who we may think are 'just doing their job', but what's important is that everyone has to do their job professionally, precisely, perfectly and passionately – in order to deliver the miracle. And every day they do.

"So on behalf of all those recipients of transplanted tissue and organs, let me thank you for your efforts, your skill and your thoughtfulness. Next I'd like to thank all those people who have never been involved in delivering a miracle, but have made a vital decision that they care about the lives of other human beings, care about them enough to have performed three functions:

- They've made the decision to become an organ and tissue donor should the circumstance arise.
- They've ticked and signed their drivers licences to confirm their decision.
- They have discussed their wishes with their family so that they understand the decision they've made for their future and the future of others.

"Organ donation is one of the greatest gifts people can bestow on another human being. In many instances those people have died. Yet, through their planning and their love of life, a part of them continues to provide life and quality of life to another human being. Every day I give thanks to the two people who loved enough to give me, a total stranger, a heart that beats, without missing a beat. So I can see a sun rise. I can feel the warmth of a hug. I can smell the fragrance of a flower. I can taste the freshness of a fruit and I can hear the laughter of a child.

"And finally, let me acknowledge and thank the families of all donors. People, who often in times of trauma unimaginable to most, have had the strength and compassion to see beyond the tragedy, who respected the decisions of their loved ones or made decisions on their behalf. To let life go on. To allow others to live a life and have a quality of life that otherwise would not have been possible.

"Through my circumstances, I've met thousands of people who have expressed their personal feelings openly and emotionally to me. Some of the words they often use are 'courage' and 'inspiration'.

"It's ironic that they attribute these words to me because I've never felt courageous or inspirational; rather I've attributed those words to the thousands of people who've been the links in the chain of the miracle of life. Thank you to all of you for encouraging and inspiring me to enjoy and appreciate every moment."

EPILOGUE

Epilogue

ROB ZADOW

At David's Mum's funeral, less than a year ago, Denis Brien related a story about Pat. She had a dearly loved car, which she always parked in his driveway but one night she forgot to put the hand brake on.

Pat was told the car was going down the drive but she refused to move, saying it must be something they did in the car service. In her eyes, despite the fact the car was heading for a stobie pole on the other side of the road, she was right.

You can gather from that little snippet that, shall we say, strong character traits ran in David's family. Indeed some 11 years ago, when Leonie my now wife, but then friend, heard we were going to have dinner with David she burst into tears – and she'd only ever seen him at a distance, such was the impression he made.

Yet about two years later, having come to know Hook so much better, I found her ringing 5AA to correct him while he was on air because his pronunciation of a word was wrong. You see, you scratched the surface of David Hookes and you may have gotten bitten, but if you kept going you would always hit gold.

Hook was a man of intense passion. That is why he could seem to be cutting. Yet, that is why he did so well on talkback radio – because he actually did care about others' opinions, but wasn't shy about stating his own. And I think that's why he and I gelled.

I think because I enjoyed taking a contrary view. Like if we were eating out, he'd say, "I'm going to have fish," and I'd say, "What's wrong with a steak?" or he'd say, "Can I place a little bet on the Melbourne Cup?" to which I would say, "You might as well give it to me." Our relationship endured despite that contrariness, because the other thing we did agree on was that you don't learn very much about life if you are always agreeing with everyone.

Hook was a man of powerful loyalties. It was that which gave him confidence in a crowd and may have seemed like arrogance to some – because he really did know who his friends were and we knew when he was our friend. Mind you, you always knew if he was mad with you, too. I guess that's the price of real friendship.

Many of you know Hook didn't like hospitals but such was his loyalty to me that when my first wife Kay was dying, Hook would just pop in at the hospice – and usually find some way to make me argue with him, just to lift me out of myself.

Hook was a man with a family whom he loved. That is why he sometimes shunned the media with a vengeance. It is why the last 12 months were so hard, as he struggled to come to terms with the death of his first coach in life, Pat, his Mum.

It is why Caprice and Kristofer, Robyn's children, became his kids when Robyn and David married, and why they stand as a unit today grieving for the man they all loved so dearly.

Hook knew his limits. You know, we would be exploring some business concept together and he'd get so far with it and then just say, "Zad's, that's understood. You fix it." Believe it or not, I think it was this capacity that helped him to scale – and I use that word on purpose, because it wasn't an easy ride for him – the heights in his sporting, media and personal lives.

But, of course, heights have their traps. You fall down, and everyone can see you do it. But Hook knew better than most; he knew what it was to fall off his horse. Asked why he didn't ever really succeed at Test cricket he just looked hard into the camera and said, "Because I wasn't good enough." He might have said that about other things, too, but that never made him give up.

I cannot hope to convey to you today what David meant to me, or me to him. I don't dare think about it yet. But one of the drivers whose car fleet David often used, shared a Greek saying with me the other night as I travelled to the airport:

Zoë se mus (pron: zoee say muss)

It means:
Life to the rest of us.

It seems so apt to finish with that because that is what Hook gave to those who knew him, or of him and it is what he would want for each one of us right now.

Zoë se mus

STATISTICS

The Magnificent Eight

ROSS DUNDAS

The Centenary Test between Australia and England was played at the Melbourne Cricket Ground from 12th-17th March 1977. England won the toss and sent Australia into bat. David Hookes was the only Test debutant in either team. He came to the crease in the first innings at 11.51am when Gary Cosier was dismissed. The score was three for 23. Hookes scored 17 runs in 32 minutes and faced 19 balls. He hit two fours, an edge past third slip then a cover drive. He was caught at second slip by Tony Greig trying to fend off a short rising ball from Chris Old. He was fourth man out and the score was 45. In England's first innings Hookes took one catch (Mike Brearley) at third slip off the bowling of Dennis Lillee. In Australia's second innings, Hookes came to the crease on day three at 11.46am with Australia four for 132.

At lunch, he was 20 not out and Doug Walters 66. Walters was out immediately after lunch, without adding. Hookes's famous tilt with Greig began at 2.18pm, the 57th over of the innings. Australia were five for 223, Hookes on 36, Marsh 19.

This is how history unfolded:

1st ball – no score
2nd ball – no score
3rd ball – four through mid off
4th ball – four backward of square leg
5th ball – four through the covers
6th ball – four through mid wicket
7th ball – four through the covers
8th ball – no score

When Hookes was out at 2.25pm his 56 runs had come from 69 balls in 122 minutes. He had hit nine fours. Australia won the Test by 45 runs at 5:12pm on the last day.

David William HOOKES
Born: May 3, 1955 Mile End (South Australia)
Died: January 19, 2004 Melbourne (Victoria)
Left-hand batsman – Left-arm slow "chinaman" bowler

First-class Career
Debut: 1975-76 South Australia v West Indians, Adelaide

Season	Country	M	Inn	NO	Runs	HS	0s	50	100	Avrge	Ct	Balls	Mdns	Runs	Wkts	Avrge	Best
1975-76	Australia	10	13	1	395	55	1	3	-	32.92	6	48	1	25	2	12.50	1/8
1976-77	Australia	6	12	-	861	185	-	1	5	71.75	8	120	1	62	-	-	-
1977	England	17	26	1	804	108	1	6	1	32.16	4	24	-	18	1	18.00	1/17
1979-80	Australia	5	9	1	343	88	-	3	-	42.88	2	108	3	64	1	64.00	1/18
1979-80	Pakistan	3	6	-	10	5	3	-	-	1.67	3	-	-	-	-	-	-
1980-81	Australia	7	14	1	387	73*	2	3	-	29.77	-	234	6	152	-	-	-
1981-82	Australia	11	17	1	703	106	-	5	1	43.94	13	351	16	131	3	43.67	1/13
1982-83	Australia	13	23	1	1424	193	1	9	4	64.73	17	222	6	123	3	41.00	2/33
1982-83	Sri Lanka	2	2	1	163	143*	-	-	1	163.00	6	-	-	-	-	-	-
1983-84	Australia	7	12	-	563	142	-	2	2	46.92	5	592	21	282	5	56.40	2/19
1983-84	West Indies	9	18	2	623	103*	-	4	1	38.94	4	252	1	216	4	54.00	3/114
1984-85	Australia	11	20	-	664	151	1	4	1	33.20	10	556	16	341	8	42.63	2/38
1985-86	Australia	12	22	1	1001	243	2	3	3	47.67	19	390	8	256	4	64.00	1/3
1986-87	Australia	10	16	1	811	306*	4	4	2	54.07	15	324	12	172	3	57.33	3/58
1987-88	Australia	11	20	1	1149	132	-	7	4	60.47	18	162	5	63	3	21.00	2/22
1988-89	Australia	12	21	3	762	133	1	5	1	42.33	18	138	2	93	-	-	-
1989-90	Australia	11	18	1	823	159	2	3	3	48.41	4	469	19	201	3	67.00	2/89
1990-91	Australia	11	18	-	655	195	4	1	2	36.39	10	180	8	103	1	103.00	1/6
1991-92	Australia	10	17	-	530	156	-	2	1	31.18	4	120	3	77	-	-	-
Total		178	304	16	12671	306*	22	65	32	44.00	166	4290	128	2379	41	58.02	3/58
Test Cricket		23	41	3	1306	143*	4	8	1	34.37	12	96	4	41	1	41.00	1/4
Sheffield Shield		120	205	9	9364	306*	14	44	26	47.78	128	3204	100	1676	26	64.46	2/22
Other First-class		35	58	4	2001	128	4	13	5	37.06	26	990	24	662	14	47.29	3/58

Opponents	M	Inn	NO	Runs	HS	0s	50	100	Avrge	Ct	Balls	Mdns	Runs	Wkts	Avrge	Best
Barbados	1	2	1	125	103*	-	-	1	125.00	-	30	1	17	1	17.00	1/17
BCCP President's XI	1	2	-	8	5	-	-	-	4.00	1	-	-	-	-	-	-
Derbyshire	1	1	-	19	19	-	-	-	19.00	1	-	-	-	-	-	-
ENGLAND	11	19	1	700	85	-	7	-	38.89	4	48	2	20	-	-	-
Essex	1	2	1	89	69*	-	1	-	89.00	-	-	-	-	-	-	-
England XI	3	6	-	249	104	1	1	1	41.50	3	168	7	92	5	18.40	3/58
Glamorgan	1	2	-	11	11	1	-	-	5.50	-	-	-	-	-	-	-
Guyana	1	2	1	64	61	-	1	-	64.00	1	78	-	71	-	-	-
Indians	1	2	-	4	4	1	-	-	2.00	-	30	-	42	-	-	-
INDIA	2	3	-	76	42	1	-	-	25.33	1	12	-	4	1	4.00	1/4
Leeward Islands	1	2	-	90	66	-	1	-	45.00	1	-	-	-	-	-	-
Leicestershire	1	1	-	59	59	-	1	-	59.00	-	-	-	-	-	-	-
MCC	1	2	-	11	8	-	-	-	5.50	1	-	-	-	-	-	-
Middlesex	1	1	-	34	34	-	-	-	34.00	3	-	-	-	-	-	-
NEW ZEALAND	2	4	1	59	38*	1	-	-	19.67	-	6	-	2	-	-	-
Northamptonshire	1	2	-	100	53	2	1	-	50.00	-	18	-	17	1	17.00	1/17
New South Wales	25	42	1	1833	243	2	6	5	44.71	25	548	8	304	2	152.00	1/3
New Zealanders	3	6	1	266	128	-	-	2	53.20	4	84	4	65	1	65.00	1/43
PAKISTAN	1	2	-	0	0	2	-	-	0.00	-	-	-	-	-	-	-
Punjab Governor's XI	1	2	-	2	2	1	-	-	1.00	2	-	-	-	-	-	-
Pakistanis	2	3	-	181	91	2	2	-	60.33	3	276	10	126	2	63.00	2/19
Queensland	23	40	1	2385	195	2	15	7	61.15	26	737	26	360	2	180.00	1/10
SRI LANKA	1	1	1	143	143*	-	-	1	-	2	-	-	-	-	-	-
SL Board President's	1	1	-	20	20	-	1	-	20.00	4	-	-	-	-	-	-
Sri Lankans	1	1	-	50	50	-	-	-	50.00	-	-	-	-	-	-	-
Somerset	1	2	-	111	108	-	1	-	55.50	1	6	1	0	-	-	-
Surrey	1	1	-	-	-	-	-	-	-	-	-	-	-	-	-	-
Sussex	1	-	-	-	-	-	-	-	-	-	-	-	-	-	-	-
Tasmania	19	28	2	1503	306*	1	2	6	57.81	17	586	18	325	7	46.43	2/22
Victoria	24	45	4	1901	193	5	10	5	46.37	38	667	31	313	7	44.71	2/38
Western Australia	29	50	1	1742	146	4	11	3	35.55	22	666	17	374	8	46.75	2/49
WEST INDIES	6	12	-	328	51	-	1	-	27.33	2	30	2	15	-	-	-
West Indians	6	10	-	325	67	-	2	-	32.50	4	150	1	103	1	103.00	1/17

Opponents	M	Inn	NO	Runs	HS	0s	50	100	Avrge	Ct	Balls	Mdns	Runs	Wkts	Avrge	Best
Windward Islands	1	2	-	96	74	-	1	-	48.00	-	144	-	128	3	42.67	3/114
Worcestershire	1	2	-	12	8	-	-	-	6.00	-	6	-	1	-	-	-
Yorkshire	1	2	-	75	67	-	1	-	37.50	-	-	-	-	-	-	-

		Inn	NO	Runs	HS	0s	50	100	Avrge	Ct	Balls	Mdns	Runs	Wkts	Avrge	Best
First Innings		100	3	4004	185	5	22	8	41.28	67	1208	34	711	12	59.25	3/114
Second Innings		73	1	3898	306*	5	15	14	54.14	47	1147	36	601	14	42.93	2/22
Third Innings		89	8	3532	195	8	19	9	43.60	25	929	38	543	9	60.33	3/58
Fourth Innings		42	4	1237	107	4	9	1	32.55	27	1006	20	524	6	87.33	1/8

Venues in Australia	M	Inn	NO	Runs	HS	0s	50	100	Avrge	Ct	Balls	Mdns	Runs	Wkts	Avrge	Best
Adelaide	78	132	5	6664	306*	7	31	20	52.47	78	2209	62	1243	22	56.50	3/58
Brisbane	13	23	2	1178	195	1	9	2	56.10	16	487	20	240	2	120.00	1/10
Devonport	4	7	-	535	142	1	1	3	76.43	6	286	8	132	4	33.00	1/11
Geelong	2	4	1	163	73*	-	1	-	54.33	2	162	11	48	1	48.00	1/22
Hobart (Bellerive)	3	3	-	34	15	-	-	-	11.33	4	18	-	21	-	-	-
Hobart (TCA)	1	1	-	35	35	-	-	-	35.00	-	96	4	50	1	50.00	1/49
Launceston	2	3	-	39	26	-	-	-	13.00	2	-	-	-	-	-	-
Melbourne	11	22	2	770	133	3	6	1	38.50	13	174	8	79	2	39.50	2/38
Newcastle	1	2	-	57	42	-	-	-	28.50	1	30	-	15	-	-	-
Perth	17	28	-	850	146	2	5	2	30.36	13	336	8	205	4	51.25	2/49
St Kilda	2	3	-	193	193	2	2	1	64.33	3	-	-	-	-	-	-
Sydney	13	24	2	553	87	2	2	-	25.14	11	216	6	112	-	-	-
Total	147	252	12	11071	306*	18	55	29	46.13	149	4014	127	2145	36	59.58	3/58

Venues in England	M	Inn	NO	Runs	HS	0s	50	100	Avrge	Ct	Balls	Mdns	Runs	Wkts	Avrge	Best
Bath	1	2	-	111	108	-	1	1	55.50	1	-	-	-	-	-	-
Chelmsford	1	2	1	89	69*	-	1	-	89.00	1	-	-	-	-	-	-
Chesterfield	1	1	-	19	19	-	-	-	19.00	1	-	-	-	-	-	-
Hove	1	-	-	-	-	-	-	-	-	-	-	-	-	-	-	-
Leeds	1	2	-	45	24	-	-	-	22.50	-	-	-	-	-	-	-
Leicester	1	1	-	59	59	-	1	-	59.00	-	-	-	-	-	-	-
Lord's	3	5	-	106	50	-	1	-	21.20	1	-	-	-	-	-	-
Manchester	1	2	-	33	28	-	-	-	16.50	-	-	-	-	-	-	-

Opponents	M	Inn	NO	Runs	HS	0s	50	100	Avrge	Ct	Balls	Mdns	Runs	Wkts	Avrge	Best
Northampton	1	2	-	100	53	-	1	-	50.00	-	18	-	17	1	17.00	1/17
Nottingham	1	2	-	59	42	-	-	-	29.50	1	-	-	-	-	-	-
Scarborough	1	2	-	75	67	-	1	-	37.50	-	-	-	-	-	-	-
Swansea	1	2	-	11	11	1	-	-	5.50	-	-	-	-	-	-	-
The Oval	2	1	-	85	85	-	1	-	85.00	-	6	-	-	-	-	-
Worcester	1	2	-	12	8	-	-	-	6.00	-	-	-	1	-	-	-
Total	17	26	1	804	108	1	6	1	32.16	4	24	-	18	1	18.00	1/17

Venues in Pakistan	M	Inn	NO	Runs	HS	0s	50	100	Avrge	Ct	Balls	Mdns	Runs	Wkts	Avrge	Best
Karachi	1	2	-	0	0	2	-	-	0.00	2	-	-	-	-	-	-
Multan	1	2	-	2	2	1	-	-	1.00	-	-	-	-	-	-	-
Rawalpindi	1	2	-	8	5	-	-	-	4.00	1	-	-	-	-	-	-
Total	3	6	-	10	5	3	-	-	1.67	3	-	-	-	-	-	-

Venues in Sri Lanka	M	Inn	NO	Runs	HS	0s	50	100	Avrge	Ct	Balls	Mdns	Runs	Wkts	Avrge	Best
Kandy	1	1	1	143	143*	-	-	1	-	2	-	-	-	-	-	-
Moratuwa	1	1	-	20	20	-	-	-	20.00	4	-	-	-	-	-	-
Total	2	2	1	163	143*	-	-	1	163.00	6	-	-	-	-	-	-

Venues in West Indies	M	Inn	NO	Runs	HS	0s	50	100	Avrge	Ct	Balls	Mdns	Runs	Wkts	Avrge	Best
Basseterre	1	2	-	90	66	-	1	-	45.00	1	-	-	-	-	-	-
Bridgetown	2	4	1	164	103*	-	-	1	54.67	-	30	1	17	1	17.00	1/17
Castries	1	2	-	96	74	-	1	-	48.00	-	144	-	128	3	42.67	3/114
Georgetown	2	4	1	106	61	-	1	-	35.33	1	78	-	71	-	-	-
Kingston	1	2	-	43	36	-	-	-	21.50	1	-	-	-	-	-	-
Port-of-Spain	1	2	-	44	23	-	-	-	22.00	-	-	-	-	-	-	-
St John's	1	2	-	80	51	-	1	-	40.00	1	-	-	-	-	-	-
Total	9	18	2	623	103*	-	4	1	38.94	4	252	1	216	4	54.00	3/114

Batting Position	Inn	NO	Runs	HS	0s	50	100	Avrge
1/2	5	-	137	107	2	-	1	27.40
3	12	-	180	67	2	1	-	15.00
4	131	8	5986	306*	9	26	17	48.67
5	85	3	4395	193	6	26	12	53.60

Batting Position	Inn	NO	Runs	HS	0s	50	100	Avrge
6	56	4	1553	111	3	9	2	29.87
7	13	1	368	67	-	3	-	30.67
8	2	-	52	28	-	-	-	26.00

Team	M	Inn	NO	Runs	HS	0s	50	100	Avrge	Ct	Balls	Mdns	Runs	Wkts	Avrge	Best
AUSTRALIA	23	41	3	1306	143*	4	8	1	34.37	12	96	4	41	1	41.00	1/4
Australian XI	19	30	3	926	108	2	7	2	34.30	12	276	1	234	5	46.80	3/114
South Australia	136	233	10	10439	306*	16	50	29	46.81	142	3918	123	2104	35	60.11	3/58

Highest Score:- 306* South Australia v Tasmania, Adelaide, 1986-87

Centuries	Team	Opponent	Venue	Season
163*	South Australia	Victoria	Adelaide	1976-77
185	South Australia	Queensland	Adelaide	1976-77
105	South Australia	Queensland	Adelaide	1976-77
135	South Australia	New South Wales	Adelaide	1976-77
156	South Australia	New South Wales	Adelaide	1976-77
108	Australian XI	Somerset	Bath	1977
106	South Australia	New South Wales	Adelaide	1981-82
137	South Australia	Victoria	Adelaide	1982-83
107	South Australia	Victoria	Adelaide	1982-83
146	South Australia	Western Australia	Perth	1982-83
193	South Australia	Victoria	St Kilda	1982-83
143*	AUSTRALIA	SRI LANKA	Kandy	1982-83
142	South Australia	Tasmania	Devonport	1983-84
111	South Australia	Western Australia	Perth	1983-84
103*	Australian XI	Barbados	Bridgetown	1983-84
151	South Australia	Tasmania	Adelaide	1984-85
106	South Australia	New Zealanders	Adelaide	1985-86
102	South Australia	Queensland	Adelaide	1985-86
243	South Australia	New South Wales	Adelaide	1985-86
104	South Australia	England XI	Adelaide	1986-87
306*	South Australia	Tasmania	Adelaide	1986-87
128	South Australia	New Zealanders	Adelaide	1987-88

Centuries	Team	Opponent	Venue	Season
132	South Australia	Tasmania	Devonport	1987-88
112	South Australia	Queensland	Brisbane	1987-88
112	South Australia	Tasmania	Adelaide	1987-88
133	South Australia	Victoria	Melbourne	1988-89
139	South Australia	Tasmania	Devonport	1989-90
118	South Australia	Western Australia	Adelaide	1989-90
159	South Australia	Queensland	Adelaide	1989-90
195	South Australia	Queensland	Brisbane	1990-91
178	South Australia	Queensland	Adelaide	1990-91
156	South Australia	New South Wales	Adelaide	1991-92

Best Bowling:- 3/58 South Australia v England XI, Adelaide, 1986-87

First-class Career

Game	Start Date	Team	Opp	Venue	Inn	Pos	How Out	Runs	O	M	R	W	Ct
1	31/10/1975	S.A	WIN	Adelaide	2	7	c Fredericks b Roberts	55	-	-	-	-	1
2	07/11/1975	S.A	NSW	Adelaide	4	7	b Colley	15	-	-	-	-	-
					1	6	lbw b Gilmour	35	-	-	-	-	1
3	14/11/1975	S.A	QLD	Adelaide	3	6	cwk Maclean b Francke	53	-	-	-	-	-
4	05/12/1975	S.A	VIC	Melbourne	2	7	not out	54*	-	-	-	-	1
5	21/12/1975	S.A	WIN	Adelaide	1	6	cwk Robinson b Bright	1	-	-	-	-	-
					3	6	b Julien	44	-	-	-	-	1
6	16/01/1976	S.A	W.A	Perth	2	6	c Hughes b Alderman	44	-	-	-	-	-
					4	5	-	-	4.0	1	17	1	-
7	14/02/1976	S.A	W.A	Adelaide	1	5	b Brayshaw	20	-	-	-	-	2
					4	6	cwk Marsh b Lillee	18	-	-	-	-	-
8	20/02/1976	S.A	VIC	Adelaide	1	7	cwk Robinson b Walker	32	-	-	-	-	-
					3	6	c Stillman b Higgs	0	2.0	0	8	1	2
9	27/02/1976	S.A	NSW	Sydney	2	7	st Rixon b O'Keeffe	24	-	-	-	-	-
					4	7	-	-	-	-	-	-	-
10	05/03/1976	S.A	QLD	Brisbane	2	6	-	-	-	-	-	-	-
11	30/10/1976	S.A	W.A	Adelaide	4	5	cwk Marsh b Malone	25	-	-	-	-	1
					2	7	b Yardley	6	-	-	-	-	-
12	09/01/1977	S.A	W.A	Perth	1	5	cwk Marsh b Clark	1	-	-	-	-	-
					3	6	cwk Marsh b Clark	3	-	-	-	-	-
13	04/02/1977	S.A	VIC	Adelaide	2	5	c Broad b Higgs	163	-	-	-	-	2
					3	5	b Callen	9	-	-	-	-	-
14	11/02/1977	S.A	QLD	Adelaide	1	5	b Dymock	185	-	-	-	-	1
					3	4	b Carlson	105	2.0	1	1	0	1
15	18/02/1977	S.A	NSW	Adelaide	1	5	b Pascoe	135	8.0	0	41	0	2
					3	4	lbw b Watson	156	5.0	0	20	0	-

Game	Start Date	Team	Opp	Venue	Inn	Pos	How Out	Runs	O	M	R	W	Ct
16	12/03/1977	AUS	ENG	Melbourne	1	5	c Greig b Old	17	-	-	-	-	1
17	30/04/1977	AXI	SUR	The Oval	3	6	c Fletcher b Underwood	56	-	-	-	-	-
18	07/05/1977	AXI	SUS	Hove	2	4		-	-	-	-	-	-
					4	4		-	-	-	-	-	-
19	14/05/1977	AXI	GLA	Swansea	2	6	lbw b Nash	0	-	-	-	-	-
					4	6	b Cordle	11	-	-	-	-	-
20	18/05/1977	AXI	SOM	Bath	1	6	b Botham	3	-	-	-	-	-
					3	6	b Burgess	108	-	-	-	-	1
21	25/05/1977	AXI	MCC	Lord's	1	6	cwk Lyon b Hendrick	3	-	-	-	-	-
					3	6	cwk Lyon b Hendrick	8	-	-	-	-	-
22	28/05/1977	AXI	WOR	Worcester	1	6	c Neale b Cumbes	4	-	-	-	-	-
					3	6	b Gifford	8	-	-	-	-	-
23	11/06/1977	AXI	ESS	Chelmsford	1	4	cwk Smith b Turner	20	-	-	-	-	-
					3	4	not out	69*	1.0	0	1	0	-
24	16/06/1977	AUS	ENG	Lord's	2	6	c Brearley b Old	11	-	-	-	-	-
25	29/06/1977	AXI	DER	Chesterfield	2	4	c and b Willis	50	-	-	-	-	-
					4	4	lbw b Hendrick	19	-	-	-	-	1
26	02/07/1977	AXI	YOR	Scarborough	1	4	cwk Bairstow b Stevenson	8	-	-	-	-	-
					3	4	b Carrick	67	-	-	-	-	-
27	07/07/1977	AUS	ENG	Manchester	1	6	cwk Knott b Lever	5	-	-	-	-	-
					3	6	c Brearley b Miller	28	-	-	-	-	-
28	16/07/1977	AXI	NOR	Northampton	1	5	lbw b Mushtaq Mohammad	53	3.0	0	17	1	-
					3	5	b Willey	47	-	-	-	-	-
29	23/07/1977	AXI	LEI	Leicester	1	5	c Shuttleworth b Taylor	59	-	-	-	-	-
30	28/07/1977	AUS	ENG	Nottingham	1	4	c Hendrick b Willis	17	-	-	-	-	1
					3	4	lbw b Hendrick	42	-	-	-	-	-
31	11/08/1977	AUS	ENG	Leeds	2	4	lbw b Botham	24	-	-	-	-	-
					3	4	lbw b Hendrick	21	-	-	-	-	-
32	20/08/1977	AXI	MID	Lord's	2	4	b Emburey	34	-	-	-	-	1
					4	4		-	-	-	-	-	-

Game	Start Date	Team	Opp	Venue	Inn	Pos	How Out	Runs	O	M	R	W	Ct
33	25/08/1977	AUS	ENG	The Oval	2	5	cwk Knott b Greig	85	-	-	-	-	-
34	03/11/1979	S.A	TAS	Devonport	2	4	lbw b Hadlee	88	4.0	0	16	0	-
					4	3	run out	9	6.0	1	18	1	-
35	16/11/1979	S.A	WIN	Adelaide	1	4	run out	3	3.0	0	15	0	-
					3	4	c Garner b Parry	67	-	-	-	-	-
36	01/12/1979	AUS	W.I	Brisbane	1	6	c Holding b Croft	43	5.0	2	15	0	-
					3	6	b Roberts	37	-	-	-	-	-
37	28/12/1979	S.A	W.A	Adelaide	1	5	not out	32*	-	-	-	-	-
38	19/01/1980	S.A	W.A	Perth	1	5	c Malone b Porter	12	-	-	-	-	-
					3	5	c Shipperd b Porter	52	-	-	-	-	1
39	22/02/1980	AXI	BPX	Rawalpindi	1	6	cwk Taslim Arif b Aftab Baloch	5	-	-	-	-	1
					3	5	c Azmat Rana b Aftab Baloch	3	-	-	-	-	-
40	27/02/1980	AUS	PAK	Karachi	1	5	c Majid Khan b Iqbal Qasim	0	-	-	-	-	-
					3	5	lbw b Iqbal Qasim	2	3.0	1	15	0	-
41	13/03/1980	AXI	PGX	Multan	1	3	c Sultan Rana b Amin Lakhani	0	-	-	-	-	-
					3	3	cwk Salim Yousaf b Rashid Khan	21	6.0	2	13	0	1
42	23/10/1980	S.A	TAS	Adelaide	2	4	cwk Woolley b Allanby	6	-	-	-	-	-
					4	4	st Woolley b Saunders	17	5.0	0	42	0	-
43	30/10/1980	S.A	NSW	Adelaide	2	4	c Pascoe b Lawson	0	-	-	-	-	-
					3	4	cwk Rixon b Lawson	35	5.0	0	23	0	-
44	13/11/1980	S.A	NSW	Sydney	1	3	c McCosker b Lawson	17	-	-	-	-	-
					3	3	c Chappell b Holland	4	-	-	-	-	-
45	29/11/1980	S.A	IDS	Adelaide	3	6	c Viswanath b Kapil Dev	0	-	-	-	-	-
46	08/01/1981	S.A	W.A	Adelaide	1	7	b Malone	33	-	-	-	-	-
					3	7	lbw b Porter	67	-	-	-	-	-
47	17/01/1981	S.A	QLD	Adelaide	2	6	cwk Phillips b Dymock	26	10.0	2	22	0	-
					4	6	c Border b Rackemann	53	3.0	1	16	0	-
48	07/03/1981	S.A	VIC	Geelong	1	6	c Walker b Higgs	35	5.0	0	12	0	-
					3	6	not out	73*	2.0	0	9	0	-
49	16/10/1981	S.A	W.A	Perth	2	5	b Alderman	7	-	-	-	-	-
					4	5	c Serjeant b Yardley	10	-	-	-	-	-

Game	Start Date	Team	Opp	Venue	Inn	Pos	How Out	Runs	O	M	R	W	Ct
50	07/11/1981	S.A	NSW	Adelaide	1	5	c Wellham b Chappell	106	-	-	-	-	-
51	13/11/1981	S.A	WIN	Adelaide	2	5	c Croft b Clarke	8	-	-	-	-	-
52	10/12/1981	S.A	NSW	Sydney	4	5	cwk Murray b Marshall	42	-	-	-	-	-
					2	4	b Holland	11	5.0	0	16	0	1
53	17/12/1981	S.A	QLD	Brisbane	4	4	not out	7*	-	-	-	-	-
					2	4	c Dymock b Hohns	51	-	-	-	-	1
54	26/12/1981	S.A	PKI	Adelaide	4	4	c De Jong b Lillie	32	-	-	-	-	2
					2	5	cwk Wasim Bari b Sikander	91	9.0	0	18	0	1
					4				4.0	0	27	0	2
55	08/01/1982	S.A	QLD	Adelaide	1	4	b Maguire	88	-	-	-	-	1
56	15/01/1982	S.A	VIC	Geelong	4	4	c Moss b Hughes	21	13.0	5	22	1	-
					1	4	cwk Maddocks b Callen	34	7.0	5	5	0	1
57	12/02/1982	S.A	TAS	Launceston	3	4	cwk Woolley b Wilson	26	-	-	-	-	1
					2	5	b Saunders	9	-	-	-	-	-
58	19/02/1982	S.A	W.A	Adelaide	4	5	c Shipperd b Malone	97	4.0	0	13	1	-
					1				7.0	1	15	0	-
59	26/02/1982	S.A	VIC	Adelaide	4	5	b Graf	63	9.3	5	15	1	3
60	15/10/1982	S.A	QLD	Brisbane	2	5	b Hohns	53	-	-	-	-	-
61	22/10/1982	S.A	VIC	Adelaide	4	5	c Chappell b Henschell	87	3.0	1	8	1	2
					1	2	cwk Sacristani b Cox	137	2.0	1	6	0	1
62	31/10/1982	S.A	EXI	Adelaide	3	2	c Green b McCurdy	107	12.0	2	33	2	-
					2	5	c Randall b Hemmings	74	1.0	0	1	0	2
63	06/11/1982	S.A	NSW	Adelaide	4	4	b Cook	39	-	-	-	-	-
					2	5	lbw b Chappell	65	7.0	0	25	0	2
64	12/11/1982	AUS	ENG	Perth	4	5	c Bennett b Lawson	60	-	-	-	-	-
					1	6	lbw b Miller	56	-	-	-	-	-
65	26/11/1982	AUS	ENG	Brisbane	3	6			1.0	0	2	0	-
					2	6	cwk Taylor b Miller	28	2.0	0	4	0	-
					4	6	not out	66*	-	-	-	-	1
66	03/12/1982	S.A	NSW	Sydney	2	5	b Whitney	35	-	-	-	-	3
					4	4	c Toohey b Whitney	42	1.0	0	12	0	2

Game	Start Date	Team	Opp	Venue	Inn	Pos	How Out	Runs	O	M	R	W	Ct
67	10/12/1982	AUS	ENG	Adelaide	1	7	c Botham b Hemmings	37	-	-	-	-	-
68	17/12/1982	S.A	W.A	Perth	4	7	c Clark b Lillee	10	3.0	1	9	0	-
					1	4	c Hogan b MacLeay	146	3.0	0	18	0	1
69	26/12/1982	AUS	ENG	Melbourne	3	4	cwk Taylor b Pringle	53	-	-	-	-	-
					2	6	c Willis b Cowans	68	-	-	-	-	1
70	02/01/1983	AUS	ENG	Sydney	4	5	c Botham b Hemmings	17	2.0	1	5	0	1
					1	5	lbw b Miller	19	-	-	-	-	2
71	18/02/1983	S.A	VIC	St Kilda	3	5	c Bright b McCurdy	193	-	-	-	-	1
72	25/02/1983	S.A	W.A	Adelaide	2	6	b Hogan	32	-	-	-	-	1
					4	5	b Yardley	0	-	-	-	-	-
73	17/04/1983	AXI	SBP	Moratuwa	3	5	c Mendis b De Silva	20	-	-	-	-	2
74	22/04/1983	AUS	S.L	Kandy	3	5	not out	143*	-	-	-	-	2
75	21/10/1983	S.A	TAS	Adelaide	1	5	b Beven	13	-	-	-	-	-
76	28/10/1983	S.A	PKI	Adelaide	4	4	c (s)Ashraf Ali b Mudassar Nazar	55	11.0	1	38	0	2
					2	4	b Abdul Qadir	35	8.0	3	19	2	-
77	25/11/1983	S.A	VIC	Adelaide	4	5	cwk Hyde b McCurdy	41	25.0	7	62	0	-
					1	4	run out	5	4.0	0	15	0	2
78	02/12/1983	S.A	W.A	Adelaide	3	4	cwk Marsh b MacLeay	57	5.0	2	8	0	-
					2	5	c Alderman b Hogan	22	7.0	2	25	1	1
79	09/12/1983	S.A	TAS	Devonport	4	2	c Faulkner b Williams	142	3.0	1	11	0	1
					4	5	b Clough	25	4.4	2	14	1	-
80	16/12/1983	S.A	NSW	Newcastle	2	6	c McCosker b Matthews	15	21.0	2	61	1	1
					4	6	c McCosker b Holland	42	5.0	0	15	0	-
81	06/01/1984	S.A	W.A	Perth	1	6	c MacLeay b Alderman	111	-	-	-	-	-
82	18/02/1984	AXI	L.I	Basseterre	3	6	b Baptiste	66	3.0	2	1	0	1
					1	5	c Lawrence b Guishard	24	2.0	0	13	0	-
83	24/02/1984	AXI	GUY	Georgetown	1	5	st Pydanna b Butts	61	4.0	0	23	0	1
					3	7	not out	3*	9.0	0	48	0	-

Game	Start Date	Team	Opp	Venue	Inn	Pos	How Out	Runs	O	M	R	W	Ct
84	02/03/1984	AUS	W.I	Georgetown	1	6	cwk Dujon b Harper	32	-	-	-	-	-
					3	6	b Garner	10	-	-	-	-	-
85	16/03/1984	AUS	W.I	Port-of-Spain	1	6	b Garner	23	-	-	-	-	-
					3	7	c Richardson b Gomes	21	-	-	-	-	-
86	24/03/1984	AXI	BAR	Bridgetown	1	5	b Estwick	22	-	-	-	-	-
					3	5	not out	103*	5.0	1	17	1	-
87	30/03/1984	AUS	W.I	Bridgetown	1	6	cwk Dujon b Garner	30	-	-	-	-	-
					3	7	b Holding	9	-	-	-	-	-
88	07/04/1984	AUS	W.I	St John's	1	6	c Richardson b Baptiste	51	-	-	-	-	1
					3	6	c Greenidge b Holding	29	-	-	-	-	-
89	14/04/1984	AXI	WIS	Castries	1	6	st Cadette b Hinds	22	-	-	-	-	1
					3	5	lbw b Kentish	74	21.0	0	114	3	1
90	28/04/1984	AUS	W.I	Kingston	1	6	b Harper	7	-	-	-	-	1
					3	6	cwk Dujon b Marshall	36	3.0	0	14	0	-
91	19/10/1984	S.A	NSW	Adelaide	2	4	c Matthews b Marks	1	-	-	-	-	1
					4	4	c Dyson b Marks	12	7.0	0	32	1	2
92	26/10/1984	S.A	WIN	Adelaide	2	3	c Gomes b Walsh	27	-	-	-	-	-
					4	8	c Greenidge b Gomes	24	12.4	0	43	0	1
93	16/11/1984	S.A	QLD	Brisbane	1	3	cwk Phillips b Rackemann	5	1.0	0	10	1	-
					3	5	cwk Phillips b Maguire	79	6.0	2	31	1	-
94	22/11/1984	S.A	TAS	Adelaide	2	5	c Bennett b Brown	151	3.0	0	22	0	-
					4	5	c (s)Bradshaw b Brown	4	-	-	-	-	-
95	30/11/1984	S.A	NSW	Sydney	2	5	cwk Rixon b Imran Khan	1	2.0	1	2	0	-
					4	6	c Imran Khan b Holland	15	-	-	-	-	1
96	14/12/1984	S.A	VIC	Melbourne	1	5	c Robinson b Davis	9	-	-	-	-	-
					3	5	run out	62	14.0	5	38	2	1
97	20/12/1984	S.A	TAS	Hobart	2	6		-	3.0	2	1	0	-
					4	7	c and b Brown	35	-	-	-	-	-
98	10/01/1985	S.A	W.A	Perth	2	5	cwk Zoehrer b Alderman	0	13.0	1	49	1	-
					4	5	cwk Zoehrer b Spalding	73	12.0	1	49	2	-
99	17/01/1985	S.A	VIC	Adelaide	2	6	c Richardson b King	25	1.0	0	1	0	-
					4	6		-	-	-	-	-	-
100	22/02/1985	S.A	W.A	Adelaide	1	5	cwk Zoehrer b Reid	83	4.0	1	7	0	2
					4	3	b Reid	6	2.0	0	13	0	1

Game	Start Date	Team	Opp	Venue	Inn	Pos	How Out	Runs	O	M	R	W	Ct
101	01/03/1985	S.A	QLD	Adelaide	1	5	c Barsby b Maguire	18	9.0	1	32	0	-
					3	5	c Trimble b Thomson	34	3.0	1	11	0	1
102	17/10/1985	S.A	W.A	Adelaide	1	4	c Reid b Clough	40	-	-	-	-	2
					3	4	c Bush b Reid	82	-	-	-	-	-
103	26/10/1985	S.A	NZS	Adelaide	1	4	c Coney b Brown	106	9.0	4	22	0	-
					3	4	lbw b Boock	14	5.0	0	43	1	2
104	15/11/1985	S.A	QLD	Adelaide	1	4	c Kerr b Frei	47	-	-	-	-	1
					3	4	c Trimble b Frei	102	7.0	0	30	0	1
105	22/11/1985	AUS	N.Z	Sydney	2	6	run out	0	-	-	-	-	-
					4	6	not out	38*	-	-	-	-	1
106	30/11/1985	AUS	N.Z	Perth	1	6	c Bracewell b Coney	14	1.0	0	2	0	2
					3	6	b Bracewell	7	-	-	-	-	-
107	13/12/1985	AUS	IND	Adelaide	1	6	b Yadav	34	2.0	0	4	1	-
					3	6		-	-	-	-	-	-
108	20/12/1985	S.A	QLD	Brisbane	2	4	cwk Phillips b Trimble	7	14.0	2	49	0	1
					4	4	c Wessels b Trimble	72	9.0	2	17	0	1
109	26/12/1985	AUS	IND	Melbourne	1	5	b Shastri	42	-	-	-	-	1
					3	4	c Srikkanth b Shastri	0	-	-	-	-	-
110	16/01/1986	S.A	NSW	Adelaide	2	4	cwk Dyer b Blizzard	243	2.0	0	3	1	1
					4	4		-	5.0	0	22	0	-
111	25/01/1986	S.A	VIC	Melbourne	2	4	run out	23	4.0	0	14	0	1
					4	4	run out	9	-	-	-	-	-
112	21/02/1986	S.A	VIC	Adelaide	1	4	b Hickey	62	1.0	0	10	0	2
					3	4	cwk Dimattina b Hickey	11	4.0	0	20	1	-
113	28/02/1986	S.A	W.A	Perth	1	4	cwk Cox b Matthews	20	1.0	0	4	0	-
					3	8	c (s)Harris b Andrews	28	1.0	0	16	0	3
114	23/10/1986	S.A	W.A	Perth	3	5	b Marks	33	-	-	-	-	1
					3	5	c Breman b Marks	77	-	-	-	-	-
115	31/10/1986	S.A	EXI	Adelaide	1	5	c Whitaker b Edmonds	0	-	-	-	-	3
					3	5	c Richards b Emburey	104	15.0	5	58	3	-
116	07/11/1986	S.A	QLD	Adelaide	2	4	lbw b McDermott	20	-	-	-	-	1
					4	2	c Kerr b Frei	0	-	-	-	-	-
117	28/11/1986	S.A	VIC	Adelaide	2	4	b Bright	6	3.0	2	3	0	2
					4	5	b Hughes	54	-	-	-	-	-

Game	Start Date	Team	Opp	Venue	Inn	Pos	How Out	Runs	O	M	R	W	Ct
118	05/12/1986	S.A	TAS	Launceston	2	5	c Woolley b Ellison	4	–	–	–	–	2
119	18/12/1986	S.A	NSW	Sydney	4	5	b Whitney	0	6.0	1	18	0	–
120	02/01/1987	S.A	QLD	Brisbane	1	4	c Inwood b Tazelaar	52	12.0	0	43	0	–
					2	5	c and b Polzin	78	3.0	1	7		1
121	09/01/1987	S.A	NSW	Adelaide	1	4	c Bower b Bennett	45	13.0	2	39	0	–
122	27/02/1987	S.A	VIC	Melbourne	1	5	c Quinn b Bright	32	–	–	–	–	–
123	06/03/1987	S.A	TAS	Adelaide	3	4	st Dimattina b Jackson	0	–	–	–	–	4
					2	4	not out	306*	2.0	1	4	0	1
124	14/11/1987	S.A	NSW	Sydney	1	4	c O'Neill b Lawson	11	–	–	–	–	–
					3	5	c Waugh b Matthews	14	–	–	–	–	–
125	20/11/1987	S.A	QLD	Adelaide	1	4	c Courtice b Botham	89	–	–	–	–	1
					3	3	c Trimble b Henschell	67	–	–	–	–	–
126	27/11/1987	S.A	NZS	Adelaide	2	4	c Crowe b Bracewell	128	–	–	–	–	1
					4	7	b Bracewell	7	–	–	–	–	–
127	11/12/1987	S.A	VIC	Melbourne	1	4	c Whatmore b Dodemaide	93	–	–	–	–	1
					3	4	not out	42*	–	–	–	–	–
128	01/01/1988	S.A	W.A	Adelaide	3	4	cwk Zoehrer b Capes	4	–	–	–	–	–
129	15/01/1988	S.A	TAS	Devonport	2	4	c Shipperd b Matthews	29	7.0	1	17	0	3
					4	4	c Cooley b Harris	132	8.0	3	11	1	2
130	22/01/1988	S.A	NSW	Adelaide	1	4	c Matthews b Gilbert	82	1.0	0	1	0	–
					3	4	run out	9	–	–	–	–	–
131	06/02/1988	S.A	QLD	Brisbane	2	4	c Maguire b Henschell	112	2.0	1	1	0	1
					4	4	st Healy b Hohns	26	–	–	–	–	2
132	18/02/1988	S.A	TAS	Adelaide	2	4	c Cooley b Lillee	112	5.0	0	22	2	1
133	24/02/1988	S.A	VIC	Adelaide	2	4	c Jones b Davis	60	–	–	–	–	–
					4	4	c (s)Ayres b Dodemaide	65	4.0	0	11	0	1
134	02/03/1988	S.A	W.A	Perth	1	4	cwk Zoehrer b Alderman	2	–	–	–	–	3
					3	4	cwk Zoehrer b Matthews	65	–	–	–	–	2

Game	Start Date	Team	Opp	Venue	Inn	Pos	How Out	Runs	O	M	R	W	Ct
135	28/10/1988	S.A	VIC	Adelaide	2	4	c and b Jackson	58	-	-	-	-	2
					4	4	not out	39*	2.0	0	5	0	2
136	04/11/1988	S.A	WIN	Adelaide	2	4	c Dujon b Walsh	8	4.0	0	28	0	2
					3	4	c Richards b Walsh	47	1.0	0	7	0	-
137	18/11/1988	S.A	TAS	Hobart	1	4	cwk Soule b Faulkner	15	-	-	-	-	2
					3	5		-	-	-	-	-	-
138	25/11/1988	S.A	W.A	Adelaide	2	4	c Veletta b Mullally	28	-	-	-	-	2
					4	4	cwk Zoehrer b Alderman	18	-	-	-	-	-
139	10/12/1988	S.A	QLD	Brisbane	2	4	b Cantrell	16	-	-	-	-	-
					3	4	not out	7*	-	-	-	-	1
140	17/12/1988	S.A	W.A	Perth	1	4	cwk Zoehrer b Alderman	6	4.0	0	10	0	-
					3	3	c Marsh b MacLeay	15	-	-	-	-	1
141	06/01/1989	S.A	NSW	Adelaide	1	4	run out	21	4.0	1	15	0	-
					3	5		-	-	-	-	-	-
142	09/02/1989	S.A	NSW	Sydney	1	4	cwk Emery b Lawson	83	3.0	1	5	0	1
					3	4	lbw b Lawson	1	-	-	-	-	-
143	15/02/1989	S.A	QLD	Adelaide	3	4	c Clifford b McDermott	71	-	-	-	-	1
					2	4	run out	73	4.0	0	14	0	-
144	22/02/1989	S.A	VIC	Melbourne	4	4	cwk Dimattina b Dodemaide	133	-	-	-	-	1
					2	2	run out	0	-	-	-	-	-
145	10/03/1989	S.A	TAS	Adelaide	1	4	cwk Soule b De Winter	66	1.0	0	9	0	-
					3	4	not out	33*	-	-	-	-	-
146	25/03/1989	S.A	W.A	Perth	2	4	c Alderman b Capes	24	-	-	-	-	1
147	03/11/1989	S.A	QLD	Brisbane	3	4	cwk Healy b Inwood	39	8.1	-	28	0	-
					2	4	c McDermott b Rackemann	67	-	-	-	-	-
148	10/11/1989	S.A	NSW	Adelaide	2	5	lbw b Whitney	99	10.0	2	24	0	1
					4	5		-	-	-	-	-	-
149	17/11/1989	S.A	NZS	Adelaide	1	4	c Greatbatch b Snedden	8	-	-	-	-	-
					3	4	not out	3*	1.0	1	-	0	1
150	01/12/1989	S.A	SLS	Adelaide	2	4	c Ratnayeke b De Silva	50	-	-	-	-	-
151	08/12/1989	S.A	VIC	Melbourne	1	4	c Watts b O'Donnell	18	3.0	2	1	0	-
					3	4	run out	23	-	-	-	-	-

Game	Start Date	Team	Opp	Venue	Inn	Pos	How Out	Runs	O	M	R	W	Ct
152	15/12/1989	S.A	W.A	Perth	2	5	lbw b Capes	0	27.0	5	89	2	-
153	19/01/1990	S.A	TAS	Devonport	2	7	c Tucker b Gilbert	139	3.0	1	11	0	2
					4	4	lbw b Tucker	0					-
154	26/01/1990	S.A	W.A	Adelaide	1	4	cwk Zoehrer b Alderman	118	5.0	1	9	1	-
155	15/02/1990	S.A	NSW	Sydney	2	4	c Marks b Lawson	10	1.0	1			-
					3	4	c Whitney b Lawson	20					-
156	02/03/1990	S.A	TAS	Adelaide	1	4	lbw b De Winter	27	1.0	1	12	0	-
					3	4	c Cooley b McPhee	38	5.0	2			-
157	09/03/1990	S.A	QLD	Adelaide	3	4	b McDermott	5	14.0	3	27	0	-
					4	4	b Cantrell	159					1
158	02/11/1990	S.A	QLD	Brisbane	2	4	c Hick b McDermott	0	9.0	6	6	0	-
					3	4	c Border b McDermott	195			6		-
159	09/11/1990	S.A	EXI	Adelaide	1	4	c Gower b Lewis	6	4.0	1	14	1	3
					4	4	st Russell b Hemmings	26					-
160	16/11/1990	S.A	W.A	Adelaide	1	4	cwk Zoehrer b Reid	0	2.0	0	6		-
					3	4	lbw b MacLeay	64			14		-
161	06/12/1990	S.A	TAS	Hobart	2	5	c Hick b Tazelaar	178					1
162	14/12/1990	S.A	QLD	Adelaide	1	4	c Phillips b Jackson	10	15.0	1	77	0	-
					3	4	b Jackson	11					-
163	11/01/1991	S.A	VIC	Adelaide	1	4	cwk Emery b Whitney	24					-
					3	4	c Taylor b Matthews	16					-
164	19/01/1991	S.A	NSW	Sydney	2	4	b Holdsworth	38					1
165	15/02/1991	S.A	NSW	Adelaide	4	3	c Holdsworth b Lawson	2					1
166	22/02/1991	S.A	TAS	Adelaide	1	3	b Robertson	24					1
					3	4	b Buckingham	43					1
167	07/03/1991	S.A	VIC	St Kilda	1	4	cwk Berry b Reiffel	0					-
					3	4	c O'Donnell b Fleming	0					-
168	14/03/1991	S.A	W.A	Perth	1	4	c Lavender b McCague	18					-
					4	4		-					-

Game	Start Date	Team	Opp	Venue	Inn	Pos	How Out	Runs	O	M	R	W	Ct
169	01/11/1991	S.A	QLD	Brisbane	2	6	c Wellham b Rackemann	26	9.0	2	33	0	-
170	08/11/1991	S.A	TAS	Adelaide	4	6	c Buckingham b Tucker	16	-	-	-	-	1
					1	5		-	-	-	-	-	-
171	15/11/1991	S.A	VIC	Melbourne	3	6	c Jones b Reiffel	26	2.0	0	10	0	-
					2	5	c Ramshaw b Reiffel	9	-	-	-	-	-
172	22/11/1991	S.A	W.A	Adelaide	3	6	c Martyn b Zoehrer	75	6.0	0	23	0	1
					1	5	b Zoehrer	13	3.0	1	11	0	-
173	20/12/1991	S.A	NSW	Adelaide	3	4	c Taylor b Holdsworth	156	-	-	-	-	1
					4	5		-	-	-	-	-	-
174	31/01/1992	S.A	NSW	Sydney	1	5	lbw b Waugh	87	-	-	-	-	-
					3	5	c Waugh b Matthews	26	-	-	-	-	-
175	07/02/1992	S.A	QLD	Adelaide	2	5	c Taylor b McDermott	5	-	-	-	-	1
					4	5	c Border b McDermott	3	-	-	-	-	-
176	13/02/1992	S.A	TAS	Hobart	2	5	c Boon b Matthews	14	-	-	-	-	1
					4	2	lbw b Gilbert	5	-	-	-	-	-
177	21/02/1992	S.A	VIC	Adelaide	2	6	cwk Berry b Dodemaide	4	-	-	-	-	-
					4	5	c Nobes b Jackson	49	-	-	-	-	-
178	28/02/1992	S.A	W.A	Perth	1	6	cwk Zoehrer b Alderman	5	-	-	-	-	-
					3	6	cwk Veletta b McCague	11	-	-	-	-	-

Test Career
Debut:- 1976-77 v England, Melbourne

Season	Opponent	Venue	M	Inn	NO	Runs	HS	0s	50	100	Avrge	Ct	Balls	Mdns	Runs	Wkts	Avrge	Best
1976-77	England	Australia	1	2	-	73	56	-	1	-	36.50	1	-	-	-	-	-	-
1977	England	England	5	9	-	283	85	-	2	-	31.44	1	-	-	-	-	-	-
1979-80	West Indies	Australia	1	2	-	80	43	-	-	-	40.00	-	30	2	15	-	-	-
1979-80	Pakistan	Pakistan	1	2	-	0	0	2	-	-	0.00	-	-	-	-	-	-	-
1982-83	England	Australia	5	8	1	344	68	-	4	-	49.14	2	48	2	20	-	-	-
1982-83	Sri Lanka	Sri Lanka	1	1	1	143	143*	-	-	1	-	2	-	-	-	-	-	-
1983-84	West Indies	West Indies	5	10	-	248	51	-	1	-	24.80	2	-	-	-	-	-	-
1985-86	New Zealand	Australia	2	4	1	59	38*	1	-	-	19.67	3	6	-	2	-	-	-
1985-86	India	Australia	2	3	-	76	42	1	-	-	25.33	1	12	-	4	1	4.00	1/4
Total			23	41	3	1306	143*	4	8	1	34.37	12	96	4	41	1	41.00	1/4

Opponents	M	Inn	NO	Runs	HS	0s	50	100	Avrge	Ct	Balls	Mdns	Runs	Wkts	Avrge	Best
ENGLAND	11	19	1	700	85	-	7	-	38.89	4	48	2	20	1	4.00	1/4
INDIA	2	3	-	76	42	1	-	-	25.33	1	12	-	4	1	-	-
NEW ZEALAND	2	4	1	59	38*	1	-	-	19.67	3	6	-	2	-	-	-
PAKISTAN	1	2	-	0	0	2	-	-	0.00	-	-	-	-	-	-	-
SRI LANKA	1	1	1	143	143*	-	-	1	-	2	-	-	-	-	-	-
WEST INDIES	6	12	-	328	51	-	1	-	27.33	2	30	2	15	-	-	-

Highest Score:- 143* v Sri Lanka, Kandy, 1982-83
Best Bowling:- 1/4 v India, Adelaide, 1985-86

International Limited-Overs Career

Debut:- 1977 v England, Manchester

Season			M	Inn	NO	Runs	HS	50	100	Avrge	Stk/Rt	Ct	Balls	Runs	Wkts	Avrge	Best
1977	England v Australia	ENG	2	2	-	14	11	-	-	7.00	24.56	1	-	-	-	-	-
1979-80	World Series Cup	AUS	2	2	-	9	9	-	-	4.50	31.03	-	6	10	-	-	-
1981-82	World Series Cup	AUS	2	2	-	18	17	-	-	9.00	54.55	-	23	18	1	18.00	1/2
1982-83	World Series Cup	AUS	12	11	2	391	76	4	-	43.44	78.51	5	-	-	-	-	-
1982-83	Aus v New Zealand	AUS	1	1	-	18	18	-	-	18.00	66.67	1	-	-	-	-	-
1982-83	SL v Australia	SL	4	4	-	99	49	-	-	24.75	96.12	3	-	-	-	-	-
1983	World Cup	ENG	6	6	-	133	56	1	-	22.17	72.34	1	-	-	-	-	-
1983-84	World Series Cup	AUS	5	4	-	103	37	1	-	25.75	70.55	1	-	-	-	-	-
1983-84	W.Indies v Aust.	WI	3	3	-	36	22	-	-	12.00	83.72	-	-	-	-	-	-
1985-86	World Series Cup	AUS	2	1	-	5	5	-	-	5.00	31.25	-	-	-	-	-	-
Total			39	36	2	826	76	5	-	24.29	72.75	11	29	28	1	28.00	1/2

Opponents	M	Inn	NO	Runs	HS	50	100	Avrge	Stk/Rt	Ct	Balls	Runs	Wkt	Avrge	Best
England	7	7	1	237	76	3	-	39.50	73.15	4	12	16	-	-	-
India	3	3	-	7	5	-	-	2.33	31.82	1	-	-	-	-	-
New Zealand	9	7	1	186	68	1	-	31.00	72.09	3	11	2	1	2.00	1/2
Pakistan	3	2	-	62	37	-	-	31.00	84.93	1	-	-	-	-	-
Sri Lanka	4	4	-	99	49	-	-	24.75	96.12	-	-	-	-	-	-
West Indies	11	11	-	205	56	1	-	18.64	63.49	-	6	10	-	-	-
Zimbabwe	2	2	-	30	20	-	-	15.00	71.43	2	-	-	-	-	-

Highest Score:- 76 v England, Adelaide, 1982-83
Best Bowling:- 1/2 v New Zealand, Melbourne, 1982-83

Sheffield Shield Career

Debut:- 1975-76 South Australia v New South Wales, Adelaide

Season	Team	M	Inn	NO	Runs	HS	0s	50	100	Avrge	Ct	Balls	Mdns	Runs	Wkts	Avrge	Best
1975-76	South Australia	8	11	1	296	54*	1	2	-	29.60	4	16	-	8	1	8.00	1/8
1976-77	South Australia	5	10	-	788	185	-	-	5	78.80	7	120	1	62	-	-	-
1979-80	South Australia	3	5	-	193	88	-	2	-	48.25	2	60	1	34	1	34.00	1/18
1980-81	South Australia	6	12	1	383	73*	1	3	-	34.82	-	204	6	110	-	-	-
1981-82	South Australia	9	14	1	562	106	1	4	1	43.23	10	273	16	86	3	28.67	1/13
1982-83	South Australia	7	13	-	967	193	-	4	4	74.38	15	96	2	69	1	69.00	1/8
1983-84	South Australia	6	10	-	473	142	-	1	2	47.30	5	394	11	201	3	67.00	1/14
1984-85	South Australia	10	18	-	613	151	1	4	1	34.06	10	480	16	298	8	37.25	2/38
1985-86	South Australia	7	13	-	746	243	-	3	2	57.38	13	288	4	185	2	92.50	1/3
1986-87	South Australia	9	14	1	707	306*	3	4	1	54.38	12	234	7	114	-	-	-
1987-88	South Australia	10	18	1	1014	132	-	7	3	59.65	17	162	5	63	3	21.00	2/22
1988-89	South Australia	11	19	3	707	133	1	5	1	44.19	16	114	2	65	-	-	-
1989-90	South Australia	9	15	-	762	159	2	2	3	50.80	3	463	18	201	3	67.00	2/89
1990-91	South Australia	10	16	-	623	195	4	1	2	38.94	10	180	8	103	1	103.00	1/6
1991-92	South Australia	10	17	-	530	156	-	2	1	31.18	4	120	3	77	-	-	-
Total		120	205	9	9364	306*	14	44	26	47.78	128	3204	100	1676	26	64.46	2/22

Opponents		M	Inn	NO	Runs	HS	0s	50	100	Avrge	Ct	Balls	Mdns	Runs	Wkts	Avrge	Best
New South Wales		25	42	1	1833	243	2	6	5	44.71	25	548	8	304	2	152.00	1/3
Queensland		23	40	1	2385	195	2	15	7	61.15	26	737	26	360	2	180.00	1/10
Tasmania		19	28	2	1503	306*	1	2	6	57.81	17	586	18	325	7	46.43	2/22
Victoria		24	45	4	1901	193	5	10	5	46.37	38	667	31	313	7	44.71	2/38
Western Australia		29	50	1	1742	146	4	11	3	35.55	22	666	17	374	8	46.75	2/49

Highest Score:- 306* South Australia v Tasmania, Adelaide, 1986-87
Best Bowling:- 2/22 South Australia v Tasmania, Adelaide, 1987-88

Australian Domestic Limited-Overs Career

Debut:- 1975-76 South Australia v New South Wales, Adelaide

Season		M	Inn	NO	Runs	HS	50	100	Avrge	Stk/Rt	Ct	Balls	Runs	Wkt	Avrge	Best
1975-76	South Australia	2	2	-	76	45	-	-	38.00	71.03	3	-	-	-	-	-
1976-77	South Australia	1	1	-	45	45	-	-	45.00	70.31	1	-	-	-	-	-
1979-80	South Australia	2	2	-	105	83	1	-	52.50	126.51	1	-	-	-	-	-
1980-81	South Australia	4	4	-	152	84	1	-	38.00	65.52	1	210	141	3	47.00	2/45
1981-82	South Australia	2	2	-	56	56	1	-	28.00	78.87	1	78	79	1	79.00	1/27
1982-83	South Australia	1	1	-	30	30	-	-	30.00	88.24	-	28	23	-	-	-
1983-84	South Australia	4	2	-	17	9	-	-	8.50	36.17	2	-	-	-	-	-
1984-85	South Australia	4	4	-	195	101	1	1	48.75	111.43	2	78	69	2	34.50	2/46
1985-86	South Australia	2	2	-	5	4	-	-	2.50	25.00	2	54	49	1	49.00	1/27
1986-87	South Australia	4	4	-	101	48	-	-	25.25	95.28	1	6	11	-	-	-
1987-88	South Australia	4	4	1	158	57*	1	-	52.67	72.48	4	6	7	-	-	-
1988-89	South Australia	2	2	-	36	35	-	-	18.00	54.55	1	60	45	5	9.00	5/41
1989-90	South Australia	4	4	-	64	45	-	-	16.00	72.73	1	12	21	-	-	-
1990-91	South Australia	2	2	-	80	52	1	-	40.00	133.33	1	6	6	-	-	-
1991-92	South Australia	2	2	-	29	17	-	-	14.50	45.31	2					
Total		38	38	1	1149	101	6	1	31.05	80.07	22	538	451	12	37.58	5/41

Opponents	M	Inn	NO	Runs	HS	50	100	Avrge	Stk/Rt	Ct	Balls	Runs	Wkt	Avrge	Best
New South Wales	6	6	-	127	45	-	-	21.17	66.15	7	147	138	5	27.60	5/41
Queensland	6	6	-	121	48	2	-	20.17	75.63	2	68	66	-	-	-
Tasmania	6	6	1	215	84	2	-	43.00	78.18	3	67	33	1	33.00	1/16
Victoria	9	9	-	309	78	2	-	34.33	81.75	4	90	72	3	24.00	2/45
Western Australia	11	11	-	377	101	2	1	34.27	87.67	6	166	142	3	47.33	2/46

Highest Score:- 101 South Australia v Western Australia, Adelaide, 1984-85
Best Bowling:- 5/41 South Australia v New South Wales, Adelaide, 1989-90

World Series Cricket

Debut:- 1977-78 Australian XI v West Indians, (VFL Park) Waverley

Season	Opponent	Venue	M	Inn	NO	Runs	HS	50	100	Avrge	Ct	Balls	Mdns	Runs	Wkts	Avrge	Best
1977-78	West Indians	Australia	2	3	1	144	81+	2	-	72.00	3	32	-	20	1	20.00	1/6
1977-78	World XI	Australia	1	2	-	110	57	2	-	55.00	-	-	-	-	-	-	-
1978-79	World XI	New Zealand	1	2	-	18	10	-	-	9.00	-	-	-	-	-	-	-
1978-79	World XI	Australia	2	4	-	151	96	1	-	37.75	-	36	1	17	-	-	-
1978-79	West Indians	Australia	2	3	1	241	116	2	1	80.33	-	48	5	16	-	-	-
1978-79	West Indies	West Indies	5	10	1	124	28	-	-	13.78	3	42	-	41	-	-	-
Total			13	24	2	788	116	7	1	35.82	6	158	6	94	1	94.00	1/6

Highest Score:- 116 Australian XI v West Indians, Waverley, 1978-79
Best Bowling:- 1/6 Australian XI v West Indians, Waverley, 1977-78

First-class Career

Game	Start Date	Opp	Venue	Inn	Pos	How Out	Runs	O	M	R	W	Ct
1	02/12/1977	WI	Waverley	1	5	b Holding	0	2.0	0	6	1	1
				3	5	c Lloyd b Roberts	63	2.0	0	14	0	2
2	16/12/1977	WI	Sydney	1	6	retired hurt	81+	-	-	-	-	-
				3	11		-	-	-	-	-	-
3	09/02/1978	WXI	Waverley	1	5	c Asif Iqbal b Greig	57	-	-	-	-	-
				3	5	c Daniel b Garner	53	-	-	-	-	-
4	04/11/1978	WXI	Auckland	1	5	b Rice	8	-	-	-	-	-
				3	5	c Padmore b Hadlee	10	-	-	-	-	-
5	08/12/1978	WXI	Waverley	2	6	cwk Knott b Le Roux	15	3.0	0	7	0	-
				4	5	c Procter b Underwood	7	-	-	-	-	-
6	12/01/1979	WI	Waverley	1	5	lbw b Garner	116	8.0	5	16	0	-
				3	5	c Austin b Roberts	56	-	-	-	-	-
7	21/01/1979	WI	Sydney	2	5	c Greenidge b Croft	69	-	-	-	-	-
				4	5		-	-	-	-	-	-
8	02/02/1979	WXI	Sydney	1	5	cwk Knott b Procter	33	3.0	1	10	0	-
				3	5	b Le Roux	96	-	-	-	-	-

Game	Start Date	Opp	Venue	Inn	Pos	How Out	Runs	O	M	R	W	Ct
9	23/02/1979	WI	Kingston	2	6	b Daniel	23	-	-	-	-	-
10	09/03/1979	WI	Bridgetown	4	4	c (s)King b Daniel	15	7.0	0	41	0	2
11	16/03/1979	WI	Port-of-Spain	1	5	c Austin b Holding	4	-	-	-	-	1
				3	5	run out	6	-	-	-	-	-
				1	5	cwk Murray b Holding	2	-	-	-	-	-
12	26/03/1979	WI	Georgetown	3	5	c Lloyd b Padmore	6	-	-	-	-	-
				1	6	b Croft	28	-	-	-	-	-
13	06/04/1979	WIN	St John's	3	4	not out	23*	-	-	-	-	-
				1	6	c Rowe b Roberts	1	-	-	-	-	-
				3	6	lbw b Holding	16	-	-	-	-	-